LET THE
PEOPLE
SPEAK

SHEILLA JONES

LET THE PEOPLE SPEAK

OPPRESSION IN A TIME OF **RECONCILIATION**

With a foreword by Sheila North

Let the People Speak
first published 2019 by J. Gordon Shillingford Publishing Inc.
© 2019 Sheilla Jones

Cover design by Doowah Design.

Photo of Sheilla Jones and Sheila North by Cheryl Struss Photography.

The foreground image depicts King George VI and Queen Elizabeth greeting chieftains of the Stoney Indian Tribe, who have brought a photo of Queen Victoria, during the royal visit to Canada in 1939. The treaties were originally signed by representatives of the British Crown acting in Queen Victoria's name. Library and Archives Canada, National Film Board, accession number 1971-271 NPC, PA-131185.

The background image is a section from the original Treaty 1 document, signed on August 3, 1871 by Chippewa and Swampy Cree Tribes and Commissioner Wemyss M. Simpson for Queen Victoria, which included a $3 annuity for every band member. Library and Archives Canada, reproduction copy number e004156539, IT 255.

This book was printed on 100% post-consumer recycled paper.
Printed and bound in Canada by Hignell Printing.

We acknowledge the support of The Canada Council for the Arts and the Manitoba Arts Council for our publishing program.

All rights reserved. No part of this book may be reproduced, for any reason, by any means, without the permission of the publisher. This book is fully protected under the copyright laws of Canada and all other countries of the Copyright Union and is subject to royalty. Changes to the text are expressly forbidden without written consent of the author.

Library and Archives Canada Cataloguing in Publication

Title: Let the people speak : oppression in a time of reconciliation / Sheilla Jones.
Names: Jones, Sheilla, author.
Description: 1st edition.
Identifiers: Canadiana 20190137088 | ISBN 9781927922569 (softcover)
Subjects: LCSH: Indigenous peoples—Canada—Politics and government. | LCSH: Indigenous peoples—
   Canada—Government relations. | CSH: Native peoples—Canada—Politics and government. | CSH: Native
   peoples—Canada—Government relations.
Classification: LCC E98.T77 J66 2019 | DDC 323/.04208997071—dc23

J. Gordon Shillingford Publishing
P.O. Box 86, RPO Corydon Avenue, Winnipeg, MB Canada R3M 3S3
www.jgshillingford.com

This book is dedicated to Jean Allard, a tenacious man who, chained to a statue of Louis Riel, came up with the idea of modernizing treaty annuities as a means of empowerment for ordinary Indigenous people, an idea he never let die.

CONTENTS

15	Chapter 1: The Voices of the People
26	Chapter 2: Indigenous Affairs, Power and Secrecy
36	Chapter 3: IA+, Canada's "Super-Province"
44	Chapter 4: The Small Politics of '66
56	Chapter 5: The "Great Thunderclap" of '69
69	Chapter 6: The Best Voices Money Can Buy
77	Chapter 7: The Rise of the Village Tyrant
92	Chapter 8: The Buffalo Jump Policy of '85
101	Chapter 9: If the People Had Decided
110	Chapter 10: Unleashing the Fury of Mothers
120	Chapter 11: Calm at the Edge of the Storm
129	Chapter 12: Testing a Revolutionary Idea
136	Chapter 13: Escaping the Reach of IA
149	Chapter 14: The New PM Takes Charge
154	Chapter 15: A New Picture of Annuities
164	Chapter 16: Crunching the Annuity Numbers
172	Chapter 17: Failing Upward at a Spectacular Rate
186	Chapter 18: Buffalo Jump 2.0
194	Chapter 19: Breaking the Tyranny of Silence
202	Chapter 20: Let the People Speak

FOREWORD

I was raised in Bunibonibee Cree Nation, an isolated community in northern Manitoba filled with mostly other Cree people, and it shaped who I am. It structured how I think. When I was growing up, I thought the rest of the world was just as nurturing and loving as my own community—a place where all people helped each other in times of need, a place where people respected each other and shared what they had with each other. Bad things sometimes happened, but somehow it always felt like there was more good than bad.

However, in some ways it was all a facade. My parents, one a residential school survivor and the other a day school survivor, made a choice to be the best parents they could be in spite of what they experienced as children who grew up in a world that was being colonized—in spite of their parents, grandparents and great-grandparents being told that everything they knew about themselves and their world was wrong and unclean.

There are many other Indigenous families who have been irreparably damaged by the intentional undermining and derogation of their culture and identity. There is ample evidence of that in urban areas, where many people are openly struggling to survive on the streets and in poorer neighbourhoods, as well as in too many First Nations reserves in Canada.

I am thankful for my resilient parents, who, like many other Indigenous parents, found a way to shield my siblings and me from the hardships of life, at least in our formative years. Because of parents like them, we are seeing many healthy Indigenous people who are thriving today, in spite of what happened to them and their families. It is important to remember that all families, including Indigenous families in this country, want what many Canadians already enjoy—a good life. A life that allows us to care for everyone in our families and communities in the most positive and healthy way.

But right now, in this bountiful country we now know as Canada, the original people of this land, with a few exceptions, are living in Third World conditions, treated with disdain and disrespect and forced to live in abject poverty. The questions we all need to ask ourselves are the four w's and the h! What, When, Where, Why and How.

Let the People Speak: Oppression in a Time of Reconciliation will start you on a path to answering those questions for yourself—where you as a Canadian citizen fit into all of this, and how you may find a way to help change the course of history, starting from where you are. If you are hoping our country is truly that place where everyone is getting what they need to be healthy contributing members of society, you should be involved.

Let the People Speak sets out in plain English what a treaty is and what the sacred agreements signed generations ago have to do with what is happening today. The sacred agreements signed between the British Crown and the First Nations of this land—agreements that essentially formed what Canada is today—laid out how original inhabitants and newcomers should live peaceably with one another. You will clearly see how the acknowledgement of sharing the land and seeing the treaties fulfilled can help this country live sustainably and be the beacon of human rights protection it portrays itself to be.

Indigenous history is finally being taught in many schools in Canada and even shared at dinner tables and book club meetings. But not everyone has had the chance to learn about the remarkable history of the First Peoples and how things came to be the way they are today. Sheilla Jones does an incredible job summarizing federal Indigenous political history in Canada over the past 150 years, with a particular focus on the past fifty years. Reading the results of her in-depth research on the subject, including how treaties come into play, will help get you up to speed on what you need to understand if you are interested in being part of a country that cares for all of its people. Others have written extensively on historical Indigenous issues. The Royal Commission on Aboriginal Peoples contributed five volumes; the Truth and Reconciliation Commission illuminated a sorry chapter in Canada's treatment of Indigenous children, and the Missing and Murdered Indigenous Women and Girls Inquiry Report has added more. The question still to be answered: what do we do to keep old patterns from repeating themselves?

The place I came from is what Canada can and should be for all of us—a country that cares for all of its citizens, willingly helps others in times of need, and knows the value of sharing. But more than that, the country I would like to see for my children, grandchildren and great-grandchildren is most likely the same country you want to see, too. A country where all children receive the best education that allows them to compete for opportunities and become the self-sustaining citizens we all want to be, while understanding the importance of helping others who struggle.

The discussion about raising treaty annuities explored in this book can lead to a real path of reconciliation, one that does not oppress anyone. While First Nations citizens are resilient and have the ability to overcome great tragedies, their voices in their own homelands are not being heard. We hear some of the leaders and advocates who know how to get media attention, but the average citizen who is the most impacted by Canada's colonial policies is largely ignored. To me, I see the strength and winds of change contained in these voices.

As natural stewards of the land, ordinary Indigenous citizens have this country's best interests at heart, and have an outstanding capacity to welcome others. The time to include the original people of this land in decision-making on all aspects of this country, especially in how it affects their daily lives, is now. What is the alternative? To keep living in denial that Indigenous people deserve better? To keep spending money on problems that seem unsolvable?

Let the People Speak: Oppression in a Time of Reconciliation will challenge you as you see the repeated patterns of how the Government of Canada has intentionally tried to do away with the Treaties through assimilation and termination policies—even to this day with Canada's "Rights Recognition Framework"—in order to keep denying the original people of this land their fair share of resources as intended in the treaties. To live in ignorance is bliss, but at what cost? If you would like to see everyone in Canada contributing to enriching our society, in whatever unique way people might choose, then this book is for you.

Sheila North
Former Grand Chief of Manitoba Keewatinowi Okimakanak (MKO)

**We realize the importance of our voices
only when we are silenced.**

– Malala Yousafzai

1
THE VOICES OF THE PEOPLE

"For too long, the voices of Aboriginal people have not been heard in the councils of government or in the management of their own economic, social and cultural affairs. Too many still live in grinding poverty and lack the tools necessary to improve their quality of life. To overcome these challenges we must enter into a true dialogue and a true partnership with the goal of building a better future."

Although this quotation might sound like it's been pulled directly from a news story today, it is actually from a speech made by Prime Minister Chrétien nearly two decades ago in 2001.[1] Frankly, the exact same statement could have been made fifty years before by a much younger Chrétien in 1968, which strikes directly at the heart of a conundrum that has long caused frustration, confusion and anger among ordinary Canadians. Why are we still talking about "grinding poverty"? Or the need for a "true dialogue" and a "true partnership"? Why have these not been resolved yet?

Since Indian Affairs (IA) became a stand-alone government department in 1966,[2] a great many men and women of goodwill and enthusiasm — Indigenous and non-Indigenous — have expended considerable time and energy attempting to "fix" the seemingly intractable issues of poverty and despair facing so many Indigenous people and their communities. The Indigenous Affairs (IA) department is still struggling with the same issues.[3]

IA is a unique department in Canada's federal government. Other departments, such as Justice, Transportation or Public Safety, provide specific government services for the benefit of all Canadians. IA does the opposite. It provides nearly all government services to a specific group of Canadians. However, that "specific group of Canadians" has no meaningful influence over what services the department decides to provide. Ordinary Indigenous people are uniquely powerless when it comes to federal Indigenous policy. They are left with the options of protest, civil disobedience or the courts to influence the government department that has control over almost all aspects of their lives, especially those living in First Nations communities. It is not a battle of equals.

The Indigenous Affairs department has long been viewed by those who have fallen away, bloodied and bruised, in their battles against the institution and its policies as an immutable monolith that is impervious to change. There is an old saying in Indigenous politics: You don't change Indian Affairs; Indian Affairs changes you.

The only people who have clearly shown that they have the power to drive change at Indigenous Affairs are prime ministers. Justin Trudeau did exactly that in 2017 when he announced the first significant restructuring of IA since it became a stand-alone department.[4] That change involved hiving off some 80 percent of the existing IA department dealing with programs and services to create the new Indigenous Services (IS) department, with a new minister. The previous IA minister was left with a reduced portfolio covering mainly governance issues in the renamed Crown-Indigenous Relations (CIR) department. But splitting the department wasn't the only change. The Northern Affairs part of the portfolio was severed from Indigenous Affairs altogether and transferred to the Internal Trade department. And then Health Canada's programs and services for Indigenous people were rolled into the new Indigenous Services department, shrinking the Health Canada portfolio by about 80 percent.

Time and again over the past half-century, we've seen prime ministers who use the weight of their office to shift Indigenous policy, with mixed results.

Liberal prime minister Pierre Trudeau, for instance, used the clout of his office in 1969 when he ordered IA minister Jean Chrétien to scrap the *Indian Act*, terminate all special Aboriginal rights, turn over responsibility for services on reserves to the provinces, and eliminate the Indian Affairs department.[5] The PM's "termination policy" was developed in secret, with input from selected IA bureaucrats but without any input from Indian band chiefs or the handful of regional Indian political leaders who did not yet have a national voice. The dramatic policy change publicly backfired on Trudeau, and in the face of public opposition led by Indian leaders, he had to withdraw it.

Conservative prime minister Brian Mulroney tried the same tactic fifteen years later in 1984 when he ordered his deputy PM Erik Nielsen to conduct a hush-hush review of IA.[6] The review resulted in a plan to devolve most of IA's responsibility for services and programs to the provinces, allocate the remaining federal responsibilities to other government departments and eliminate the Indian Affairs department altogether. However, the policy that was jokingly named "Buffalo Jump of the 1980s" by Nielsen's team had a darker agenda. The plan was to squeeze band governments financially until they accepted the status of ethnic municipal governments. To sweeten the pot, band governments were to be offered the financial relief of five-year block funding, but only in exchange for voluntarily surrendering their peoples' now constitutionally protected Aboriginal rights. An explosive leaked memo detailing this new variation of a "devolution-and-then-termination policy" triggered a public backlash. The IA department once again survived. However, unlike the Trudeau back-down, the Mulroney cabinet quietly set in motion the devolution and termination priorities of the Buffalo Jump policy.

In 2004, Liberal prime minister Paul Martin took a different path. He oversaw closed-door, by-invitation-only meetings to develop a multi-billion-dollar accord that he hoped would set the stage for a new relationship between the federal government and Indigenous people.[7] By this time, the federal government was funding three Aboriginal Representative Organizations (AROs) that it had sanctioned as the official and sole voices of First Nations, Inuit and Métis people at the federal table. There were two smaller AROs specifically for Indigenous women and girls and for Indigenous people not represented by the three main organizations. In the Martin negotiations, the five AROs all got to sit at the table with senior IA bureaucrats, some Members of Parliament and a few other selected people.

The process was a success, insofar as it resulted in an accord that provided a framework for devolution of more powers and responsibilities from IA to band governments. However, it's not clear what effect the new devolution policy would have had since it was never enacted by Stephen Harper, the Conservative prime minister who followed Martin.

Liberal prime minister Justin Trudeau adopted Martin's successful methodology in 2017 in negotiating the newest, new relationship between Indigenous people and the Crown, but this time it was a much tighter circle of people sitting at the table in the secretive, closed-door meetings. It was almost entirely bureaucrats from IA and a range of other departments delivering Indigenous programs, and representatives from only one ARO, the Assembly of First Nations, which represents First Nations chiefs. Some regional chiefs' groups were also consulted, while others boycotted the process. The new plan that slowly emerged in 2018 called for the gradual elimination of the *Indian Act* and Indigenous Services, after the devolution of most of the Indigenous Services responsibilities to provincial governments and to band governments. The band governments would then take the form of municipal-style entities, complete with a ten-year block funding plan. At the time of this writing, the requirement that chiefs sign away their people's rights in exchange for gaining block funding and freedom from the *Indian Act* was still government policy.

There is a certain irony in Justin Trudeau's promising the elimination of Indian Affairs and the *Indian Act*; his father promised the same thing nearly fifty years earlier, but Pierre Trudeau's 1969 termination policy triggered a national outrage, not a national move to reconciliation. And yes, the current Trudeau plan gives off more than a whiff of the Mulroney Buffalo Jump policy. However, it is not what is in the policy plan that is cause for immediate concern. It's what is missing — the voices of ordinary Indigenous people.

Why are the voices of Indigenous people still not heard in the councils of government or in their own affairs? The simple answer is that ordinary Indigenous people have no political power, and hence, no political voice. They don't have a seat at the table when their futures are being negotiated by others. They didn't have a voice when the *Indian Act* was established in 1876; they do not have a voice today. And since ordinary Indigenous people are voiceless and powerless, they are shut out of the very policy decisions and governance issues that could provide the means to empower them.

There is an old saying attributed to Lord Acton that power tends to corrupt. A corollary to that saying, played out in Indigenous politics, is that powerlessness tends to destroy. Is it possible that the well-documented social inequities in Indigenous communities—high levels of poverty, suicide, incarceration, children in care, family violence—are, in fact, the *symptoms* of institutionalized powerlessness?

If that is the case, then all the public inquiries, royal commissions, compensation awards for government-sanctioned historical abuses and prime ministerial apologies will ultimately be futile if the root cause of hopelessness, powerlessness and despair are not addressed.

Ordinary Indigenous people have no political power, and no political voice.

At first blush, this statement may seem absurd. In the mainstream media, it may appear as if Indigenous voices are omnipresent, whether it is commentary about murdered and missing Indigenous women, pipeline protests, announcements of federal/provincial funding to address boil-water orders, housing, child care services or another controversial court case on Indigenous rights.

Ordinary Indigenous people certainly have plenty of organizations to speak for them. There are the five national Aboriginal Representative Organizations, with nearly seventy regional and territorial counterparts.[8] There are also some eighty tribal councils across Canada to advocate for Indigenous interests.[9] And there are more than 4,000 Indigenous groups and organizations across the country funded by IA and Canadian Heritage,[10] mainly in culture, arts, women's issues and support for Indigenous media. And then there are all the Indigenous musicians, artists, actors and writers who are giving voice to the pain, beauty and drama of their lives and cultures.

In the face of such significant media, political and cultural coverage, it may seem ridiculous to suggest that ordinary Indigenous people are voiceless and powerless. Yet when it comes to being heard at the federal political level, they are exactly that.

Power from the top down

In its simplest terms, power in Indigenous politics—and the money that goes with it—flows entirely from the top down, with IA at the top and ordinary Indigenous people firmly entrenched at the bottom of the power hierarchy. There is no mechanism for power to flow from the bottom upwards, and no means for ordinary Indigenous people to hold the department that controls almost all aspects of their lives accountable to them.

The *Indian Act* was passed by Parliament in 1876 to give the Indian Affairs branch rules and regulations by which bureaucrats could administer the provisions of the historic treaties signed between Indian bands and the Crown. For roughly the first 100 years of the Act, Indian Agents employed by IA had dictatorial control over what happened on the reserves they were assigned to manage. The Act did allow for chiefs and councils to be elected, but this colonial governance system had little meaning for ordinary Indians, other than it provided a chief with an extra $25 a year and a new suit of clothes every three years, and an extra $15 for councillors. Chiefs had no real power and neither did ordinary band members. The power was all held by the Indian Affairs branch.

That changed in the 1960s when the new, stand-alone IA department recognized that its century-old assimilation policy had not worked, as evidenced by the fact that nearly 80 percent of Status Indians still lived on reserves.[11] IA shifted to a policy of devolution of power and responsibility to band councils, with an eye to turning bands into provincial responsibilities. The chiefs were granted new powers to deliver IA programs in their communities and, for the first time, they received core funding for band operations so that the positions of chiefs, councillors and administrators came with actual paycheques. It turned those positions into highly coveted jobs. However, the band governments were not accountable to band members; they were beholden to IA, the source of their power and money.

The Aboriginal Representative Organizations established by the federal government in the 1970s were in the same position. They were totally reliant on federal funding to run their offices, pay for telephones and Gestetner machines, and to pay their directors and staff. If the AROs stepped out of line, IA was prepared to reassert its control by slashing their funding and returning it only when assured of the ARO's willingness to comply with IA's agenda.

The reality for both AROs and band governments on reserves was a simple, immutable truth. What Indian Affairs had the power to dispense, it had the power to take back. What Indian Affairs had the power to bestow, it had the power to withhold. That same power dynamic continues to this day, with the exception of a handful of First Nations communities that have developed enough of their own economic resources to free themselves from IA dependency.

Indigenous political/representative groups like the Assembly of First Nations (AFN) and its provincial/territorial counterparts deserve a great deal of credit for what they have been able to achieve for Indigenous people, despite being deeply compromised by their own dependency on IA. Protection of Indigenous rights and the historic treaties, for instance, would never have been enshrined in the Constitution in 1982 were it not for their determined efforts.

However, AROs are fundamentally flawed organizations that are politically weakened by their dependency on IA and undermined by the internal friction among their leaders about whether the organization is too cozy with IA officials or too confrontational. But it is the claim that AROs are the legitimate political voices of their people that is their greatest weakness.

It has long been an open secret in Indigenous politics that the AFN does not speak for all ordinary First Nations (FN) people. It is an organization of reserve chiefs. However, more than half of FN people today no longer live on reserves and the chiefs do not represent their concerns in the AFN. The AFN sought to address this political vulnerability in 2005 by deciding to allow all eligible First Nations members across the country to vote for the AFN's national chief from a selection of candidates chosen by the chiefs. It would, finally, be a mechanism for ordinary First Nations people to make their voices heard within the AFN, albeit in a very limited fashion. By 2008, however, the AFN had dropped the idea as too expensive and too complicated to deliver.

But, you might ask, are not chiefs empowered through elections by band members who still live on reserves to represent their interests? For the first 100 years under the *Indian Act*, band elections were largely irrelevant. The Indian Agent had the power to appoint a chief and councillors if communities didn't bother with elections. That changed with the IA devolution policy in the 1960s. Elections suddenly became very important because whoever was elected had complete control of the power and money dispensed to the band by IA. It quickly became apparent that there was a big problem with elections. The *Indian Act* had no requirement that elections on reserves be free and fair. The Act did, however, give IA the authority to unilaterally nullify election results and simply replace troublesome chiefs and councillors with people of IA's choosing who were valued for their compliance.

IA never bothered itself about how the lack of free and fair elections affected ordinary band members because ordinary Indians were of no political value to the department, other than as a continuously suffering client base for IA's ever-expanding programs and services. Chiefs, on the other hand, had the legal authority to sign "self-government" agreements and sign away their people's rights. Whether chiefs were legitimately elected by their people was generally irrelevant to IA in advancing the Buffalo Jump policy objectives of squeezing bands financially to force them into signing termination papers.

Because elections have so long been considered irrelevant, or served as snake pits for feuding factions to fight it out over which one controls the band's power and money, First Nations communities have not institutionalized accountability through elections in place of the traditional, consensus-based form of governance. Band governments answer to IA, not to the community. However, the willingness of the federal government, the IA department, the AROs and the chiefs and councillors (who may or may not be fairly elected) to sustain the pretense that ordinary Indigenous people have a voice in Indigenous politics at the federal level has served to institutionalize their powerlessness. As a result, it has been, to all intents and purposes, a government policy of oppression that renders ordinary Indigenous people voiceless.

It is worth repeating. *Ordinary Indigenous people have no political power, and no political voice.*

There is another segment of the Canadian population that is shut out of Indigenous politics. Ordinary non-Indigenous people also have no say in policy decisions made by Indigenous Affairs or its AROs that affect them and their communities. The difference is that, for most of the past 150 years, ordinary non-Indigenous Canadians have demonstrated a casually callous lack of interest in the concerns of Indigenous people. The exception was a brief spurt of attention during the civil rights era in the 1960s and 1970s, and again now, as talk turns to reconciliation.

Let's pause for a moment and be clear about who we mean when we talk about ordinary Indigenous people and ordinary non-Indigenous people. Indigenous people in Canada are defined constitutionally as First Nations (Indian), Métis and Inuit. Canadians, whatever their ancestry or ethnicity who are not First Nations, Métis or Inuit are, by definition, non-Indigenous. That's the easy part. The word "ordinary" as used here could well be describing people who, in their everyday lives, are extraordinary, one-of-a-kind, remarkable, tragically broken, genius, outrageous, or any other adjective that conveys anything-but-ordinary. However, if they are not the power brokers, political players and decision-makers in the power hierarchy of Indigenous politics, they are ordinary people. Even many of the people employed by Indigenous Affairs, the Indigenous political organizations, or who work for band councils could be considered "ordinary" in the sense that they have no power to affect the laws, policies and rules that impact the lives of Indigenous people. They have jobs; they do not have power. There is a difference.

How do ordinary Indigenous people feel about this state of affairs? The obvious thing to do is ask. Many of the people I interviewed from First Nations across North America who had made a pilgrimage to the shore of Lac Ste. Anne near Edmonton in the summer of 1999 made their views clear. "Our leaders are deaf. No one listens," they said, sometimes with bitterness and sometimes with a resigned shrug. "No one speaks for us."[12] Almost two decades later, when I interviewed people at the Treaty tent at The Forks in Winnipeg in the summer of 2017, they were still saying the same thing.

When PM Justin Trudeau announced the massive restructuring of IA in the summer of 2017, he called it "an important step in building a true nation-to-nation, Inuit-Crown, and government-to-government relationship with First Nations, Inuit, and Métis peoples in Canada" that would work toward "making our national journey of reconciliation a reality."[13]

The goal of reconciliation between Indigenous and non-Indigenous people is certainly an admirable one. It offers the promise of an end to fighting, resentment, guilt and anger. A coming together in peace. Solving once and for all the tragic poverty and despair in so many of Canada's Indigenous communities so that we can live in collegial harmony. How can we not want that?

Trudeau raised the political stakes for delivering on reconciliation in his address before world leaders at the United Nations General Assembly in the fall of 2017. "The good news is that Canadians get it. They see the inequities. They're fed up with the excuses. And that impatience gives us a rare and precious opportunity to act."[14]

He is correct in saying that Canadians are impatient to get on with reconciliation. A national poll conducted by Environics in 2016 asked 2,000 non-Indigenous people how they viewed reconciliation with Indigenous people.[15] Not only were non-Indigenous people strongly in favour of reconciliation, more than 80 percent felt that they, personally, "have a role to play in bringing about reconciliation."[16]

We are currently witnessing an unprecedented willingness by ordinary Canadians (Indigenous and non-Indigenous) to invest their time and energy to support reconciliation. We saw it when 70,000 people took to the streets in the Walk for Reconciliation in Vancouver in the fall of 2017. It's there when people participate in the emotionally challenging Blanket Exercises hosted by KAIROS, in healing ceremonies, in Circle groups and other events across the country. It's there at church events, book launches, NHL hockey games and university conferences where events begin with "We acknowledge that this event is taking place on Treaty lands…"

Sometimes, it's about more than just talk. The RCMP in Nova Scotia in 2017 began providing eagle feathers to its detachments so that victims, witnesses and police officers would have the option of swearing legal oaths on a feather.[17] The feathers have the same legal standing as a Bible for sworn statements to the RCMP. Manitoba, the province with the highest per capita Indigenous population, did the same in early 2019.[18]

Sometimes, it exactly that—talking. In January 2019, Cree MP Robert-Falcon Ouellette became the first person to speak in an Indigenous language (Plains Cree) in the House of Commons with a live interpreter.[19] The Senate has offered simultaneous translation of Inuktitut (an Inuit language) in the chamber since 2008.[20]

People are looking for a way to do their part for reconciliation, even if they're not quite sure what that is. This is a rare political opportunity when the public mood and the government agenda appear to be aligned on the complex and emotionally fraught topic of Indigenous issues, but is reconciliation where we're actually heading? If one party to reconciliation has been rendered voiceless by institutionalized oppression, how is meaningful reconciliation supposed to happen?

Indigenous leaders, on their own, are helpless to change the political status quo inside which they are trapped. If they could have found a way to liberate themselves from IA's controls so they could speak honourably for their people, they would have.

The power for change lies in the hands of the federal government, specifically the prime minister and cabinet. However, politicians are far more likely to cling to the safety of the status quo than rock the boat on a contentious issue like the oppression of ordinary Indigenous people—unless they are assured that they have the political support of enough Canadian voters.

However, before Canadians raise the considerable power of their voices to advocate for change, it is important to understand how the world of Indigenous politics arrived at this impasse, recognize the cost of entrenched powerlessness and consider meaningful solutions that address the problems rather than the symptoms.

Endnotes to Chapter 1

1. Prime Minister Jean Chrétien, in a letter sent to delegates to the first Indigenous Peoples Summit of the AmErikas, Ottawa, March 2001, quoted in *Resolving Aboriginal Claims: A Practical Guide to Canadian Experiences*, 2003, INAC, 35.

2. Prior to 1966, the Department of Indian Affairs and Northern Development (DIAND) was a branch of the Department of Citizenship and Immigration; prior to 1949 it was a branch of the Department of Mines and Resources; prior to 1936, it was part of the Department of the Interior.

3. For simplicity, the acronym IA will be used interchangeably for Indian Affairs and Indigenous Affairs, as both are names commonly used for the same department.

4. Prime Minister's Office (PMO), August 28, 2017, New Ministers to support the renewed relationship with Indigenous Peoples, https://pm.gc.ca/eng/news/2017/08/28/new-ministers-support-renewed-relationship-indigenous-peoples.

5. Statement of the Government of Canada on Indian Policy 1969, more commonly referred to as The White Paper, 1969. Available online at https://www.aadnc-aandc.gc.ca/eng/1100100010189/1100100010191.

6. The Nielsen Task Force was announced by Prime Minister Brian Mulroney on September 18, 1984, just one day after his Conservative party was sworn into office. Deputy PM Erik Nielsen was mandated to review five key spending areas in government, one of which was "Indian and native programs."

7. *Strengthening the Relationship: Report on the Canada-Aboriginal Peoples Roundtable*, April 19, 2004, Government of Canada, http://publications.gc.ca/site/eng/9.819383/publication.html.

8. The five AROs are: Assembly of First Nations, Métis National Council, Congress of Aboriginal Peoples, Inuit Tapirit Kanatami, and Native Women's Association of Canada. Based on their respective websites in March 2019, they collectively identify 69 regional, provincial and territorial counterparts.

9. Tribal Council Funding, Indigenous and Northern Affairs Canada, https://www.aadnc-aandc.gc.ca/eng/1100100013812/1100100013813.

10. Yale D. Belanger, David R. Newhouse, and Kevin Fitzmaurice, 2008, "Creating a Seat at the Table: A Retrospective Study of Aboriginal Programming at Canadian Heritage," *The Canadian Journal of Native Studies*, XXVIII, 1 (2008): 41. Prior to 2012, Canadian Heritage was funding some 4,000 Indigenous groups and organizations, primarily Indigenous women's and artists' organizations, friendship centres, and cultural and media organizations. After 2012, many of those programs were transferred to Indigenous Affairs.

11. Indian Affairs and Northern Development Annual Report, Fiscal Year 1966–67, Government of Canada, p 55. Note that off-reserve Status Indians were not the responsibility of IA at that time.

12. Based on interviews by the author in 1999 and 2017.

13. PMO, New Ministers, August 28, 2017.

14. Bruce Campion-Smith, "Canada struggles to improve conditions for Indigenous people, Trudeau tells the UN," *The Toronto Star*, September 21, 2017.

15. "Canadian Public Opinion on Aboriginal Peoples," June 2016, The Environics Institute, with partners Canadians for a New Partnership, The Circle on Philanthropy and Aboriginal People in Canada, The Inspirit Foundation, Institute on Governance, National Centre for Truth and Reconciliation, Reconciliation Canada and Tides Canada, 35.

16. Ibid.

17. "Nova Scotia RCMP introduce eagle feather as new option to swear legal oaths," Media Release, October 30, 2017, Royal Canadian Mounted Police, http://www.rcmp-grc.gc.ca/en/news/2017/nova-scotia-rcmp-introduce-eagle-feather-new-option-swear-legal-oaths.

18 "Manitoba RCMP announces eagle feather as option to swear legal oaths," Media Release, January 22, 2019, Royal Canadian Mounted Police, http://www.rcmp-grc.gc.ca/en/news/2019/manitoba-rcmp-announces-eagle-feather-option-swear-legal-oaths.

19 "Robertson, Dylan, Ouellette, interpreter bring Cree voice to House of Commons," January 28, 2019, *Winnipeg Free Press*, https://www.winnipegfreepress.com/local/ouellette-interpreter-bring-cree-voice-to-house-of-commons-504990672.html.

20 Wilbert J. Keon, Chair, The Standing Committee on Rules, Procedures and the Rights of Parliament, April 9, 2008, https://sencanada.ca/en/Content/Sen/chamber/392/journals/048ap_2008-04-09-e.

2
INDIGENOUS AFFAIRS, POWER AND SECRECY

Most ordinary Canadians (Indigenous and non-Indigenous) have little idea of just how powerful the Indigenous Affairs (IA) department is within Canada's national government. IA has jurisdictional reach over 90 percent of Canada's landscape, as well as authorities that reach into every single federal department and agency. All of them. Splitting IA into Indigenous Services and Crown-Indigenous Relations does not change this power dynamic because it constitutes little more than putting some new labels on the same authorities.

IA's mandate gives the department responsibility under the *Indian Act* of 1876 for managing the obligations in historic treaties and for negotiating modern treaties. The historic treaties, signed primarily in the 1800s and early 1900s, cover about 50 percent of Canada's land mass.[1] The modern treaties, signed after 1975, cover another 40 percent, primarily in the North.[2] Only southern Quebec, a bit of Labrador and Newfoundland, and most of British Columbia remain outside IA's mandate, with the exception of the portion of the 3 million hectares of reserve lands[3] and 200 or so reserves that lie outside the historic and modern treaty areas.

As the push for self-government in the form of modern treaties has accelerated, IA has extended its reach into all government departments and agencies.

"Modern treaties are unique in the world," states an IA 2014 training manual for federal officials on the modern treaty process, "...virtually every federal organization's mandate will intersect with Aboriginal treaty rights at some point, from natural resource development to heritage to procurement."[4]

The manual noted that "*all* departments and agencies have obligations" with respect to modern treaties and "*all* departmental activities, programs, policies and legislation must be developed and implemented in a manner that complies with modern treaty provisions."⁵ (IA's emphasis.) To ensure compliance, IA has taken the role of coordinating and guiding all federal departments and agencies in fulfilling treaty responsibilities. IA admits this intrusion into other departments' jurisdiction "creates a horizontal management challenge for Canada."⁶

The department is currently involved in implementing nearly 30 modern treaties, each of which creates hundreds of obligations for federal departments and agencies.⁷ New treaties in the form of self-government agreements will have impacts across federal government departments and across the country once they are negotiated and signed. They will affect Canadians just about everywhere. Yet ordinary Canadians—Indigenous and non-Indigenous—are not involved in this process. Since the implementation of the *Indian Act* in 1876, the federal government has shown little interest in involving Canadian society in working out policies that have legal, social and economic implications for the relationship between Indigenous and non-Indigenous people. The policy decisions continue to be made inside the bureaucratic bubble of Indigenous Affairs and its selected Aboriginal Representative Organizations, with ordinary Canadians—Indigenous and non-Indigenous—finding out about the deals being negotiated when they are completed and publicly announced.

And now, self-government/modern treaty issues are going to get even more complicated. The relationship between Canada's Indigenous and non-Indigenous people was supposed to undergo a dramatic shift as the Trudeau government moved to deliver on its explicit goal of "accelerating a move to self-government and self-determination of Indigenous Peoples."⁸ This included a suite of legislative changes that are intended to "de-colonize" the management of Indigenous issues and prepare the ground to eliminate the *Indian Act*.

The move to "accelerated self-government" could see the potential creation of somewhere between forty and eighty new self-governing nations, all negotiated on behalf of Canada by the staff of the IA governance programs, under the new Crown-Indigenous Relations portfolio. But how much trust should ordinary Canadians—Indigenous and non-Indigenous—have in IA's ability to effectively deliver on such vast and far-reaching negotiations?

Let's take a look at some recent efforts.

Newfoundland gets its second official band

When Newfoundland entered Confederation in 1949, Premier Joey Smallwood declared that no Indians lived on the island.⁹ There were, of course, Mi'kmaq people who had migrated there from the mainland over several centuries. They weren't officially recognized by Indigenous Affairs until 1987 with the creation of the 2,500-member Miawpukek Reserve on the southern coast of the island.¹⁰ The Federation of Newfoundland Indians wanted to get the province's other estimated 10,000 Mi'kmaq people registered under the *Indian Act*, and in 2006, began serious negotiations with IA for the creation of the Qalipu Mi'kmaq First

Nation. (Qalipu means "caribou" and is pronounced ha-lee-boo.) Unlike the Miawpukek (Middle River) community, Qalipu was not going to have reserve land, but would have IA programs and services delivered through a central office in Corner Brook. When the landless band was officially announced in 2011, a call went out for band members. They would qualify for a Status card and all the benefits that come with it but without having to live on a reserve. More than 100,000 people applied, which threw the whole process into disarray.

In 2014, the Harper government had to rush a bill through Parliament to authorize changing the membership rules mid-stream and to give IA legal protection against the blowback.[11] It just made an even bigger mess. By the summer of 2017, thwarted membership applicants had launched a class-action lawsuit, and neighbour had turned against neighbour.

"I think we need to give up on the idea of reconciliation with the government," a bitter Kelly Anne Butler, a Mi'kmaq and Aboriginal Affairs officer at Memorial University's Grenfell Campus, told a reporter.[12] She had qualified for a Status card; her brother had not. The Mi'kmaq community, she added, would have been better off if the negotiations had never started.

For a government department that has had more than fifty years of experience in establishing new Indigenous bands and negotiating modern treaties and land claims, Indigenous Affairs was remarkably inept at rolling out the creation of the Qalipu FN. This was a fairly simple and straightforward deal to accept a known group of Newfoundland Mi'kmaq for registration under the *Indian Act*. However, IA should not have been taken by surprise at the rush for membership. It was, after all, offering incentives in the form of immediate benefits that come with a Status card, such as free supplemental health and dental care, selected tax breaks and the ability to live and work in the USA without a Green Card. And there was no requirement that anyone had to move from their condo in St. John's or Ottawa to live on a reserve with boil-water orders and mouldy houses. Why wouldn't lots of people apply, if they could see immediate financial benefits for themselves and their families?

A new Western nation for the Métis

The negotiations underway in 2018 for a new Métis Nation were not likely to catch IA negotiators off-guard. It has been in the works for nearly forty years.

In early 2017, the long-sought dream of creating a Métis Nation came tantalizingly closer to realization when the Indigenous Affairs minister and the president of the Manitoba Métis Federation (MMF) signed a Memorandum of Understanding to work out the negotiating strategy for nationhood.[13]

The MMF, which is the most powerful of the Métis political organizations in Canada, had nearly gotten its own nation in 1992. It was part of a secret deal with Prime Minister Brian Mulroney in exchange for Métis support of the Charlottetown Accord, after the Assembly of First Nations withdrew its support.[14] The Métis Nation deal promised that the Métis would have their own legislature, equalization payments from Ottawa, control of membership and jurisdiction to enact legislation governing all Métis people in a new nation stretching west from Northwestern Ontario to British Columbia and north from Montana and North Dakota to the Northwest Territories. As the date of the 1992 referendum vote approached, the MMF negotiators struggled to hash out the details ahead of Mulroney's promised announcement of the $10 billion Métis settlement.[15]

When the Charlottetown Accord went down to defeat in the October referendum, the Métis Accord was thought dead, too. But the MMF didn't give up. It pushed the claim of nationhood to the Supreme Court of Canada, which delivered a favourable ruling in 2013.[16] How many people would be citizens of this new nation? Maybe 600,000. Maybe only 60,000. The terms of the negotiations? Also unknown. The Memorandum of Understanding (MOU) between the MMF and Canada stated all discussions would be *in camera* and confidential.[17] The groundwork for this self-governance agreement, just like the Métis Accord before it, was being negotiated in secret.

The negotiations between Indigenous Affairs and the Manitoba Métis Federation may have been all above board and scrupulously fair, but we don't know that. Negotiations held in secret, especially those that involve a great deal of power and money, are too easily clouded by suspicion. We all understand human nature and how it can bend unwisely in the presence of such temptation. And it doesn't help that the MMF, from its troubled early years after it was set up in 1969, had earned a reputation for its hard-edged brand of politics.[18]

The Riel rebellion annuity confusion

The resolution of a long-standing wrong against a Saskatchewan First Nation, dating back to the North-West Rebellion, seemed straightforward enough at the start. There was nothing secretive going on, but there were some surprising twists.

The treaties negotiated between the Crown and Indian bands from 1850 to 1929 all contained a single provision for empowerment of individuals within the band collective: the payment of an annuity to every man, woman and child in the band in perpetuity. Prime Minister John A. Macdonald ordered the $5 annuity payments revoked for fourteen bands located between Saskatoon and the Battlefords as punishment for their having allegedly aided the 1882 uprising led by Louis Riel. The annuity was reinstated in 1886, but in 2011, the Beardy's & Okemasis band (Beardy's for short) near Duck Lake filed a claim with the Indigenous Affairs Specific Claims Tribunal. The band's chief wanted compensation for the $4,250 the band members had been wrongfully denied, and compensation for losses.

There was little evidence that people in the Beardy's band had supported Riel's rebels and thus violated treaty terms. The sticky issue was whether a claim about annuities—an individual right—could be heard by the tribunal, which was mandated to hear only claims about collective rights. The tribunal judge eventually ruled in 2012 that the annuity was both an individual *and* a collective right,[19] heard the case, and awarded Beardy's $4.5 million in compensation.[20] The band council immediately established a trust for the money, and provided the roughly 300 individual band members with a one-time payment of $250 in March 2017. The band paid off the bank loan taken out to fund the claim and retained the rest to consolidate the band's debts and remodel the band's service station.[21]

The problem with this case is that it brought to the surface a conflict in First Nations communities that pitted the ephemeral individual rights against the might of collective rights. The chiefs and councils across Canada had largely ignored annuities over the past fifty years when they campaigned for modernization of health, education and economic development benefits for the collective. As long as the annuity was a piddling $4 or $5 (and it still is) being paid directly to individuals and hence not controlled by the band government, it was of little interest. The Beardy's case opened the door for the collective to claim the annuity, but the chiefs and councils of treaty bands weren't interested in going after the $5 annuities. They were claiming that the treaty annuity should have been modernized all along, and the Crown defaulted in not increasing the payments over time. This created a brand new source of claims against the Crown—compensation for annuity arrears.

By Indigenous Affairs' own policy, annuities could not be paid to the band (the collective) because "the treaties stipulate that the annuity must be paid in cash to members on an individual and annual basis."[22] However, IA's Tribunal on the Beardy's case ruled that the "mechanics of payment does not alter the nature of the right"[23] and found in favour of the collective.

Are annuities an individual right or a collective right? To clarify the issue, a spokesperson for Indigenous Affairs supplied this helpful response in the fall of 2017: "annuities are both a collective and individual rights issue."[24] With the current *Indian Act* silent on treaty annuities,[25] it appears that IA and its tribunal are relying on the language of treaties directing annuity payments to individuals (individual right), and on IA's policy that those individuals must be members of a treaty band to be eligible for the annuity (collective right).

Because ordinary First Nations people have no political voice at the federal level, there are no groups or organizations that they can count on to step up and defend the right of individuals to the annuity. There have been only government-funded organizations (AROs) that fight for collective rights. New legal actions being taken by chiefs and councils are signalling that ordinary men, women and children eligible for treaty annuities might well be on track to lose the sole individual right provided for them in the treaties.

Paying the piper

These three cases hardly cover Indigenous Affairs negotiators in glory, but there is more to be concerned about here than questionable negotiation skills. There's that old saying: he who pays the piper calls the tune. In other words, whoever is providing the money gets to call the shots. So, let's look again at the three examples to see who has been paying for what.

In the Qalipu Mi'kmaq First Nation negotiations, IA provided the Federation of Newfoundland Indians with funds so the small organization could hold up its end of the negotiations. But how much say did the Federation truly have in setting the terms and conditions for the new band, given the dramatic power imbalance between the two parties?

Regardless of how the Qalipu's toxic membership dispute ultimately gets sorted out, the band is now one of the largest First Nation groups in Canada, funded by IA and its multitude of federal co-delivery partners to the tune of about $12 million a year.[26] With that money, the Qalipu band, like all bands in Canada, is turned into an agent of Indigenous Affairs, with core funding from IA to staff the band office in Corner Brook and its three satellite offices. Their jobs are to deliver the multitude of programs and services from IA and other government departments to band members.

In the Métis Nation negotiations, there was no mystery about who was paying for what because it was spelled out in the MOU.[27] Indigenous Affairs was paying for the MMF's part of the negotiations, just as it had for the Federation of Newfoundland Indians. Unlike the tiny Newfoundland organization, however, the MMF had an annual budget of about $33 million in 2016. More than half was provided by IA and its co-delivery partners, and the rest came primarily from the Manitoba government.[28] Indigenous Affairs had also been actively helping to build the Métis Nation by funding recruitment and registration, as well as funding both sides of the negotiations. In the fall of 2018, IA provided $40 million to the provincial organization "to help the MMF transition from a special-interest advocacy group into a self-governing Indigenous Nation, the details of which still have to be negotiated with Ottawa."[29]

Who was calling the tune? Were the two parties actually in opposition or were they both on the same side of the table working out a chummy deal? Then you have to ask: who was representing the interests of Canada's ordinary Métis people in these negotiations? The Métis Nation of Ontario, for instance, was furious about being shut out of the new Métis Nation because the Manitoba organization was drawing boundaries that excluded all the Métis in central Ontario,[30] as well as in Quebec and the Maritimes.

The annuity claim by the Saskatchewan Beardy's band seemed like a reasonable case for compensation, but small bands often cannot afford to take on the costs of making claims. Indigenous Affairs has a department just for that purpose. It gives bands up to $3.5 million to research and file claims against the Crown. Once a claim is filed, IA provides an interest-free loan and gets first dibs on any successful settlement award for repayment. The outstanding loans provided to bands in order to make claims against the Canadian government were nudging the $1 billion mark in 2017.[31] The Beardy's & Okemasis band, however, did not lean on IA to fund its claim before the Tribunal. It cost them $1.4 million in legal and research fees, which they covered with a loan from the Royal Bank of Canada and repaid out of the settlement money.

The financial conflict of interest is less of an issue in the Beardy's case than the somewhat incestuous relationship between Indigenous Affairs and its agents (the five AROs and the FN band governments). The Specific Claims Tribunal was set up by IA and the Assembly of First Nations, and reports to the IA minister.[32] When cases like the Beardy's decision so clearly open the door to huge financial claims for annuity arrears by the same chiefs the AFN represents — and Indigenous Affairs is helpfully right at hand with buckets of cash and loans to get the claims rolling — it can raise questions about the seemingly limitless amount of money (and jobs) tied up in the claims.

We should not lose sight of the fact that all of this money being discussed is public money. Canadian taxpayers — Indigenous and non-Indigenous — are picking up the tab for both sides of the land claims and self-government negotiations, along with the settlements awarded as a result of those claims ($55.8 million in 2017).[33]

The lack of transparency around IA negotiations makes them vulnerable to suspicions about whether the people at the negotiating tables are acting in good faith. And it raises some legitimate questions about whose interests are really being served. We simply don't know, and that's a huge problem.

Deciding for themselves

In the aftermath of the surprise announcement in August 2017 that the Trudeau government was accelerating the move to self-governance as a means of reconciliation, former prime minister Paul Martin was adamant that whatever form of governance was going to be created, it had to be decided by Indigenous people themselves.

"It starts with the inherent right to self-government," said Martin. "Then what you begin to deal with is how are they going to effect it, how are they going to do it? And this has to be their decision. One of the first things First Nations will have to decide is if it is 614 communities or is it going to be 50 or 60 nations. All the decisions that have to be made in this area are theirs to make."[34]

If ordinary Indigenous people have no political power and no political voice at the federal level, it stands to reason that they will most certainly *not* be the ones deciding for themselves about reconciliation through self-governance and modern treaties. It will be Indigenous Affairs and the AROs and band representatives it funds that will be "negotiating" with each other.

In fact, the push for negotiations for self-government will mainly involve only one of the AROs, the Assembly of First Nations. The self-governance negotiations for the Inuit are largely signed off, complete with surrendering their rights to any further claims. And the Métis political leaders are focussing their energy on creating a Métis Nation that they will run. It is the future governance of nearly all the First Nations communities that is taking centre stage at the negotiation table, and there is no place at the table for the voices of ordinary Indigenous and non-Indigenous Canadians to be heard.

We are at a crucial turning point in the evolution of the relationship between Indigenous and non-Indigenous Canadians, and the scope of the self-governance negotiations has the potential to impact the lives of people all across the country. However, the impediment to change is more than the expansive powers of Indigenous Affairs, no matter how it rearranges the office furniture and changes the labels on the doors. It's also about money.

Endnotes to Chapter 2

1. INAC's Mandate, Presentation to the Natural Energy Board Modernization Expert Panel, January 20, 2017, Indigenous and Northern Affairs Canada, Annex A, 13.
2. Ibid., Annex B, 14.
3. Ibid., 3.
4. Modern Treaty Implementation: Implications for Federal Departments and Agencies, Aboriginal Affairs and Northern Development Canada, Modern Treaty Training for Federal Officials, February 26, 2014, 5.
5. Ibid., 6.
6. Ibid.
7. Ibid.
8. Prime Minister's Office, New Ministers to support the renewed relationship with Indigenous Peoples, August 28, 2017, http://pm.gc.ca/eng/news/2017/08/28/new-ministers-support-renewed-relationship-indigenous-peoples.
9. Suzanne Owen, 2017, "Unsettled Natives in the Newfoundland Imaginary," in *Handbook of Indigenous Religion(s)*, Greg Johnson and Siv Ellen Kraft, eds., Brill, 223.
10. Ibid., 224.
11. Read more about Bill C-25, the Qalipu Mi'kmaq First Nation Act, May 1, 2014, openparliament.ca/bills/41-2/C-25.
12. Justin Brake, "Qalipu enrolment outcome 'next big reconciliation issue' in Canada: Chief," theindependent.ca/2017/02/24/qalipu enrolment, February 24, 2017.
13. Memorandum of Understanding [MOU] on Advancing Reconciliation between the Manitoba Métis Federation Inc. and Her Majesty the Queen in Right of Canada, 2017.
14. Sheila Jones Morrison, 1995, *Rotten to the Core: The Politics of the Manitoba Métis Federation*, 101060 (an imprint of J. Gordon Shillingford Publishing), 11.
15. Ibid., 21.
16. Manitoba Métis Federation *v* Canada (Attorney General), 2013 SCC 14 [2013] 1 S.C.R. 623, Docket 33880, March 8, 2013.
17. Ibid., Section 10, Section 12.
18. Jones Morrison, 1995.
19. Reasons for Decision, Beardy's & Okemasis band #96 and #97 *v* Her Majesty the Queen in the Right of Canada, Claim SCT-5001-11, 2012, 5.
20. Ibid., 45.
21. "Beardy's First Nation distributes, invests Specific Claims Tribunal treaty funds," *Clark's Crossing Gazette*, February 15, 2017, http://ccgazette.ca/2017/02/15/beardys-first-nation-distributes-invests-specific-claims-tribunal-treaty-funds/.
22. Section 6.3.3, Alternative delivery models, Evaluation of Indian Moneys, Estates and Treaty Annuities, Indigenous and Northern Affairs Canada, April 2013, 64.
23. Reasons for Decision, Beardy's & Okemasis band #96 and #97 *v* Her Majesty the Queen in the Right of Canada, Claim SCT-5001-11, 2015, 74.
24. Media Relations, Indigenous and Northern Affairs Canada, email communication with the author, September 8, 2017.
25. The *Indian Act* of 1985 contains a single sentence (Section 72) stating that "Treaty money" is payable out of the federal government's Consolidated Revenue Fund. It is silent on terms and

conditions of annuity payments in general. Annuities are mentioned only twice: once in relation to spousal support (Section 68) and once regarding payouts when a person ceases being a band member (Section 15).

26 Qalipu Mi'kmaq First Nation, 2017–18, Annual Report, p 10, http://qalipu.ca/qalipu/wp-content/uploads/2018/08/AR%202017-2018_web.pdf.

27 MOU MMF and Canada, 2017, Section 8.

28 Non-Consolidated Financial Statement, Manitoba Métis Federation, March 31, 2016, 5.
The MMF generates about $1.5-million of own-revenue, including fundraising, rents and investments.

29 Gloria Galloway, 2018, "Ottawa moves forward with historic plans for Métis self-government," *The Globe and Mail*, September 22, 2018, https://www.theglobeandmail.com/politics/article-ottawa-moves-forward-with-historic-plans-for-metis-self-government/.

30 Tony Balfour, 2013, "For the Record… On Métis Identity and Citizenship Within the Métis Nation," in *aboriginal policy studies*, Vol. 2, no. 2: 128–141.

31 Financial Statements for the Year Ended March 31, 2017 (unaudited), Indigenous and Northern Affairs Canada, Loans and interest receivable, https://www.aadnc-aandc.gc.ca/eng/1506088853301/1506088945817#chp12.

32 Preamble, *Specific Claims Tribunal Act*, 2008, 1.

33 INAC Financial Statements 2017.

34 Paul Martin interview on CBC Radio's *The House*, September 2, 2017.

3
IA+, CANADA'S "SUPER-PROVINCE"

The Indigenous Affairs department didn't start out with far-reaching powers. It didn't even exist as a separate department until 1966. Before that, the Indian Affairs Branch was part of the Department of Citizenship and Immigration, having been moved previously from the departments of the Interior and of Mines and Resources.[1]

When the Department of Indian Affairs and Northern Development (DIAND) became a stand-alone department, it had three branches: Indian Affairs, Northern Administration and Parks. The Indian Affairs Branch continued with the responsibilities it had for Canada's "Indian and Eskimo people" under the Citizenship department.[2] The Northern Administration Branch was in charge of services to Northerners, including assisting with administration of the territorial governments of the Yukon and North-West Territories.[3] The Parks Branch looked after National Parks and Historic Sites, the National Battlefields Commission and the Canadian Wildlife Service.[4]

In 1966–67, the IA Branch within DIAND had a client base of about 192,000 people: 180,000 Status Indians living on reserves,[5] which accounted for about 80 percent of all Status Indians in Canada,[6] and about 12,000 northern Inuit.[7] Métis people were not the IA Branch's responsibility at that time, nor were off-reserve Status Indians, non-Status Indians or southern Inuit.

The new DIAND department had a modest budget of $197.4 million,[8] of which just over half ($104.7 million)[9] was allocated to the IA Branch for delivering programs and services to its Indian and Inuit client base. The IA Branch also had two federal co-delivery partners for that fiscal year. The Medical Services Branch of Health and Welfare Canada covered health care for Indians and Inuit at some $25 million per year,[10] and Central Mortgage and Housing Corporation (CMHC) was contributing about $2 million for on-reserve housing.[11] That meant that IA plus its two co-delivery partners (IA+) were spending about $131.7 million in 1966–67 on delivering programs and services for 192,000 people, or about $690 per client.

Fast-forward fifty years to 2017–18. Much had changed. The Indigenous Affairs Branch had become Indigenous Affairs (IA). The responsibilities for parks and wildlife were long gone; the territorial governments were managing their own affairs. Non-Indigenous programming, which accounted for less than two percent of the department's budget,[12] was transferred to another department in 2018.

IA's budget for 2017–18 was $10.056 billion.[13] However, the number of federal co-delivery partners had jumped to thirty-three. How much were IA plus its co-delivery partners (IA+) spending on delivering Indigenous programs and services that fiscal year? That turns out to be a challenging question to answer.

Indigenous Affairs stopped identifying the department's multiple co-delivery partners, with the last publicly available list in the IA Estimates for 2004–05.[14] At that time, IA had thirteen co-delivery partners: Health Canada, Human Resources Development Canada (HRDC), CMHC, Solicitor General, Canadian Heritage, Fisheries and Oceans, Industry, Correctional Services, Natural Resources, Justice, Privy Council, National Defence and Public Safety. Spending on Indigenous programs and services for Indigenous Affairs plus thirteen co-delivery partners (IA+) totalled $8.8 billion, of which $5.8 billion came from IA and another $3 billion from the other federal departments and agencies.[15]

Up until 2006, which coincided with the election of the Stephen Harper government, IA provided a breakdown of how much each co-delivery partner spent on delivering Indigenous programs and services, as well as contact information for each department and agency. Perhaps there were political reasons, either in cabinet or in the IA department, to want to obscure program spending. In the thirteen years between 2004–05 and 2017–18, IA's spending nearly doubled from $5.8 billion to more than $10 billion.[16] The number of co-delivery partners had jumped from thirteen to thirty-three.

A fog of confusion over how much is being spent and by which government departments can serve as a useful shield against accountability and politically problematic questions. According to a spokesperson for IA (Indigenous Services and Crown-Indigenous Relations) in 2018, no "official" list of co-delivery partners is available.[17] There must, however, have been an official list somewhere for the department to specify in 2017 that IA had thirty-three co-delivery partners.[18] When I pressed for more information in 2019, the Policy and Strategic Direction Branch responded by providing a link to the government's Main Estimates covering all 320 departments and agencies, and suggested, more or less, that I go figure it out for myself.[19]

It is possible, in the absence of assistance from IA officials, to arrive at a reasonable approximation of the total IA+ spending for 2017–18 by extrapolating from the known spending in 2004–05 and 2017–18. For instance, we know that IA's budget for 2017–18 was $10.057 billion. Health Canada remained the largest co-delivery partner, spending $3.364 billion delivering Indigenous health care programs that same year. For brevity, the calculation of spending for the other thirty-two co-delivery partners, totalling about $5,680 billion, is detailed in Appendix A. The result, admittedly rudimentary, puts the total spending in 2017–18 for IA+ (IA plus Health Canada plus its thirty-two other co-delivery partners) at about $19.1 billion.

Counting the clients

In 1966, the IA+ client base — the Indigenous people eligible for IA+ programs and services — covered 192,000 Indian and Inuit people. In 2017–18, the number was significantly higher, partly because of population growth, an expansion of services to a wider range of Inuit and First Nations people, and the inclusion of Métis people in 1982 as one the three constitutionally recognized Aboriginal groups in Canada.

By the 2016 Census conducted by Statistics Canada, more than 1.6 million people self-identified as Aboriginal (Indigenous), or about 4.9 percent of Canada's population.[20] However, not all of them were included in the IA client base, which is the same client base as for IA+.

The numbers used by IA are more precise than Stats Canada numbers. Status (Registered) and Treaty Indians (who must also be Status to be eligible for treaty annuity payments) are all clients of IA, whether they live on or off reserves. According to IA, the Registered Indian population was 970,562 people as of December 31, 2016.[21] This aligns fairly closely with the 977,230 people who self-identified as First Nations in the 2016 census.

The same census lists 65,025 Inuit in Canada, with about half living in Nunavut. However, programs and services for the Inuit living in Nunavut are provided through federal transfers to the Nunavut territorial government, not through IA. Subtracting the Nunavut Inuit population of about 32,300[22] from the national Inuit population means about half of Inuit (about 32,730) remain IA clients.

Calculating the Métis client base is particularly difficult because there is considerable disagreement across the country over Métis identity. Different Métis organizations have different definitions of who qualifies as Métis.

There are five provincial Métis organizations that receive a significant portion of their funding from the provinces, with additional programs funded by IA+. If we consider participation in programs and services delivered by IA+ as a requirement for people to be considered part of its client base, we are not much farther ahead. There is no centralized, intra-provincial database or information-sharing mechanism for Métis programs and policies that can produce hard numbers.[23]

Many of the 587,545 Métis who self-identified in the 2016 Census may have had nothing to do with the Métis political organizations, or if they did, they might be accessing only provincially funded programs. For instance, Ontario had the largest number of self-identified Métis, at 120,585 people.[24] However, the provincial Métis representative organization, the Métis Nation of Ontario, had a registry of only 20,000 Métis citizens[25] who may or may not have been receiving federally funded IA+ programs and services. Similarly, according to the Census, 89,355 Manitobans identified as Métis,[26] however the Manitoba Métis Federation reportedly had about 36,000 people as members.[27] There could be some 50,000 Métis people in Canada who receive federal services from IA+, or maybe 150,000. It is a guess, at best.

Using the numbers from IA on First Nations people and for Inuit outside Nunavut, and a guesstimate of 150,000 Métis, we arrive at a client base for IA+ of about 1.15 million people, or about 3.1 percent of Canada's population of 36.7 million people.[28]

In 1966–67, IA+ spending per client averaged about $690. In 2017–18, IA+ spending of an estimated $19.1 billion for 1.15 million people averaged about $16,609 per client.

Having arrived at an approximation of IA+ spending and the number of people eligible for Indigenous programs and services, what does it tell us—beyond the obvious fact that spending has increased significantly over the past fifty years—to help us better understand the world of Indigenous politics?

Accounting for a Canadian "super-province"

Like all federal government departments, Indigenous Affairs answers to the Prime Minister and Cabinet of the government of the day. However, it is unique in Canada in terms of its mandate and how it operates. Unlike other government departments, IA does not provide specific services to Canadians in general as do, for instance, the departments of Justice, Natural Resources or Oceans and Fisheries. Rather IA provides a wide range of services to a specific Indigenous client base, and this is where all the co-delivery partners come in.

It doesn't really matter that IA has been divided into Indigenous Services and Crown-Indigenous Relations, or if more or fewer federal departments and agencies are co-delivery partners. Nor is it significant that 80 percent of Health Canada's budget and its Indigenous programs were transferred to Indigenous Services for 2018–19.[29] The IA departments and all the co-delivery partners still constitute the same Indigenous Affairs Plus (IA+).

IA+ provides a vast range of birth-to-death services for its Indigenous client base, from infant care[30] to settlement of estates for the deceased.[31] It delivers education, health care and social services, which are typically provincial responsibilities. Given that more than 80 percent of its spending in First Nations communities is for "basic, province-type services,"[32] IA+ is more like a federally run "province."

This idea is worth examining. If all the federal Indigenous programs and services were gathered together and administered by the "province" of IA+, how would it stack up against Canada's real provinces and territories?

In 2017–18, the Canadian government paid out $72.9 billion in annual federal transfers to provinces and territories for health transfers, equalization payments and more.[33] If we go with the $19.1 billion figure as the equivalent of a federal transfer to IA+, it would sit just behind Ontario ($21.1 billion) and Quebec ($22.7 billion) in federal transfers,[34] and way ahead of fourth place British Columbia at $6.7 billion.[35] In other words, if IA+ were a province, it would be the third-largest province in Canada in terms of federal spending.[36]

The per capita spending for IA+ of $16,609 might sound high, but consider that the per capita federal transfers in 2017–18 to the Yukon ($25,229), North West Territories ($29,044) and Nunavut ($41,745) were significantly higher.[37] These numbers reflect the high cost of delivering territorial governance, programs and services to a small population spread out over the vast regions of the North.

It is not unreasonable to question the soundness of the $19.1 billion figure for IA+ spending when it is not backed by hard numbers provided by the federal government. However, consider that Indigenous Affairs and Health Canada together accounted for $13.4 billion[38] in Indigenous spending in 2017–18. Those are hard numbers. And that still leaves spending by thirty-two more co-delivery partners to account for.

An estimate of spending by IA+ of about $19.1 billion could be a bit less or a bit more. That number does not, for instance, include new spending announced in the spring of 2018 of $4.8 billion for IA+ over five years.[39] Nor does it include another $1.7 billion over ten years for Indigenous Early Learning and Child Care Framework announced in the fall of 2018.[40]

The Trudeau government was promising more "investment" in Indigenous programs and services, over and above what had already been announced. It was setting up a scenario where, over the next few years, IA+ could surpass Quebec to become Canada's largest "province."

With jurisdictional reach over almost all of Canada and spending rivalling Quebec and Ontario, IA+ can indeed be considered a uniquely powerful "super-province." But it is one whose citizens are uniquely powerless.

"Citizens" who don't count

Even though IA+ holds inordinate power over the lives of people in First Nations and Inuit communities from birth to death, the "citizens" of IA+ have no say in how it operates. Not a single person in the IA+ administration is elected by ordinary Indigenous people to represent their interests. Not one.

Indigenous people cannot express their dissatisfaction with the IA+ administration by throwing it out and electing one more to their liking. There are no structural mechanisms built into the federally run "province" of IA+ whereby its "citizens" can demand their voices be heard or hold the administration accountable to them. They are voiceless and powerless.

It would be as if citizens of, say, New Brunswick or Saskatchewan were governed by a bureaucracy in Ottawa, without any elected officials chosen by the people to represent them. Such a situation would justifiably be considered an outrageous affront to democracy.

From the time of Prime Minister John A. Macdonald and the imposition of the *Indian Act* of 1867, the federal government has treated Indigenous people as wards of the state deemed incapable of making informed decisions for themselves. Policy was imposed from the top down. It still is.

Prime Minister Justin Trudeau was right when he told the UN leaders in 2017 that there was "a rare and precious opportunity to act" on reconciliation.[41] However, reconciliation as envisioned in the fine words of the Trudeau government and its ministers may not be the long-awaited and much-discussed road to reconciliation. It is entirely possible that negotiations over self-governance and Indigenous nation-building—one that currently excludes the very people who will be governed by the new system—will have the opposite effect. Instead, we may well be seeing the ground laid for a future prime minister to stand in the House of Commons and apologize, yet again, for the harm done to Canada's Indigenous people for what, as was the case with Indian Residential Schools, the federal government thought seemed like a good idea at the time.

The modern history of Indigenous politics in Canada is only a half-century deep. Once we walk through the rocky political landscape of the past fifty years, we will have a better understanding of how ordinary Indigenous people lost their political voice and their power…and how they can get it back.

Endnotes to Chapter 3

1. Federal Departments of Indigenous and Northern Affairs (edited July 18, 2018), https://www.thecanadianencyclopedia.ca/en/article/aboriginal-affairs-and-northern-development-canada/.
2. DIAND, Indian Affairs and Northern Development Annual Report, Fiscal Year 1966–67, Government of Canada.
3. Ibid., 79.
4. Ibid., 113.
5. G. Graham-Cumming, 1966, Medical Liaison Officer, *Highlights of Indian Vital Statistics 1966*, Medical Services, Department of National Health and Welfare, Government of Canada, 1. Total Indian population, 1966: 225,372.
6. DIAND 1966–67, 55. Note that off-reserve First Nations people were not considered the responsibility of Indian Affairs.
7. Saku, James C., 1999, Aboriginal Census Data in Canada: A Research Note, *The Canadian Journal of Native Studies* XIX, 2 (1999): 370. Note that census data varied, depending on how ethnicity questions changed. The census identified 11,835 Inuit in 1961 and 17,550 Inuit in 1971.
8. DIAND, 1966–67, 113.
9. Ibid.
10. Public Health, Welfare and Security, Statistics Canada, 1963–64, 310. Reliable information for 1965–66 does not appear to be readily available. https://www66.statcan.gc.ca/eng/1963-64/196303340310_p.%20310.pdf.
11. DIAND, Press Release, January 4, 1968, volume 8881, file 55/29-2. Indian Affairs Minister Arthur Laing announces that almost $2 million would be spent that year to build houses on Indian reserves.
12. The construction of the Canadian High Arctic Research Station, for instance, does not count as Indigenous program spending.
13. INAC, Indigenous and Northern Affairs Canada: 2017–18 Departmental Plan, Government of Canada, https://www.aadnc-aandc.gc.ca/eng/1483561566667/1483561606216.
14. INAC, 2004–05 Estimates, Federal Partners, 14, http://publications.gc.ca/collections/collection_2015/aadnc-aandc/R1-42-2004-eng.pdf.
15. Ibid.
16. INAC, 2017–18 Departmental Plan, 51, https://www.aadnc-aandc.gc.ca/eng/1483561566667/1483561606216#ps.
17. Public Affairs, Department of Crown-Indigenous Relations and Northern Affairs (CIRNA) and the Department of Indigenous Services Canada (ISC), Government of Canada, email communication with author, October 9, 2018.
18. INAC's Mandate, Presentation to the Natural Energy Board Modernization Expert Panel, January 20, 2017, Indigenous and Northern Affairs Canada, 2.
19. Public Affairs, ISC/CIRNA, email communications with author, March 20, 2019.
20. Aboriginal peoples in Canada: Key results from the 2016 Census, Statistics Canada, October 25, 2017.
21. INAC, 2017, Registered Indian Population by Sex and Residence, https://www.aadnc-aandc.gc.ca/eng/1523286391452/1523286414623#tbc7.
22. Nunavut Quick Facts, July 2017, http://www.stats.gov.nu.ca/en/home.aspx.

23 Yvonne Poitras Pratt, et al., 2017, *Painting a Picture of the Métis Homeland*, Rupertsland Institute, 3. http://www.rupertsland.org/wp-content/uploads/2017/11/Painting_a_Picture_of_the_Metis_Homeland.pdf.

24 Aboriginal peoples in Canada: Key results from the 2016 Census, Statistics Canada, https://www150.statcan.gc.ca/n1/daily-quotidien/171025/dq171025a-eng.htm.

25 Métis Nation of Ontario website, http://www.metisnation.org/about-the-mno/the-m%c3%a9tis-nation-of-ontario/.

26 Aboriginal peoples in Canada: Key results from the 2016 Census, Statistics Canada, https://www150.statcan.gc.ca/n1/daily-quotidien/171025/dq171025a-eng.htm.

27 Alexandra Paul, "400 Métis families get chance to buy first home," *Winnipeg Free Press*, February 15, 2019, https://www.winnipegfreepress.com/local/new-grant-offers-metis-15000-to-buy-first-homes-505907982.html.

28 Statistics Canada, Canada at a Glance 2018, https://www150.statcan.gc.ca/n1/pub/12-581-x/2018000/pop-eng.htm.

29 Indigenous Services Canada, Departmental Plan 2018–19, p 33, https://www.sac-isc.gc.ca/eng/1523374573623/1523904791460#chp9.

30 INAC, Sub-Program 2.2.3: First Nations child and Family Services, 2017–18, https://www.aadnc-aandc.gc.ca/eng/1483561667907/1483561705638#2_2_2.

31 INAC, Sub-Program 2.3.2: Estates, 2017–18. "The Indian Act provides the Minister of Indigenous and Northern Affairs Canada with exclusive jurisdiction over the administration of estates for First Nations individuals who were ordinarily resident on reserve at the time of their death" and "INAC's role includes approving a will or declaring a will to be void," https://www.aadnc-aandc.gc.ca/eng/1483561667907/1483561705638#2_3_2.

32 INAC, 2004–05 Estimates, 14.

33 Finance Canada, Federal Support for Provinces and Territories (2009–2019), https://www.fin.gc.ca/fedprov/mtp-eng.asp.

34 Finance Canada (2009–2019).

35 Ibid.

36 Appendix B: Federal transfers to IA+, provinces and territories, 2017–18.

37 Finance Canada (2009–2019).,

38 INAC, 2017–18 Departmental Plan, $10.057-billion: Health Canada Indigenous programs 3.1, 3.2 and 3.3 total $$3,133,980,043, plus 80% of Internal Services ($229,534,560) totals $3,363,514,603 or $3.364-billion, https://www.canada.ca/en/health-canada/corporate/transparency/corporate-management-reporting/report-plans-priorities/2017-2018-report-plans-priorities.html#a72.

39 Government of Canada, 2018–19 Budget: Equality + Growth, A Strong Middle Class, p145–146, https://www.budget.gc.ca/2018/docs/plan/budget-2018-en.pdf.

40 Government of Canada, News Release, September 17, 2018, Government of Canada, Assembly of First Nations, Inuit Tapiriit Kanatami and Métis National Council announce the first Indigenous Early Learning and Child Care Framework, https://www.canada.ca/en/employment-social-development/news/2018/09/government-of-canada-assembly-of-first-nations-inuit-tapiriit-kanatami-and-metis-national-council-announce-the-first-indigenous-early-learning-and-.html.

41 Bruce Campion-Smith, "Canada struggles to improve conditions for Indigenous people, Trudeau tells the UN," *The Toronto Star*, September 21, 2017.

4
THE SMALL POLITICS OF '66

There was no mistaking who held all the power in First Nations communities well into the 1960s. Under the powers of the *Indian Act* of 1876,¹ an Indian Agent could literally rule as a tyrant over the lives of the band (or bands) he managed, at a time when the majority of Status Indians (Registered Indians) lived on reserves. The Indian Agent had the power to punish and reward as he deemed fit. He could unilaterally change Indian names to European ones, prevent Indians from leaving the reserve by refusing to issue mandatory passes, ban traditional ceremonies, withhold rations as retribution, prevent reserve residents from forming political organizations, and much more.²

At that time, some three-quarters of Status Indians in Canada counted as Treaty Indians.³ The bands signing on to treaties ceded their traditional lands to the Crown in exchange for ongoing livelihood supports in the form of annuities and the freedom to continue hunting, fishing and trapping, along with other treaty provisions. Some of the land was specifically reserved for them, and thus began the formalized rule of the Indian Agent on reserves.

In 1869, the Indian Affairs Branch introduced an act authorizing the election of a chief and councillors for each band every three years,⁴ with only men over the age of twenty-three allowed to vote. The electoral system was a way for IA to displace traditional tribal governance that included women's councils and consensus decision-making. It would, according to the act, "pave the way to the establishment of simple municipal institutions."⁵

This was certainly not the model of traditional governance practised by First Nations prior to settlement, when individuals and families had considerable autonomy within the collective. The community members relied on each other to survive and to thrive, and carefully chose wise leaders. Noted Indian leader Big Bear, for instance, was groomed from the time he was a child to succeed his father as chief, and his leadership qualities were recognized early on. A leader's success would be measured by the number of followers in his band, and should he abuse his position or fail his followers, they were free to vote with their feet and move to a community with better leadership.⁶ That freedom ended with the imposition of the *Indian Act* of 1876, and the regulation of reserves under the control of Indian Agents. Elections were an alien adversarial governance system that reserve residents had no choice but to accept, since IA or its agents simply appointed chiefs and councils if they didn't.

People living under the rule of the Indian Agent had little recourse in the face of abuses of authority, not when Indian Affairs required that all complaints and inquiries by band members be directed to IA through the local agent. Later amendments to the Act gave strengthened control of government officials over elections by giving Indian Agents powers to call elections, oversee them, and to cast the deciding vote in band council elections in the event of a tie.⁷

The *Indian Act* was not a treaty or alliance between the Crown and Indians. It was legislation written by the federal government to clarify the powers of the Crown over Indians and reserve lands, and legal authority to enact the terms of the treaties and the policy priorities of the government of the day. The lines of authority flowed only in one direction—from the top down. There was no provision in the act through which individuals or collectives living under the *Indian Act* could demand their voices be heard. Indian Affairs was accountable to the government of the day; it was not accountable to the people living under the Act.

The chiefs and band councils were given very limited powers by Indian Affairs, such as keeping down the weeds on the reserve and preventing the trespass of cattle. If the chief and council got ideas about making changes on the reserve, even simple ones, they had to first be approved by the Superintendent of Indian Affairs (later by the Indian Affairs minister). The need to get written authorization from Ottawa tended to slow everything down long enough to drain away any enthusiasm or initiative, and give the Indian Agent time to deal with "troublemakers" in his own way.

One band in northern Alberta did not have to deal with an Indian Agent until 1957.⁸ Even though the Slavey people of Hay Lake, near the border with the Northwest Territories, signed onto Treaty 8 in 1899, they remained a nomadic people, following the moose and trapping for furs to trade with the Hudson's Bay Company. Leading the Slavey people was Chief Harry Chonkolay, a hereditary leader who had been trained from youth for the role he finally assumed in 1938.⁹

The people of the Slavey community depended on each other for survival, as did all the bands before the settlers came. Everybody had a valued role to play, even the children.

"We lived happily," Chonkolay said in the 1970s,¹⁰ speaking through an interpreter, recalling that band members lived in Alberta in the summer and moved into British Columbia for the winter. As a traditional headman, he was not paid for his leadership. He hunted, trapped, fished, ranched and logged, along with the other men in the band.¹¹

But life changed for Chonkolay and his people when they got reserve land and the Oblate missionaries built a large residential school there in 1952.

Indian Affairs wanted the Slavey children in school, which meant families had to stay put in the community. IA built 100 one-room log cabins and an Indian Agent moved in. He took over administering the rations, pensions, family allowance payments and other tasks that had been performed by the Hudson's Bay Company on behalf of Indian Affairs since the 1920s.[12]

By 1963, the entire remote community was living on monthly welfare of about twenty dollars per family. They had switched from a subsistence-based, nomadic lifestyle of living on the land to a subsistence-based, fixed lifestyle on the reserve that was completely dependent on government handouts. The entire process of conversion from independence to total dependency had taken only ten years.[13]

The band's medicine man Willie Denechoan lamented at the time, "We are different than we used to be. The government has us in a little box, with a lid on it. Every now and then they open the lid and do something to us and close it again."[14]

Fed up with being invisible, trapped on the reserve and living in the abject poverty of welfare dependency, every able-bodied Slavey man from Hay Lake made the long trip south to Edmonton in early February 1965. There was no road to the reserve, so more than 100 men boarded school buses and rode the sixty miles of winter ice roads out to a gravel road, and then south 600 miles to the city. Few of the men spoke English, including the chief, and most had never been in a city before. But once there, they followed Chief Chonkolay in a silent, frozen march, down the middle of the street in downtown Edmonton to the Alberta legislature to confront Premier Ernest Manning. The men marched because they wanted jobs, they said, not welfare.[15]

The roughly dressed men in their oil-stained coats marching four abreast were, no doubt, a strange sight in the city's main thoroughfare, but it is unlikely many people knew what to make of the parade. Indians were largely invisible to most of Canadian society.

Manning met Chonkolay and a couple of the younger men who could speak English and act as interpreters. The premier politely reminded them that the band was the responsibility of the federal government, not the province, but Manning did agree to send a telegram to Prime Minister Lester Pearson demanding action from the federal government.[16]

Indian Affairs investigators flew into Hay Lake a week later and, according to author Heather Robertson, what they found was infinitely worse than what the Slavey men had described to the premier:

"Houses had no furniture but metal tubs on wood stoves for melting snow for drinking water, a few squalid, sagging beds covered with coats and dirty blankets, plywood and cardboard peeling off the floors, leaky roofs. Children, ragged and dirty, often half-naked at below-zero temperatures, pulled sleds loaded with firewood. A smell of rot, filth, smoke, wet clothes, permeated the fetid air in the log homes, large one-room buildings housing ten to fifteen people... From the rafters, inside, hung strips of smoked moose meat and dried fish — the staple diet of the people."[17]

The attention drawn by the march in Edmonton, said Robertson, was intended to shout out to the rest of the country to look at the conditions in which they lived. They wanted to be seen and acknowledged.

"This was the second phase of the march — an explanation, at least in part, of why the Indians went to Edmonton. Their main purpose was not jobs, not training, not angry demands but just to say: 'Look at me.'"[18]

A few things had stayed the same after the Slavey people were anchored to a single piece of land because of the Oblate missionary school. Chonkolay continued as hereditary chief, and he still fit into his treaty suit,[19] given to him by Indian Affairs in 1939 to honour the treaty term that the chief of each band receive a new suit.

"The way of life had changed only in one respect," wrote Robertson, "Work was missing now. The people were forced to live in an idleness they'd never experienced before. Their only apparent value or use was to produce children to fill the school. The value of the children changed. Out on the trap line, children had been valuable and useful, but now they were a liability, increasing the rations required without being able to contribute to the productivity of the family. This was the little box the Slaveys found themselves in in 1963. There was no prospect that this way of life would ever change."[20]

The Indian Affairs investigators took a good look at the Hay Lake reserve over three days, fired the Indian Agent and left. They had looked inside the box, but quickly closed the lid. They had no solution for men who no longer had a role as providers to their families, and no role as warriors to protect their families and fellow band members. Those roles were now covered by Indian Affairs. In many cases, the only new role available for men that preserved their dignity was working for the Indian Agent or serving on the band council. Challenging the system seemed impossible.

Cree activist Harold Cardinal was just a teenager in the 1950s when he first got involved in Indian politics in Alberta. His father had long been involved in the Indian Association of Alberta, and Cardinal knew the kind of grief faced by early Indian leaders.

"The Indian agent," said Cardinal in 1969, "dead set against any successful Indian organization, actively worked against the leaders of the day. He had many weapons and never hesitated to use them. Sometimes he openly threatened to punish people who persisted in organizational efforts. More often he used subtle weapons such as delaying relief payments or rations to show the Indians which way the wind was blowing."[21]

Still, said Cardinal, they persisted.

"The first leaders were genuine heroes. They had guts and needed them. They had no money; they had no access to skilled and trained advisors; they were harassed by white government officials and the police and they were doubted by their own people. Yet they fought on."[22]

Indians tried to organize politically in the 1920s. In response, the federal government added a new section to the *Indian Act* in 1929 prohibiting Indians from hiring lawyers or raising funds to make claims against the government without a licence from the IA superintendent.[23] The government did not outright ban political organizing, but instead criminalized seeking legal help. And it clearly signalled that the government did not want Indians gathering for political purposes or organizing in opposition of its decisions.[24] Given that travelling any distance at that time was difficult, that there was no money to pay people to attend meetings, and that people might be punished by the Agent for attending meetings, it was a struggle to get organized.

From the time the Indian Association of Alberta (IAA) was founded in 1939, the organization "was concerned, on an every-day level with treaty rights."[25] The people placed great faith in the chiefs and headmen who had negotiated the treaty terms, and held a similar faith in the power of the treaties for their security. The association also faced the challenge of moving past long-standing tribal enmities in efforts to organize, such as the bloody history of wars between the Blackfoot and Plains Cree. Not enough time had yet passed in the 1930s for people to forgive and forget.[26]

The Alberta association developed strong connections with the League of Indians of Western Canada, an offshoot of the League of Indians of Canada, which had been founded in Six Nations territory in Ontario in 1918. It also allied itself with political reform movements such as the United Farmers of Alberta and the Cooperative Commonwealth Federation (the forerunner of the New Democratic Party).[27] The IAA made its mark on the national political stage in the 1940s and 1950s. It was recognized as a leader in Indian politics, especially under the leadership of Jim Gladstone, a Cree adopted by the Blackfoot in 1887 when he was a baby. He finally succeeded in bringing both tribes together into one organization. In 1958, Prime Minister John Diefenbaker made Gladstone the first Status Indian appointed to the Senate, where he fought to get Indians the right to vote in federal elections. That right was granted in 1960, but it changed little of what was happening on the ground. At the reserve level, the chief and council still had only token powers that were routinely overridden by the Indian Agent or Indian Affairs. But it was better than nothing.

James Burke, a former staffer with the Manitoba Indian Brotherhood (MIB), also described the subsistence life on reserves in the 1960s as "better than nothing."[28] Although there was some migration to urban centres, encouraged by Indian Affairs as part of its assimilation policies, most people stayed on the reserves and held onto their faith that their protection flowed from the treaties their long-gone leaders had signed.

The promises in the treaties—livestock, farm tools, fishing nets, bullets and other tools, along with education, protection against famine and pestilence, and a medicine chest provision—were, in effect, gradually "modernized" over the years to become the many programs and services being delivered by Indian Affairs. In the mid-1960s, as the Indian Affairs branch of Citizenship and Immigration became a stand-alone department, it was spending over $130 million on supports for Indians on reserves across the county, but it was hard to tell from the shabby housing and hardscrabble living conditions.

"Given all this," said Burke, "one would think that the Indian's special status is more of a millstone than a crutch. Not from the Indian standpoint, though, for poor housing is better than no housing, inadequate education is better than no education, and inferior medical care is better than no medical care."[29]

Indian Affairs was finding it harder in the 1960s to ignore growing public awareness that people on most reserves—80 percent of Canada's Indian population—were deeply impoverished. The civil rights movement in the United States had awakened the Canadian consciousness, at least a bit, to racial oppression in their own country. People like the Slaveys were no longer quite as invisible as they used to be. To demonstrate that Indians were being consulted on policy, Indian Affairs set up provincial and national advisory councils, and paid the travel costs for band council members to attend meetings. They were, according to Harold Cardinal, pointless exercises in which IA told Indians what the branch had already decided to do, and then cranked out propaganda to Parliament and the public about how they were consulting with Indians about everything. The councils were terminated in 1968.

"The Indian people themselves insisted they be dropped," said Cardinal. "All they accomplished, for all their government doubletalk, was the embarrassment of many sincere but deceived Indian workers."[30]

Harold Cardinal was only twenty-four years old when he was elected president of the Indian Association of Alberta (IAA) in 1968, which meant dropping out of university in Quebec where he was studying sociology. The young man with a big grin, usually seen wearing a buckskin jacket, grew up on the Sucker Creek reserve near High Prairie in northwestern Alberta. He had been trained by his father and the elders about the importance of the treaties and traditional laws.

Cardinal and other Indian leaders knew that if they wanted to make themselves heard in Ottawa, they were going to need real money to do it. The old days were over. No more attempting to organize by hitching rides to neighbouring reserves, sleeping on people's sofas, and picking up a few dollars here and there for memberships. No more hiding from the Indian Agent and risking arrest for being off the reserve without a pass.

"We first approached the Department of Indian Affairs for help," Cardinal admitted. "Of course, we were promptly refused. It seems that they didn't have any money in their budget allocated for the purposes of Indian organizations."[31]

The influence of the IAA had waned since the 1950s, but the small provincial Indian organizations in Manitoba, Saskatchewan, Alberta and BC saw themselves as voices for the bands. It would have made sense for the bands to provide financial support for political organizing, but that wasn't possible. According to Cardinal, Indian Affairs had instituted a policy that limited funding for Indian organizations to twenty-five cents per person in each band.[32] Even if a few bands could scrape together the allowed amount to donate to their own organizations, it still wouldn't have amounted to a hill of beans.

Nonetheless, the provincial Indian organizations each managed to tap into funds in a roundabout way through a federal farming program set up in 1961 under the Agriculture and Rural Development Act (ARDA). Walter Deiter, leader of the Federation of Saskatchewan Indians, was able to access ARDA funding in 1966, the first time in Canadian history that an "unsupervised Indian organization" had been awarded such funding.[33] Two years later, Harold Cardinal and the Indian Association of Alberta had $180,000 in ARDA funding in hand. So did Dave Courchene, president of the newly formed Manitoba Indian Brotherhood. They had enough money to make themselves heard, and they weren't dependent on Indian Affairs for it.

"We were quite happy with the arrangement," said Cardinal. "We knew that if we had been forced to rely on direct funding from Indian Affairs, we would always have been very vulnerable to pressures from that department. This way we felt we had slipped some buffers between us and Indian Affairs."[34]

Cardinal and the Alberta association's people could finally breathe a sigh of relief. They had the financial resources to invest in ideas they wanted to pursue, like rewriting the *Indian Act* to reflect the needs and views of the people. This they did in preparation for the first-ever national consultations called by the Indian Affairs minister. But new players were moving onto the stage.

Jean Chrétien was appointed the minister for Indian Affairs by Prime Minister Pierre Trudeau in July 1968. It was not a prestige posting. Indian Affairs was a portfolio where ambitious, first-time ministers could cut their teeth before moving quickly to a better posting as soon as one presented itself. Chrétien was an ambitious thirty-four-year-old MP from Quebec with a mangled syntax and a reputation as a tough guy, first elected to office in 1963. He had no experience with Indian issues and, until the previous year, had never even been to the Prairies. Except for a few months as a junior minister in National Revenue, Indian Affairs would be his first significant cabinet position.

Chrétien recalled that Trudeau had told him that his inexperience would be an asset, and also told him, "In fact, you represent a similar background. You're from a minority group, you don't speak much English, you've known poverty. You might be the minister who understands the Indians."[35]

Chrétien was the seventh minister in just seven years to take on the Indian Affairs portfolio.[36] It *really* wasn't a prestige position.

The department Chrétien took over might have been a small one, but it had a lot on its plate. Indian Affairs was looking to divest itself of some of those responsibilities. As a pilot project, IA selected about 100 bands and provided them with grants to employ band staff, with the objective of gradually turning over the "authority, the responsibility and the financial resources which enable them to do for themselves the many things the Branch is doing for them now."[37]

IA was also looking at ways to push the provinces to take over services like education and health care, which were normally the purview of provincial governments. This generated considerable alarm within the Indian organizations. They worried IA was gradually divesting itself of responsibility for Indians, and such moves would undermine the treaties with the Crown that represented their security.

This was at a time when treaties, reserves and Indian rights were not constitutionally protected. The *Indian Act* and the Indian Affairs department could be eliminated with the stroke of pen. Of course, it would have been shameful for the Crown to simply tear up the treaties it had signed, but there was no constitutional impediment preventing the federal government from doing so.

Still, Indian leaders had cause for optimism in 1968 when Jean Chrétien was appointed. He chose to immediately proceed with the first national consultations with Indian chiefs that had been announced the previous year by his predecessor Arthur Laing. The new minister would be crossing the country and consulting with elected Indian chiefs and other political leaders on how to amend the *Indian Act*.

At the Winnipeg hearing in December 1968, the president of the Manitoba Indian Brotherhood (MIB), Dave Courchene, paused before he began his presentation. He invited Chrétien to sit with them on their side of the table, rather than be on the other side. The Indians, he said, were asking the government to be their partner.[38]

Courchene was a burly man known for his powerful and fiery speeches, and that is what he delivered.

"The status of a Canadian Indian compares unfavourably with the status of the Negro in the United States. Surely Canadian cities need not be burned and looted to evidence discontent and neglect." The first step, he said, "is the restoration of trust, crumbled by years of neglect and actual abrogation of treaty agreements. The treaty rights of the Indians in all of Canada must be restored."[39]

Courchene also called for recognition for Indian dignity with a program of guaranteed income so that people, especially the elderly lacking education or skills, should not be made to "suffer the continued indignity of living on welfare."[40] He finished his presentation with a wish that Indians would become equal citizens, both politically and economically, and hoped that at the next consultations with the Minister, they would be able to do away with the *Indian Act*.

"You say," responded Chrétien, "perhaps next time there will be no more *Indian Act*. I hope this will be possible one day, because it is the only way that you, who are really the first citizens of this land, will be part of the country."[41]

It was a satisfying meeting for the Manitoba Indian Brotherhood, with new opportunities already opening up. Indian Affairs had chosen the Brotherhood as a partner in the trial program "to invest Indians at the band level with sufficient expertise to administer their own programs," where "Indian people of Manitoba were to be involved in the decision-making process" and where they would play a significant role in creating the decentralization process that would lead to "the granting of full autonomy to the province's registered Indians."[42] Through the new Manitoba Project, IA was scaling up its plans to turn Manitoba band councils into program administrators who would be more aligned with the provincial government, with the ultimate goal of offloading program responsibilities onto the provinces.

The Manitoba Project agreement was confirmed in February 1969, and it included the Brotherhood taking over the Community Development file for Manitoba from Indian Affairs. It came with half a million dollars in funding.[43] It also provided the MIB with some tasty carrots with which to persuade band chiefs that the Brotherhood, with its growing budget, was the one and only real voice of Indians in Manitoba. It wasn't long before Courchene was being accused of living a luxurious city lifestyle while people on reserves were going hungry. Of course, "luxurious" in this context might not have been all that grand, but people were not blind to the growing gap between how their leaders lived on the salaries funded by IA and their own circumstances.

Multiple voices were trying to make themselves heard in Indian politics, but IA was picking winners, which meant it was also picking losers. One of the rivals for Indian power, Saskatchewan Cree William Wuttunee, might well have been bitter when he saw his voice diminished as IA anointed its chosen winners with big dollars and ignored groups like his. He was harshly critical of leaders like Courchene and Cardinal, and speculated publicly about whether the IA-sanctioned Indian organizations were potent instruments for change or "government-backed refuges for self-serving despots."[44]

"They are very anxious," said Wuttunee, "to maintain their executive power over the Indian people, and they resort to attacking their own people from big offices in the cities, and because most Indians are still humble, the leaders can, without much objection from their own people, step upon them as they wish."[45]

Dave Courchene was quickly making a name for himself politically. In the spring of 1969, he was approached by Ed Schreyer, the leader of the New Democratic Party in Manitoba, to run in the province's vast northern riding of Rupertsland. It was the largest riding in the province, sparsely populated, and mostly by Indians. Courchene had bigger and more lucrative fish to fry with the Manitoba Project, so he turned to Métis activist Jean Allard.

The tall, handsome Allard had the makings of a persuasive politician, motivated by a desire to make a difference. He'd grown up in the French-speaking farming community of St. François Xavier west of Winnipeg, which had once been part of the Selkirk-Peguis land grant. He'd had no trouble finding work in a lumber camp in Manitoba or on a fishing boat in Vancouver. But by the age of twenty-four, he was a widower with a small child.

"I grew up quicker than I expected," he said. "I remember vividly that beautiful May morning when I left the hospital in Vancouver. My wife had just died of leukemia. When I closed her eyes before I left, I felt like I would never be afraid of anything again."[46]

With a child to raise, he also knew he could no longer rely on a lifestyle based on brawn and not brain, so he decided to put his Jesuit education at St. Boniface College boarding school to good use.

"I went to university and got a law degree. I didn't intend to practise law. What I wanted was the small measure of respect that would come with the letters behind my name. I headed back to Manitoba, and instead of working in a lumber camp, I was running pulpwood operations for Indian Affairs."[47]

And what he discovered working for Indian Affairs infuriated him.

"I'd spent time overseeing projects for Indians, clearing hydro-line right-of-ways in the bush, running pulpwood operations. I thought these projects were intended to help Indians, but a successful project attracted the wrong kind of attention. As soon as it started being successful, some [Indian Affairs] bureaucrat changed the rules and a promising project floundered and failed."[48]

Allard had gotten his first hard lessons about the frustration and futility of going up against the IA bureaucracy, but he was not about to be bested by intransigent civil servants ensconced in their comfortable offices in Ottawa or Winnipeg.

"When I realized I could do little to change the bureaucracy that ran economic and employment programs for Indians, I thought I might make a difference if I became a politician. I figured that the bureaucrats would have to listen to me then. I thought I could make some meaningful and substantive changes to the lives of the impoverished Indians on northern reserves if I sat on the provincial government benches."[49]

Allard was prepared to use the powerful pulpit of public office to make sure Indian voices were heard in the legislature. He went up to the Fort Alexander Reserve (now the Sagkeeng First Nation) about 120 km northeast of Winnipeg, to see Dave Courchene at his home. Allard told him he was willing to run for the Rupertsland seat.

"I'd need someone to run my election campaign for me," Allard said, "and Dave told me to go see the young fellow next door and he would be able to help me. That young fellow was Phil Fontaine, and between the two of them I was elected in 1969 to the Manitoba Legislature with Schreyer as premier."[50]

To be precise, Allard was elected to office in a tight race on June 25, 1969, helping the NDP form a socialist government in Manitoba for the first time.

That same day, the world of Indian politics changed forever.

Endnotes to Chapter 4

1. Full text of *The Indian Act*, 1876, An Act to amend and consolidate the laws respecting Indians: https://www.aadnc-aandc.gc.ca/eng/1100100010252/1100100010254 (viewed July 2, 2018).

2. For an overview of the historic role and authority of Indian Agents in Canada, see: Vic Satzewich and Linda Mahood, 1994, "Indian Affairs and Band Governance: Deposing Indian Chiefs in Western Canada," *Canadian Ethnic Studies* 26:40–58; James Miller, 1996, *Shingwauk's Vision: A History of Residential Schools*, University of Toronto Press; Katherine Pettipas, 1994, *Severing the Ties that Bind*, University of Manitoba Press; Vic Satzewich, 1996, "Where's the Beef?: Cattle Killing, Rations Policy and First Nations 'Criminality' in Southern Alberta, 1892–1895," *Journal of Historical Sociology* 9: 188–212.

3. Statistics Canada, 2016, Aboriginal peoples in Canada: Key results from the 2016 Census, https://www150.statcan.gc.ca/n1/daily-quotidien/171025/dq171025a-eng.htm.

4. *An Act for the gradual enfranchisement of Indians, the better management of Indian Affairs and to extend the provisions of Act 31st*, June 22, 1869.

5. Ibid.

6. Jean Allard, 2002, "Big Bear's Treaty: The road to freedom," *Inroads*, Issue No. 11, 117.

7. *The Indian Advancement Act*, 1886, c. 44, s. 5. See also Section 9.2, Band Government and Law-Making Powers, *Royal Commission on Aboriginal Peoples*, Vol 1, Part Two, 263.

8. Rob McKinley, "Northern Alberta traditional chief passes away at 89," *Windspeaker*, Vol. 5, Issue 11, 1998.

9. Ibid.

10. Canadian Press, "Modern world move regretted," *The Citizen*, Prince George, Monday, March 12, 1979, 12.

11. McKinley, 1998.

12. Heather Robertson, 1991, *Reservations are for Indians*, 2nd edition, (first printed 1970) James Lorimer & Company, 18.

13. Ibid., 19.

14. Ibid., 1.

15. Ibid., 14.

16. Ibid.

17. Ibid.

18. Ibid., 15.

19. McKinley, 1998.

20. Robertson, 1991, 22.

21. Harold Cardinal, 1969, *The Unjust Society* (1st edition, 1969, originally published by MG Hurtig Publishers), Douglas & McIntyre, 83.

22. Ibid., 83.

23. Indian Legal Claims, *Looking Forward, Looking Back*, Vol. 1, Section 9.9, Royal Commission of Aboriginal Peoples, 272.

24. Laurie Meijer Drees, 1997, "A History of the Indian Association of Alberta, 1939–1959," PhD Dissertation, University of Calgary, 51.

25. Ibid., xiii.

26. John L Tobias, 2003, review of *The Indian Association of Alberta: A History of Political Action*, by Laurie Meijer Drees, *Canadian Historical Review* 84, no. 4, 663.

27　Meijer Drees, 1997, 52.
28　James Burke, 1976, *Paper Tomahawks: From red tape to red power*, Queenston House Publishing, 3.
29　Ibid., 3–4.
30　Cardinal, 1969, 88.
31　Harold Cardinal, 1977, *The Rebirth of Canada's Indians*, Hurtig Publishers, 171.
32　Ibid.
33　*Saskatchewan First Nations: Lives Past and Present*, 2004, Volume Editor Christian Thompson, 52.
34　Cardinal, 1977, 174.
35　Jean Chrétien, 1985, *Straight From the Heart*, Key Porter Books, 62.
36　Dick Bell, Guy Favreau, René Tremblay, John Robert Nicholson, Jean Marchand and Arthur Laing served as Indian Affairs ministers from 1962 to 1968 when Jean Chrétien was appointed. https://en.wikipedia.org/wiki/Minister_of_Crown%E2%80%93Indigenous_Relations#Cabinet_ministers.
37　DIAND, Indian Affairs and Northern Development Annual Report, Fiscal Year 1966–67, Government of Canada 1966–67, 52.
38　Report on the Indian Act Consultation Meeting, Winnipeg, Manitoba, December 18, 19, and 20, 1968, DIAND, 3.
39　Ibid., 4 and 12.
40　Ibid., 11.
41　Ibid., 13.
42　James Burke, 1976, 60.
43　Ibid., 66.
44　Ibid., 96.
45　William Wuttunee, 1971, *Ruffled Feathers: Indians in Canadian Society*, Bell Books, 10.
46　Jean Allard, 1999, interview with author.
47　Ibid.
48　Jean Allard, 2002, "Big Bear's Treaty: The road to freedom," *Inroads*, Vol. 11, 11.
49　Jean Allard, 1999, interview with author.
50　Allard, 2002, 114.

5
THE "GREAT THUNDERCLAP" OF '69

In the House of Commons on June 25, 1969, Indian Affairs minister Jean Chrétien stood before fellow Members of Parliament.

"Mr. Speaker, before reading my statement, I should like to bring to the attention of the house the presence in the Speaker's gallery of a group of Indian leaders representing all provinces. May I welcome those citizens on the occasion of their visit."[1]

The leaders in the gallery may well have been excited to be in the House and recognized by the minister, but they had no idea what was coming. The opposition parties in the House did. An hour earlier, Chrétien had provided them with copies of his statement.

"Throughout a year's consultation with Indian leaders," Chrétien announced to the House, "the government has reviewed its programs for Indians and their effects on the present situation of the Indian people. The review has shown that this is the right time to change long-standing policies. The Indian people have shown their determination that present conditions shall not persist."[2]

That, of course, would not have come as a surprise to the Indian leaders in the gallery. Most of them had participated in those consultations.

Chrétien continued. "The Indian people should have the right to manage their own affairs to the same extent that their fellow Canadians manage theirs. Under present conditions they do not have anything like this degree of control over their land, their funds, or in fact any of their responsibilities. This is the central fact about conditions today, and it must change."[3]

The minister got that right. Indian leaders did want change and the right to manage their own affairs. But the mechanism Chrétien was proposing came as a shock. The minister announced that the *Indian Act* would be repealed and provincial governments would take over responsibilities for services for Indians that were normally under provincial jurisdiction. The process would be eased by $50 million that would be made available over five years for economic development on reserves.

Chrétien finished with a flourish, stating the intent over five years "to wind up that part of my department which deals with Indian affairs; the residual responsibilities for the federal government to be transferred to other appropriate federal departments."[4]

The White Paper, or the "Statement of the Government of Canada on Indian Policy," as it was officially titled, was then revealed at a news conference, where a pleased Chrétien seemed to actually believe that Indian leaders would be on board. He assured them they would now "decide for themselves" about their equality with all other Canadians and their freedom to have reserves removed from the protection of the state.

Parliamentarians may have been surprised by this newly announced government policy, but Indian leaders were stunned. The White Paper hit like a "great thunderclap" that reverberated through the Indian community. Indian leaders were outraged. Jean Chrétien had sat through the previous year's consultations on *amending* the *Indian Act*, and he had certainly seemed like he was listening. Not once had Chrétien hinted that the plan, all along, was to pull the plug on the Act. He said nothing, not even when he sat with them on the same side of the table.

It was Harold Cardinal's worst fears coming true. The sense of betrayal was palpable, in part because the apparent reversal by the minister had come so quickly. Just five days earlier, Chrétien had been on Cardinal's home reserve of Sucker Creek in Alberta, standing right in front of the delegates to the twenty-fifth-anniversary convention of the Indian Association of Alberta.

In Chrétien's short speech, he talked of equality with non-Indigenous Canadians in terms of "advantages" and "responsibility," and how the Indians need to be "free" to make their own decisions regarding lands.[5] He might have been trying, in a roundabout way, to prepare the chiefs for what was coming in the White Paper, but a combination of Chrétien's vagueness, his convoluted way of speaking and his poor English — and the fact that some of the chiefs were not fluent in English either — left his audience baffled. If he was trying to break it to them gently, he missed the mark completely. His audience applauded politely without having a clue what the minister had been going on about. Chrétien might well have mistaken the absence of a negative reaction from the chiefs as tacit approval of the new Indian policy. It may also explain why the Indian leaders were so shocked as they sat in the Speaker's gallery listening to the minister's statement.

The very next day, the provincial Indian groups raised their voices in unison, using the name "National Indian Brotherhood," which those same provincial leaders had just created to give themselves a national presence. They issued a media release denouncing the government's intentions and made clear their sense of betrayal over the fact that the White Paper bore no relation to what was discussed during Chrétien's national consultations.

"It is apparent to us," read the release, "that while there was a show of consultation, neither the Minister nor his Department really heard and understood the Indian people. Or having heard and understood, they chose to follow the well beaten trail of the past decades and ignore our views."[6]

The White Paper was produced without any input from, or consultation with, Indian leaders, but with input from ministers, senior bureaucrats and selected civil servants from Indian Affairs. The hope was to eliminate "the Indian problem" by eliminating the *Indian Act*. This was a continuation of government policies since the 1830s designed to terminate the special status of Indians.[7]

But the new policy was really the brainchild of Prime Minister Pierre Trudeau, who professed a desire for a Just Society of participatory democracy, where individual citizens were paramount to the success of a democratic state, but not collective groups or tribal collectives.[8] This clashed head-on with the firmly held belief of Indians who saw themselves as communal societies with collective rights that were protected by the treaties.

Of most immediate concern to Indian leaders were the plans underway to hand over Indian programs and services to the provinces. Provincial governments were not legally bound to uphold any treaties or agreements that the Crown had signed with Indian chiefs. The future of the treaties was on the line.

The National Indian Brotherhood media release continued, "At all consultation meetings the Indian people expressed the desire to take on greater responsibility in running their own affairs. Yet the new policy will have the affairs of Indian people run by still another bureaucratic structure. At no time during the consultations did this Minister indicate to us that we would be thrown into the laps of the provinces, some of which have already established their chapters of a Department of Indian Affairs."[9]

The Brotherhood statement called out the Trudeau government for failing to act in good faith, and concluded, "If we accept this policy, and in the process lose our rights and our lands, we become willing partners in cultural genocide. This we cannot do."[10]

Cardinal responded to the clear attack on the treaties by sitting down and banging out a book called *The Unjust Society*. He didn't hold anything back. He took direct aim at Pierre Trudeau's justification for the White Paper — that in a Just Society, all Canadians should be subject to the same laws, and that Indians were just another ethnic group in multicultural Canada. Cardinal wanted the Canadian public to know that the trust between government and Indian leaders, as tenuous as it had been, had now been broken.

Edmonton political activist and bookstore owner Mel Hurtig, who was still finding his feet in the publishing business, got the Cardinal book onto store shelves at the speed of light (in book publishing terms). *The Unjust Society* was an immediate bestseller. Within six months, it had sold 26,000 copies, putting Cardinal right up there with Pauline Johnson as the most widely read Canadian Indian.[11]

Canadians were reading. And they were listening.

"Our people no longer believe," Cardinal wrote. "It is that simple, and it is that sad. The Canadian government can promise involvement, consultation, progressive human and economic development programmes. We will no longer believe them... They can tell us their plans for local self-government. We will shrug our disbelief. The government can create a hundred national advisory councils to advise us about our problems. We will not listen to them... We will know they have nothing new to say."[12]

What most alarmed him was what Trudeau was saying about the treaties.

"It is inconceivable," the Prime Minister had said in his defence of the White Paper, "that one section of society should have a treaty with another section of society. The Indians should become Canadians as have all other Canadians."[13]

Yet, said Cardinal, to Indian people, the treaties are considered the Indian Magna Carta.

"If our rights are meaningless, if it is inconceivable that our society have treaties with the white society even though those treaties were signed by honourable men on both sides, in good faith, long before the present government decided to tear them up as worthless scraps of paper, then we as a people are meaningless. We cannot and will not accept this... If we surrender, we die."[14]

If Harold Cardinal was the loudest voice on the Indian side and could speak with authority and confidence, it was because Cardinal was an articulate leader. But most important, the Alberta Indian Association had the money needed to be heard, thanks to its funding from the federal Agriculture Department. At least it did, right up until the moment that summer when the funding suddenly evaporated.

The Agriculture department had shifted priorities, and didn't want to be butting heads with Indian Affairs by continuing to fund the Indian organizations, especially when Indian issues had become such a political hot potato due to the White Paper. The Agriculture department hastily dumped that responsibility onto the Secretary of State department, which then ended up in a territorial battle with Indian Affairs over who would manage funding for Indian organizations. The IA department hadn't had money to support organizations when Cardinal had asked a year earlier, but if there was going to be funding for Indian political organizations, IA was determined that no other department was going to be in charge of it.

The Indian leaders were adamant that their core funding not fall under IA's control, not when they were in the midst of the battle against the White Paper. The Alberta, Saskatchewan and Manitoba organizations had to wait for six months as helpless bystanders, without knowing where their funding was going to be coming from, as Jean Chrétien battled it out over departmental jurisdiction with Secretary of State Gérard Pelletier.

"We took a hard line position," said Cardinal. "We did not want Indian Affairs to control funding for Indian organizations. In fact, we fought like hell to prevent that from happening because we well understood the implications of an Indian Affairs victory."¹⁵

Eventually, Pelletier prevailed, perhaps in some small measure due to his close friendship with the prime minister. He established the Secretary of State department as the go-to source of core funding for a whole range of political, cultural and social organizations, with a budget that jumped from $4.6 million in 1969–1970 to $44 million the following year.¹⁶ Core funding was crucial to groups that needed annual funding to rent office space, hook up telephones and buy those Gestetner machines. Indian political organizations needed that funding, too, and there was a pot of money allocated just for them.

Indian Affairs did not, however, take their jurisdictional loss of ground with grace. Its bureaucrats immediately went to the half-dozen provinces without existing Indian organizations, and to band leaders on reserves, and encouraged them to apply to the State department for a piece of the core funding pot. If they didn't, IA warned, the three main organizations would get all the money.

"The arithmetic is obvious," said Cardinal. "The more organizations that applied, the less money there was for any one. Those of us who had worked and fought hardest were rewarded with reduced resources. Those who did little or nothing got a hell of a lot without effort. Indian Affairs was buying our allies from our ranks with our money."¹⁷

Still, the Alberta association had gotten through the financial drought by leaning heavily on a bank overdraft, and in the meantime, had focussed its attention on preparing a response to the White Paper.

It was one thing to write a response to a government policy paper. It was quite another for that response to be heard in Ottawa at the cabinet level where it could have a big impact. Indian leaders typically faced an ongoing challenge in reaching out to government ministers, as bureaucrats usually intervened and redirected them to Indian Affairs without the ministers ever being made aware that they had been approached. This time was different. The backlash against the White Paper, both from Indian organizations and the public, seemed to have left Trudeau uncertain about how to proceed with Indian policy. Such a strong and coherent pushback from Indian organizations had never happened before, and they had public sympathy on their side.

"Somehow the Indian problem got stuck in Trudeau's mind," said Cardinal, "and that accounts for the build-up in ministerial interest. We were able to sit down with a minister and tell him what was on our minds. We had established at least a speaking relationship with cabinet, and we had broken the dictatorial stranglehold Indian Affairs had always held."¹⁸

The Indian Association of Alberta produced Citizens Plus, a response to the White Paper, which they dubbed the Red Paper. Of primary importance was setting up an Alberta Indian Development System, using the $50 million promised in the White Paper, through which the Alberta association would address education and economic development. The Red Paper made clear it was imperative that community members were to be in control of the programs they would develop — a bottom-up solution to poverty on reserves rather than the top-down approach that was the standard operating procedure for Indian Affairs.[19] Indians were deciding for themselves, and this was the plan they wanted.

Despite Chrétien trying to run interference at what was perceived as undermining his department's control over Indians, what the Alberta group wanted was to present the Red Paper directly to the Prime Minister and cabinet ministers. And that's what they got.

The Prime Minister didn't have to personally take the meeting. In fact, Trudeau had both a Liberal majority government and considerable personal political capital. He had been swept into power in summer of 1968 on a wave of Trudeaumania, the likes of which Canada had never seen before. However, Trudeau's politics was grounded in a well thought-out vision for the country: separation of church and state; the need to distinguish between sin and crime; the rejection of nationalism in all its forms; and the primacy of the individual.[20]

"I consider nationalism," Trudeau had said, "to have been a sinister activity in world history over the last 150 years. And that goes for English-Canadian nationalism, French-Canadian nationalism, or Gaullist nationalism, or whatever."[21]

What about Indian nationalism?

The White Paper had ignited a sleeping nationalism among Indian people, and now it was staring Trudeau in the face. He had miscalculated in his belief that the "freedom" he was offering Indian people by doing away with the constraints of the *Indian Act* and the treaties was what they, too, wanted.

Trudeau already had a nationalist fight on its hands with the Front de libération du Québec (FLQ), which had organized itself into "paramilitary cells and set out to bomb, kidnap, and ultimately murder their way" to a Quebec utopia.[22] He didn't need another war on his hands.

Government bureaucrats are typically pragmatists when it comes to devising policy. They can put forward a particular argument and test the reaction. If that argument doesn't fly with the Canadian public, they'll test another one.[23] There was no real need for Trudeau to turn the White Paper into a hill to die on.

Trudeau didn't seem to have a Plan B, but maybe a meeting with Indian leaders in a high-profile location like the Centre Block on Parliament Hill, with all the media attention it would receive, would be the opportunity to reframe a political confrontation into a meeting of honourable men trying to arrive at a better understanding.

On June 4, 1970, the Indian Association of Alberta, led by Harold Cardinal and backed by the National Indian Brotherhood, sat down across from Trudeau and thirteen government ministers in the Railway Committee Room, one of the two largest meeting rooms in the Centre Block. There they were — fourteen men in dark suits and ties on one side of a long table, facing a second long table, where sat another dozen men, many in full ceremonial dress, including massive feathered headdresses. In the metre-wide gap between the two tables, journalists' heads bobbed up and down as they thrust up cameras and microphones from where they were kneeling on the floor.[24] Behind the government table hung a massive portrait of the Fathers of Confederation, directly in the sightlines of the Indian delegation.

The room was packed. About 100 delegates had accompanied the Alberta crew, all of whom either paid their own way or had support from their bands.[25]

Harold Cardinal, in his beaded and fringed buckskin jacket and Buddy Holly–style glasses sat directly across from Jean Chrétien, Pierre Trudeau and Paul Martin, Sr., in their dark, bespoke suits. Cardinal had one hour to present the 100-page Red Paper and make his case for a different kind of governance based on respecting and delivering treaty rights. But first came a ceremonial Indian prayer. Then, one of the Alberta chiefs in full regalia stepped around the reporters crouched between the tables to personally hand Trudeau a copy of the Red Paper. Chief Harry Chonkolay then stood, dressed in his very old Treaty suit, even though he could easily have afforded a new suit after oil had been discovered on the Slavey reserve. He handed Chrétien a copy of the White Paper. Speaking Slavey, translated by Saskatchewan's Walter Deiter, Chonkolay said that they didn't need the government's policy paper anymore and were giving it back because "we have our own set of ideas as to what the Indians should be doing for themselves."[26]

Dave Courchene from the Manitoba Indian Brotherhood spoke ahead of Cardinal and laid it on the line, stating that for the first time in 100 years, Indians were united. "We are not only brothers in colour and blood, but we are brothers in purpose, intent, aspirations, hope and effort. The government of Canada has had one hundred years to prepare its White Paper. We have had but one year to prepare our views. We now have but one hour to meet with you. The hour is one hundred years."[27]

Then it was Cardinal's turn, first expressing his disappointment that after so many years, both sides had made so little apparent progress towards reaching an understanding of each other's point of view. He proceeded to dissect the proposals in the White Paper and replace them with plans laid out in the Red Paper. In a nutshell, the modernizing of treaty promises for education, health care and economic development would alleviate the sorry state of life on reserves, and the programs would be run by Indians themselves through the provincial Indian organizations and the band councils. And it would all be funded by the government as outlined in the treaties.

Cardinal received a standing ovation from the people packing the room. Even some reporters applauded.[28]

Trudeau, in his turn, admitted that it might have been better for the government to consult with Indian leaders on the White Paper and that maybe they were naïve in their approach. However, he took exception to some criticisms in the Red Paper, saying bluntly, "you can say that the government doesn't understand, that it's stupid and ignorant, but do not say that we are dishonest and that we are trying to mislead, because we're not."[29]

Courchene got in the last word. "This one hour certainly will go down in history, as far as Indian people are concerned, provided it is not all talk. I hope that this hour that we have had together will certainly be the start of a long-term plan."[30]

Both sides got the message: the Indians were there in strength and meant business. Still, the meeting wrapped up with Trudeau signing autographs.[31] Indians were no more immune to Trudeaumania than other Canadians.

It was, Cardinal said later, "our first ever working meeting with the Prime Minister and his cabinet," and they were "euphoric" to have made such a huge political breakthrough. They had won agreement in principle for regular meetings between cabinet and the National Indian Brotherhood. "Politically, it was our high point; our greatest success; our political equivalent of Little Bighorn. Chrétien himself took it as a crushing defeat."[32]

The battle between the two men hardened and it got personal.

On opposite sides of the table

As Cardinal and Chrétien faced each other across the tables that day in the Railway Committee Room, it might have appeared as if they were coming from different worlds, but they had more in common than they may have realized. The tough *petit gars* from Shawinigan, Quebec, was only nine years older than the Cree kid from the Sucker Creek reserve in Alberta, and their families had an unusual symmetry. Chrétien was one of nineteen children (ten of whom did not survive infancy), while Cardinal was one of eighteen children (eight of whom died at an early age). The two rivals were both raised as Catholics—Cardinal at the Oblate Indian Residential School near his reserve, and Chrétien at the Séminaire Saint-Joseph de Trois-Rivières.

Cardinal's father Frank was a chief on their reserve and had been politically active in the Indian Association of Alberta and farm politics.[33] He'd made sure Harold was "home-schooled" in politics and indoctrinated in the traditional knowledge by Cree elders.[34] On the other hand, Chrétien's father Wellie, a paper mill machinist, turned the family into outcasts by defying Quebec public sentiment during the Second World War and supporting military conscription.[35]

Chrétien went on to study law at Laval University; Cardinal to study sociology at St. Patrick's College (now part of Carleton University), just a few kilometres from Parliament Hill. Chrétien joined a Shawinigan law firm after completing his law degree and then successfully ran for parliament for the Liberals in 1963. Cardinal quit university to become the leader of the Indian Association of Alberta in 1968. Both men had ambition, but in terms of heart-felt ideology, Cardinal probably had more in common with Trudeau than with Chrétien.

But that day in Ottawa, Chrétien and Cardinal were both young, ambitious men getting their feet under the table with the big boys, although they were definitely on opposite sides of that table.

Flushed with a success beyond what they could have hoped for after the meeting with the prime minister and cabinet ministers, Cardinal and the other provincial leaders left Ottawa and headed back home. They had won a significant victory. Even the Trudeau government acknowledged as much.

According to an internal government post mortem on the fallout from the White Paper, "The political potency of the Indians' reaction, the near unanimity of support from them and from those segments of the Canadian public concerned with such matters... helped to produce what for the Indian...leadership was bound to be the conclusion that they had gained surrender from the government."[36]

Cardinal and the other Indian leaders were political neophytes, however, and they made a critical mistake. They left Ottawa in 1970 without taking the crucial step of consolidating their success by immediately holding follow-up meetings with ministers. It would cost them.

The Indian Affairs department had no intention of accepting defeat or surrender, having just survived a death sentence. The *raison d'être* of Indian Affairs became, in effect, the implementation of the ideas in the Red Paper. Of course, it would be managed from the top-down, just as IA had always managed its programs. IA would devolve powers to bands to operate Indian Affairs–managed programs, including millions of dollars in economic development funds. The Indian provincial organizations would also get money to deliver programs and run economic development programs, funded by Indian Affairs and closely managed by a mushrooming Indian Affairs bureaucracy.

And then Chrétien made his move against Cardinal. Hell hath no fury like a government minister whose departmental authority has been scorned. The Alberta association had its funding suspended, ostensibly over sit-ins and demonstrations about schools being closed on reserves, until Cardinal was forced to resign as president to save it.

"Indian Affairs," said Cardinal, "refusing to roll over and play dead, in spite of its crushing defeat, rallied some of their allies within the Brotherhood, and they dragged their feet long enough for us to lose vital momentum in our negotiations at the cabinet level. Within the year that agreement was all but forgotten."[37]

By 1972, other cabinet ministers in Ottawa were no longer taking meetings with Indian leaders. Their inquiries were once again being redirected to Indian Affairs. Chrétien had taken his revenge.

"The whole process," said Cardinal a few years later, "was a beautiful, almost unbelievable commentary on Chrétien's survival instinct and political ability. In two years, he had wiped out the access we had gained to other ministries, and we were, in principle, back to the pre-1968 days when Indian Affairs held all the reins."[38]

Magnanimous in victory, Chrétien at least took the calls from Indian leaders, and it was a compliment of sorts that he set about using the recipe provided by the Alberta association's Red Paper to rejuvenate the department.

The money trap

Within a short time, the provincial Indian organizations and their newly created National Indian Brotherhood (NIB) had funding from Indian Affairs to hire specialists to assist with researching Indian land claims and policy development. In 1970, the leaders of the provincial organizations had chosen George Manuel, a Shuswap leader from the BC interior, to be the NIB president. Manuel was deeply concerned about the corrupting effect of more and more money being spent—money doled out by Indian Affairs, the Privy Council, Health and Welfare and other departments—on NIB's ability to represent the interests of Canada's Indians.

"When Indian people were poor," said Manuel, "we were able to retain our Indian identity. But the more money we get, the more we seek, and the more we get entangled in the economic and political institutions of the white man and lose track of our Indian culture, identity and politics."[39]

The Union of BC Indian Chiefs had no such concern. They produced their own 1970 position paper in response to the White Paper, and so did the Manitoba Indian Brotherhood. The Brown Paper, as the BC chiefs called their paper, said it wasn't necessary for Indian Affairs to be providing programs and services on behalf of the federal government when Indian organizations could do it for them, fully funded by IA, of course. The BC chiefs did not see that running IA programs undermined their independence.

"There is no need," stated their Brown Paper, "for us to be deprived of self-determination merely because we receive federal monetary support, nor should we lose federal support because we reject federal control."[40]

Manuel's wariness was justified. For many Indians, the National Indian Brotherhood and the provincial organizations had become little more than extensions of the government, a "brown bureaucracy," with its leaders labelled "Uncle Tomahawks" by Indian activists who figured they'd sold out. Whether the Indian organizations believed they'd been co-opted or not, the effect was the same.

An alternative theory of the highly visible 1970 showdown between the provincial Indian leaders and Trudeau, Chrétien and the cabinet emerged over the next few years, and it wasn't flattering to the Indian leaders. Basically, it implied they had been played.

James Burke, author of *Paper Tomahawks*, who had worked for Manitoba Indian Brotherhood, suggested in 1976 that Indian Affairs had, for some time, wanted to establish a single authoritative voice to represent Indians across Canada. The bureaucrats could then bypass the uncooperative Indians who kept resisting the programs IA wanted to establish.

From IA's perspective, Indian Affairs programs were continually failing because it was too difficult to get Indians to agree on anything. Setting up the provincial Indian associations with programs to run, along with the funding that goes with it, seemed like their best shot for implementing IA policies. But the people were not necessarily buying into what the organizations claiming to fight for their rights were trying to sell. Even though a century had passed, the people still held onto their faith that the wise leaders who had signed the treaties had known what they were doing, and viewed the new leaders with some suspicion.

Said Burke, "The government realized these Indian leaders were on a shaky footing. Any support they had was tenuous and superficial. It was imperative that Indian people should unite behind their provincial associations."[41]

Enter the White Paper, a straw man, a fake enemy. Like most groups, said Burke, Indians would readily band together against a common threat, in this case the Indian Affairs department, which many already considered a villainous entity.

"Chrétien's white paper was intended to be a straw man which the provincial leaders would—amid a storm of publicity—knock down, demonstrating to their constituents that they were a match for the federal government and able representatives of their people."[42]

Had Cardinal and the other leaders been played? Was that why the Prime Minister and thirteen cabinet members had brought their considerable clout and status into the Railway Committee Room, assured of national media coverage, to sit across the table from the Indian leaders?

Whatever the strength of Burke's argument, when the Trudeau Liberals were up for re-election in 1974, the government made sure the National Indian Brotherhood knew its place. The organization flexed its new-found muscles by attempting to embarrass the government during the election campaign. In response, Indian Affairs cut off $1 million in funding to the provincial Indian organizations, restoring the funding just days before the NIB's own elections.[43]

If there was any confusion about who was controlling the money and who was calling the tune, the Indian organizations got the message loud and clear.

Endnotes to Chapter 5

1. Hon. Jean Chrétien, Minister for Indian Affairs and Northern Development, Routine Proceedings, Hansard, June 25, 1969, https://www.lipad.ca/full/1969/06/25/1/.
2. Ibid.
3. Ibid.
4. Ibid.
5. Jean Chrétien, June 20, 1969, Speech to the 25th Annual Convention of the Indian Association of Alberta, is preserved at Native AmErikan Studies Department at the University of Lethbridge, Alberta.
6. National Indian Brotherhood (NIB), Media Release: Statement on the Proposed New "Indian Policy," June 26, 1969, 3.
7. Sally Weaver, 1981, *Making Canadian Indian Policy: The Hidden Agenda 1968–1970*, University of Toronto Press, 125.
8. Leon Crane Bear, 2015, "The Indian Association of Alberta's 1970 *Red Paper* Published as a Response to the Canadian Federal Government's Proposed 1969 *White Paper* on Indian Policy," M.A. Thesis, University of Lethbridge, 72.
9. Ibid., 3.
10. Ibid., 5.
11. David Monture, June 1970, "An Interview with Harold Cardinal," *The Indian News*, Vol 13, No 3, Ottawa, 4.
12. Harold Cardinal, 1969 (1999 reprint), *The Unjust Society*, Hurtig Publishing, 23–24.
13. Ibid., 24.
14. Ibid., 26.
15. Harold Cardinal, 1977, *The Rebirth of Canada's Indians*, Hurtig Publishing, 177.
16. Peter R. Elson, 2011, *High Ideals and Noble Intentions: Voluntary Sector-government Relations in Canada*, University of Toronto Press, 60.
17. Cardinal, 1977, 178.
18. Ibid., 183.
19. Harold Cardinal, June 17, 1970, Report by Harold Cardinal, President of the Indian Association of Alberta: 26th Annual Convention, transcript, 1–9. Folder M7655-320, James Gladstone fonds, Glenbow Museum in Calgary, Alberta.
20. Robert Wright, 2016, *Trudeaumania: The Rise to Power of Pierre Elliott Trudeau*, HarperCollins, xiv.
21. Ibid., xii.
22. Ibid., 11.
23. Weaver, 1981, 41.
24. Monture, 1970, 4.
25. Cardinal, 1977, 183.
26. Monture, 1970, 1.
27. Ibid.
28. Ibid., 7.
29. Ibid.

30 Ibid.
31 Ibid.
32 Cardinal, 1977, 184.
33 Kathleen Flaherty, "The White Paper/Red Paper," CBC radio program *Ideas*, February 22, 2010. URL: http://www.cbc.ca/ideas/episodes/2010/02/22/white-paper-red-paper-cd/.
34 Ibid.
35 Bob Plamondon, 2017, *The Shawinigan Fox: How Jean Chrétien Defied the Elites and Reshaped Canada*, Great River Media.
36 Quoted in "Contribution Agreements: a Partial History of 'Devolution,'" 2012, http://www.thunderchild.ca/upload/documents/Why%20There%20Are%20Contributions%20Agreements[1].pdf.
37 Cardinal, 1977, 185.
38 Ibid., 186.
39 J.R. Ponting, and R. Gibbins, 1980, *Out of Irrelevance*, Butterworth & Co., 244.
40 William Wuttunee, 1971, *Ruffled Feathers*, Bell Books, 62.
41 James Burke, 1976, *Paper Tomahawks: From red tape to red power*, Queenston House Publishing, 10.
42 Ibid.
43 Ponting and Gibbins, 207.

6
THE BEST VOICES MONEY CAN BUY

When the Liberal government swept to power in 1968, Prime Minister Trudeau appointed nearly a dozen "ministers without portfolio" with no particular job to do. One of them was Robert Stanbury. Any politician welcomes the positive publicity that comes from announcing and dispensing funding, and in 1969, Stanbury was seconded to the Secretary of State department to do just that. He had been given the job of sprinkling money around the country to just about any special interest or civic group that wanted to make its voice heard. Stanbury was a very busy man.

This federal generosity with the public purse was partly informed by Canada's official move towards becoming a multicultural society, with ethnic groups wanting to be heard. It also had its roots in official bilingualism policy, and even in the fallout from the FLQ crisis in Quebec. The protests and violence around the civil rights movement in the United States had governments in Canada on edge, too. In the United States, Native protests were growing louder and angrier, led by the American Indian Movement. It was encouraging civil disobedience, and leading a national protest to bring attention to the conditions on reservations, which culminated in the deadly stand-off at Wounded Knee, South Dakota in 1973.

The message for politicians was clear. If aggrieved segments of society felt they were not being heard by government, they might feel forced to turn to violence to get their message across. Funding such groups served as a societal safety valve.

The government of Pierre Trudeau was not just handing out goodies so folks could feel that they had input into public policy. Participatory democracy was not a one-way street. The government could "manage" segments of society, ones that might otherwise become a political irritant, by turning their organizations into the political clientele of the government.[1] Designating and funding a single national voice for whatever segment of society wanted to be heard was a much more efficient way of consulting special interest groups than having to listen to a cacophony of voices with conflicting ideas and opinions. Such organizations also had the benefit, from the government's perspective, of having the organizations themselves smother the voices of their fringe elements under the weight of their larger, more moderate factions. In many respects, it was a wise investment that brought a certain tidiness to dealing with Canada's diverse and often fractious population, particularly in the aftermath of protest marches and other forms of noisy public dissent during the 1960s.

Thousands of civic groups were born in the 1970s, thanks to Secretary of State funding. Between 1968 and 1972, the State department under Gérard Pelletier became the single largest funder of volunteer organizations, and the department's budget bloomed in 1970 to $44 million. Funding flowed to create women's organizations, Indigenous political, social and cultural organizations, youth exchange programs, ethnic heritage organizations and just about any community group that felt isolated from the political process and wanted to advocate for change.[2]

It should be noted that Stanbury's prolific seeding of new organizations on behalf of State minister Pelletier did not always sit well with other government departments that had core responsibilities for the same constituency. That is what happened when Jean Chrétien, the Indian Affairs minister, had been duking it out with Pelletier over who should control funding for Indian political organizations.

The Indian political organizations fretted about the implications of accepting government funding for their operating expenses, and so did other civic groups. Relying on government funding to keep the lights on raised the very real question of how vulnerable to political whims and budget cuts this would make an organization. But it also raised the question of how the organization would be perceived.

The Union of Human Rights and Civil Liberties Associations, for instance, was formed with funding from the State department in October 1970 during a particularly touchy time for civil rights. Trudeau had just invoked the *War Measures Act* during the FLQ crisis, which had the effect of immediately suspending civil liberties across the country. But that particular furor, warned the president of the Canadian Civil Liberties Association, should not blind civil rights advocates to the risks to their credibility from accepting state funding.

"If any civil liberties group even requests Government money for its operating expenses," he said, "it will appear in the eyes of the public... to be less than independent of the very authority it must challenge. Consider, for example, the situation that might arise if such an organization requested money and then failed to oppose some subsequent Government policy. Even though the civil liberties group might decline to oppose a particular policy on perfectly legitimate grounds it would appear to the public that its decision was based on somewhat less laudable considerations."[3]

The rationale for creating and funding Indigenous political organizations emerged from the State department's Sub-committee of the Interdepartmental Committee of Indian and Eskimo Policy. This dull-as-dishwater-sounding committee was busy hammering together the foundations of a political dynamic that would shape Indigenous politics for the next fifty years. On the committee were representatives from Indian Affairs, Secretary of State, National Health and Welfare, Privy Council, and the Treasury Board to Indian Provincial and Territorial Associations.[4] Joining them were representatives from the organizations that would become the Aboriginal Representative Organizations (AROs): "the National Indian Brotherhood, Inuit organizations, Métis and non-Status Indian groups and the Native Women and Native Youth Associations."[5]

It isn't clear how much say the Indian, Inuit and Métis representatives had setting up the AROs, given that the sub-committee on Indian and Eskimo Policy described Aboriginal people as a "uniquely impoverished and disorganized" ethnic group that had yet to get a handle on how to organize politically so that they could engage effectively with Canada's modern political institutions.[6]

The ARO program was designed to "enable the Native citizens of Canada to organize their own opinion and develop program proposals of imminent concern to them. It is felt that programs developed in this manner have a higher potential for successful implementation than programs developed by non-native agencies and imposed upon Native people."[7] That sounded fine in theory, but how were "Native citizens of Canada" supposed to organize their own opinion if the federal government was pre-emptively setting up Aboriginal Representative Organizations of its own choosing?

The ARO program was the federal government's first program specifically for Indigenous political organizations. It's not that there weren't any Indian political groups around that already had deep roots. The problem was that they hadn't been raised up in the ways of modern political institutions. The Indian Association of Alberta had been around since the 1930s. Yet Harold Cardinal admitted to political naïveté when the association made some serious blunders in dealing with the federal government, not the least of which was leaving Ottawa in a state of euphoria after the showdown with Trudeau and his cabinet without consolidating their gains.

The Union of Ontario Indians had an even deeper history. The organization represented the Anishinabek Nations, and traced its roots back to the Confederacy of Three Fires in the 1600s, well before European contact. The Confederacy controlled the military and trade around the Great Lakes, and except for a few wars, generally managed to have good relations with the Iroquois Confederacy and other tribal groups. The Three Fires confederacy evolved into the Grand General Indian Council in 1870, and then into the Union of Ontario Indians in 1949. With the White Paper as a catalyst in 1969, it turned itself into a more politically focussed organization.

Despite its Indigenous political pedigree, could the Union of Ontario Indians interact effectively with all levels of government to influence the changes they wanted to see for their people? It was clear that the government was not intending to adapt its own structures to interact with Indigenous political groups. The older organizations would have to adapt. However, the ARO program had lots of brand new organizations for IA to mould to its requirements.

The National Indian Brotherhood was formed in 1969, but it couldn't very well be considered the national voice of Indians if it represented only Manitoba, Saskatchewan and Alberta, along with the newly reorganized Union of Ontario Indians. In the space of a year, NIB had provincial counterparts set up in British Columbia, Nova Scotia, New Brunswick, Prince Edward Island, Quebec and the Northwest Territories.

Robert Stanbury continued dispersing the State department's largesse. The Native Council of Canada confirmed its core funding from Stanbury in 1971. The decision to create a national council came at a meeting of the leaders of the Métis and non-Status Indian organizations from the Prairies and BC on November 16, 1970, the eighty-fifth anniversary of the hanging of Louis Riel.[8] Both groups felt they were in the same position politically—landless and without federal recognition.[9] However, like the National Indian Brotherhood, the Native Council needed to beef up its national credentials if it was going to serve as a national ARO. Representing groups in BC, Alberta, Saskatchewan and Manitoba weren't enough. The council did the same as the NIB, quickly setting up new organizations in Quebec, the Maritimes and the territories, so it could claim to represent Métis and Non-Status Indians from coast to coast.

The newly created Native Women's Association of Canada was also a beneficiary of the core-funding blitz in 1971. It became the umbrella organization of the Native women's provincial and territorial organizations, and the self-described "national voice of Native women."[10] Inuit Tapirisat of Canada was also formed that same year as an alliance of Inuit organizations representing the regions of the far North.

The Indigenous voices dealing with government at the national level were narrowed down to four: the National Indian Brotherhood, the Native Council of Canada, the Inuit Tapirisat of Canada and the Native Women's Association. They would be the sole voices of their respective Indigenous constituencies. Of course, Indian Affairs had its own agenda. The four AROs were ideal vehicles for selling IA policy to the people, and useful for orchestrating the devolution of IA responsibilities onto Indian bands.

Why did Indigenous organizations go along with it? Did they really believe they could retain their independence while being entirely financially dependent on IA for both core and program funding? One explanation might have to do with the sudden and unprecedented access to power at the federal level. The AROs had, for the first time, an official IA-sanctioned role to play as intermediaries between lower-level political organizations and IA bureaucrats.

The presidents of the provincial organizations also had, for the first time, real power and money. Each organization could use its newfound clout to prove to its constituency that it, alone, was their true voice. It also provided a juicy carrot or a big old stick to use against the continuous challenges of jealous rival political organizations.

In this rush to set up organizations to speak for Indigenous people, a key element in the discussion was missing—the people who were supposed to be represented by these organizations. Were the AROs in fact the legitimate voices of the people they claimed to speak for?

A question of legitimacy

An assistant deputy minister at Indian Affairs was wondering the same thing. Bob Connelly wasn't looking to undermine the organizations for some nefarious purpose. A great deal of public money was going to be flowing to these organizations to deliver IA programs, and he wanted to ensure their legitimacy. In 1973, Connelly called in Jack Beaver, a wealthy Ojibway businessman who was the vice-president of the Churchill Falls (Labrador) Corporation. Despite the contentiousness of the massive hydro-electric project, he still had time to serve as a "fixer" for IA.[11]

Beaver was descended from a long line of chiefs of the Ojibway Alnwick Reserve near Mississauga. He joined the Royal Canadian Air Force and flew Spitfires in the Second World War. With his veteran's allowance, Beaver enrolled in Queen's University and left with an engineering degree. He then spent four years as Alnwick chief before signing on with Ontario Hydro in 1949. He worked his way up through the ranks, and was part of the team commissioning Ontario's first nuclear power plant at Deep River before leaving Ontario Hydro in 1972 for the Churchill Falls project.[12]

As an Indian leader himself, Beaver had an ongoing concern about the access of Indigenous people to legislative power. He recommended electing an Indigenous member to Parliament for each province, chosen and elected by all Indian, Inuit and Métis people. It would, Beaver said, "alleviate the ever-present problem as to whether any Indian organization properly represents the Indians they claim to."[13]

Beaver's task was to figure out if the AROs were, indeed, legitimate voices of their people. Connelly was particularly concerned about the National Indian Brotherhood, so that is where Beaver focussed his attention. He looked at the NIB, a national political organization, to see how it compared with federal political parties.

"There is a distinct difference," wrote Beaver in his report to Connelly, "between a National Political Organization and the National Indian Brotherhood in that the Political Party can only represent those who belong to the Organization while the Brotherhood assumes to speak for all Indians simply because they are Indians. The Political Party system therefore provides a basis for varying opinion or in fact active dissent by virtue of the number of parties with differing views. The National Brotherhood appears to represent a unanimity of opinion that in all probability does not exist."[14]

In other words, the multi-party system allows for multiple, dissenting voices to be heard, whereas the Indian political system has just a single party — the NIB. As anyone familiar with Indigenous politics knows, the idea that there can be a single Indigenous group representing "a unanimity of opinion" is unrealistic. Democracy tends to be inconvenient and messy wherever you go, whether Indigenous or non-Indigenous.

The silencing of dissenting voices by upholding a one-party system was one of Beaver's criticisms of the NIB. He also identified two key weaknesses of both the national and provincial Indian organizations.

First, he said, the organizations "are not directly accountable to those whom they [claim] they represent since the people cannot effectively withdraw support."[15] The NIB might assert it was speaking for all Status Indians. However, those same Status Indians did not individually sign up to the NIB, so they couldn't quit or resign or otherwise protest what the NIB was doing. If you have no mechanism to protest actions taken in your name, what kind of power do you really have over an organization that claims to speak for you?

People have a number of ways of withdrawing their support from an organization. If they have a membership, they can cancel it. Or they can simply not renew. If they paid a fee, they can ask for a refund. They can leave an organization, such as a church, by joining one that better reflects their values. The act of joining a different church is itself a statement that they no longer endorse their previous church. In political parties, cancelling a party membership is viewed as an explicit statement of repudiation, even if ex-members do not join another party. But none of these options was available to ordinary Indigenous people.

In the days before core funding (and before computers), provincial Indigenous organizations lacked the time and resources to travel around their province to recruit members and collect membership fees. After attaining core funding from IA, such efforts were not necessary, as the organizations could simply declare themselves as the voice for the Indians or the Métis. The NIB did have a legitimate claim to speak for the leaders of the provincial organizations, as they were the people who created the NIB to be their national voice in Ottawa. The links to ordinary Indian people, however, were as insubstantial as cobwebs floating on a summer breeze.

Beaver's second point was the real kicker. Legitimacy, he said, is undermined when credence is lent "by specific recognition by Government through such funding that such Organizations do in fact represent the people."[16] The very act by government officials of selecting a specific group to become an Aboriginal Representative Organization was intended to give it legitimacy. Yet the same officials who anointed the National Indian Brotherhood could, in a fit of pique or political vengeance, set up and fund a completely different group, and then declare the new outfit to be the one and only voice of all Indians. The "legitimacy" of such organizations was, and still is, bestowed by the government.

And what about the people whose voices have been hijacked? How do they get their voices heard? They don't. They have been rendered voiceless.

The "Beaver Legitimacy Test" is an important tool for testing the legitimacy of any organization that claims to speak for a particular group. Do the people in that group have a means of withdrawing their support from the organization? Is the organization's "legitimacy" bestowed by a someone other than the people it speaks for? These are simple questions, but the answers reveal a great deal. Would any of the Indigenous political organizations be able to honestly and fairly pass the Beaver Legitimacy Test?

Still, if the purpose of AROs set up in the 1970s was actually to serve IA's interests, what did it matter if the organizations were legitimate or not? Beaver's report was quickly buried, and both Indian Affairs and the National Indian Brotherhood were prepared to continue with the pretense that the NIB was the legitimate voice for all Indians.

Even with the flurry of new national, provincial and territorial Indigenous organizations set up with core funding under the Indian and Eskimo policy, Indian Affairs had larger plans. It decided in 1974 that all Indian bands would now have core funding. The elected chiefs and councils would then have resources to set up their own municipal-style governments.

This was hardly a new idea. In 1880, IA called on regional superintendents and Indian Agents "to report whether the bands under their supervision were sufficiently enlightened to justify the conclusion that the inauguration of a simple form of municipal government among them would be a success."[17] The response? The majority of those reporting back indicated that Indian bands in their districts "were not sufficiently advanced in intelligence" to take on the responsibility.[18]

It took until the 1970s—nearly 100 years after the creation of the *Indian Act* of 1876—for IA to decide that some bands were "sufficiently advanced in intelligence" to begin handling small-scale municipal-style governance. For the first time in their lives, the men on reserves who had found some small dignity in their positions as the largely powerless elected chiefs and councillors were being handed IA-sanctioned power, along with the keys to the cash box. What could possibly go wrong?

Endnotes to Chapter 6

1. Yale D. Belanger, David R. Newhouse, and Kevin Fitzmaurice, 2008, "Creating a Seat at the Table: A Retrospective Study of Aboriginal Programming at Canadian Heritage," *The Canadian Journal of Native Studies*, Vol 28, No. 1, 37.

2. Peter R. Elson, 2011, *High Ideals and Noble Intentions: Voluntary Sector-government Relations in Canada*, University of Toronto Press, 60.

3. Dominique Clément, 2005, quoting Eamon Park in a letter to Don Whiteside, November 18, 1970, in "An Exercise in Futility? Regionalism, State Funding, and Ideology as Obstacles to the Formation of a National Social Movement Organization in Canada," *BC Studies*, No. 146 (Summer): 81.

4. Belanger et al., 53.

5. Ibid., 53–54.

6. Ibid., 38.

7. Ibid.

8. Tony Belcourt, 2013, "For the Record: On Métis Identity and Citizenship Within the Métis Nation," *aboriginal policy studies*, Vol. 2, No. 2, 129. Available online: ejournals.library.ualberta.ca/index.php/aps/article/view/19010.

9. Ibid.

10. Native Women's Association of Canada, https://www.nwac.ca/home/about-nwac/about-us/.

11. Dr. Jack Beaver, Obituary, *Queen's Alumni Review*, January-February 1990, http://images.ourontario.ca/Cobourg/48315/data.

12. Ibid.

13. John (Jack) Beaver, 1975, "The Indian—Yesterday, Today and Tomorrow," *The Empire Club of Canada Addresses*, December 4, 1975, 168.

14. Jack Beaver, 1973, in a report to ADM Robert Connelly, Indian Affairs, given by Connelly to Jean Allard, part of which is referenced in *Big Bear's Treaty*.

15. Ibid.

16. Ibid.

17. Annual Report Of The Department Of Indian Affairs For The Year Ended 31st December, 1880, Dominion Of Canada, 13, http://central.bac-lac.gc.ca/.item/?id=1880-IAAR-RAAI&op=pdf&app=indianaffairs.

18. Ibid.

7
THE RISE OF THE VILLAGE TYRANT

If Harold Cardinal was angry when he wrote *The Unjust Society* in 1969 (and he was), he was livid when he wrote *The Rebirth of Canada's Indians* eight years later. His plan for community control of programs, so carefully laid out in the Red Paper, had been turned on its head, as Indian Affairs imposed its Ottawa-designed development programs upon reserves. It was a fiasco of failures.

The Red Paper had been clear that socio-economic programs "must be completely controlled by the Indian people themselves. In this way, they can literally lift themselves up by their own bootstraps."[1]

It appeared, however, that bootstrap-lifting was not on IA's agenda. It was determined to micro-manage programs of its own design. Of course, this was hardly a surprise to people living on reserves.

In the 1950s, the Civil Liberties Section of the Canadian Bar Association raised the alarm about the dangerously dictatorial powers held by the IA minister. He — and it had always been "he" up until Ellen Fairclough was appointed IA minister in 1958[2] — had exclusive power. His decisions were not subject to review or appeal, nor was he bound by law of precedent or statute. The minister had complete control over anything happening on reserves, including all matters dealing with schools, infants and "mentally defectives," the election of chiefs and councillors, and "matters testamentary."[3] In other words, the minister had total control of an Indian's life from the moment of birth to the execution of her Last Will and Testament. No wonder legal minds concerned with civil liberties were alarmed.

IA's shift in the 1960s from a policy of assimilation to one of devolution of programs and services to band governments quickly picked up steam. By 1971, only 16 percent of bands had taken over the administration of IA programs and services. By 1982, that number had jumped to 50 percent.[4] However, IA was "granting" responsibility for administration to band councils but without the accompanying authority. IA bureaucrats just couldn't seem to let go.

Mi'kmaq (Micmac) researcher Lynda Kuhn Boudreau described in the 1980s how core funding and devolution of programs affected chiefs and councils.

"Political organizations and Band Councils which had been actively fighting bureaucratic assimilation were now unconsciously becoming the tools of the Department of Indian Affairs as, with control over funding, the Department had increased control over economic, social, educational and political affairs of the Micmac people."[5]

The focus of Indian politicians turned increasingly to figuring out how to acquire more money, thereby perpetuating a system of "government grantism" on reserves.[6]

It amazed Harold Cardinal that ordinary Indian people couldn't see that the chiefs and councils had been turned into puppets of Indian Affairs. The department, he said, was subjugating an entire group with an illusion that it was delivering democracy by allowing elected chiefs and councils some small administrative duties.

"It's a hell of a frustrating thing to explain to people that what is being played on them is a cruel and deceptive trick... Indian Affairs knows that it can give them bits of programmes; a few dollars here, a bit more power there; without ever making any substantial policy changes or having to deal with the desire to bring power back to the community level. This is undoubtedly one of the best orchestrated propaganda campaigns ever launched by a government."[7]

The increased funding of band governments and the increased number of programs that bands were allowed to administer did not lead to community empowerment. Rather, it led to the kind of power struggles on reserves that had not been seen when the Indian Agent held all the cards.

When a new chief and council were elected on a reserve, said Cardinal, "they would be full of public zeal and look every way in which to perform their duties to the most benefit of the community. Then gradually another motivation strikes their actions. The chiefs and council members grow to like the power their jobs give them... Other power groups form to try to displace what has now become the establishment. Because of the way local government has been set up, a political confrontation develops. Each side seeks power and authority over the reserve."[8]

It is not illogical for people who feel disempowered to seek vehicles to enhance their sense of self. This was particularly true of men, who had ceased to have much of a role in their communities after the fur trade collapsed and farm labour jobs became scarce after the 1950s. Indian Affairs had already usurped their roles as leaders and providers. Why wouldn't they see the power imbued by the elected office as a way of reclaiming some dignity and personal empowerment?

Cardinal realized that many Indians retained a long-held respect for the chiefs chosen in the traditional way, the wise men who had signed the treaties as the best way to look after their people. They had transferred that continuing respect onto the elected chiefs.

"Some people still think that the chief and council hold the power because they signed the treaties… Nor are they aware that at the time of treaty-signing, the Indian tribal system had its own way of choosing leaders; its own way of keeping checks and balances on those leaders, and this has been lost."[9]

Selecting a chief the traditional way involved extensive consultation within the community until a consensus on the most worthy candidate was achieved. The electoral system on reserves, as with all elected political offices in Canada, imbues the office itself with worthiness, and the person holding the office just "borrows" it for a while. On reserves, elected officials could only borrow that power if Indian Affairs approved. IA had, and continues to have, the authority to unilaterally nullify election results and replace elected officials as it chooses. This, alone, reveals how thin is the power of elected officials on reserves.

Some communities have shunned band elections. Mohawk council elections on Kahnawake First Nation near Montreal are lucky to draw a 30 percent turnout, as traditionalists believe that participating in band council elections undermines their sovereignty.[10] And most members of the Six Nations Confederacy in Ontario, which considers itself the oldest democracy in the world, refuse to participate in *Indian Act* elections. Only about ten percent bother to vote. Rather, the confederacy has its own council that operates outside the control of Indian Affairs.[11]

The authority and power on reserves lies with the IA minister, not with the elected band council. There are sections in the *Indian Act* that define the decision-making framework for band councils, but those rules maintain the overriding authority of the minister.[12] Remarkably, the Act is silent about the responsibilities of the chief and council to the people who elect them, or how the people are supposed to participate in band decision-making.[13] The band councils might be elected by band members, but they are not accountable to band members. They are accountable to Indian Affairs, the source of their power and their money.

However tenuous that power might be, chiefs and councillors are nonetheless in positions of great power over residents on reserves. The IA funding for almost everything flows through their hands, the exception being any wages earned off-reserve and the $4 or $5 treaty annuities paid out each year. When the elected officials control the reserve, they control its wealth, however modest it might be, so that the faction or kin group that wins the election wins everything. It didn't take long for many reserves to develop into a two-tier society—the wealthy elite and the powerless poor. This income disparity was even more noticeable on reserves with oil and other resource wealth.

Cardinal lamented the fact that the traditional ways that include checks and balances and the laws that governed tribal communities had been lost.

"Because contact with those laws has been lost for so long, it is nearly impossible for the Indian community to create, or even apply, any system with which to check the excesses of its own leaders and its own members."[14]

The model is not entirely lost. In his unpublished manuscript "Big Bear's Treaty: The Road to Freedom," Jean Allard held up Big Bear as the model of a wise and thoughtful leader at a time when the traditional culture was fast coming to an end in the face of waves of incoming settlers. A generation before Big Bear was born, Allard's voyageur great-great-grandfather, Jean-Baptiste Lagimodière, was trading in the Northwest, and Big Bear was but an infant when another of Allard's ancestors was constructing Fort Langley on the Fraser River.[15] Change was coming.

Big Bear (Mistahimaskwa) was groomed to succeed his father as a hereditary chief, and his leadership qualities were recognized early on.

"A leader's success," said Allard, "was measured by the number of lodges in his tribe. Leaders who abused their position, who made poor decisions about where to hunt or camp, quickly lost their tribe. A family would simply pack up their lodge and move on. A chief did not order his people to follow his wishes. He advised them of his plan, and if people disagreed with him they were free to make their own decision about whether to follow him or to join a different tribe. It was an effective check and balance on the power of leaders."[16]

At the height of his leadership, Big Bear counted 400 lodges in his band, or about 3,000 people. Big Bear was one of the last major Plains leaders to sign on to Treaty 6, and he held off signing for four years while he tried to figure out the best thing to do for his people. When he did finally sign in 1882, little more than 100 people remained with him.[17] His people were facing starvation while Big Bear sought (and failed) to create a coalition of Cree bands to press the Crown for contiguous reserves in the North West;[18] they voted with their feet.

Of course, that option no longer existed for Indians after the imposition of the *Indian Act*. The Indian Affairs branch registered Indians (thus giving them Status) based on their belonging to particular bands. There was little provision for free movement between reserves, even within the same tribe. On the Prairies where Big Bear's people had once roamed, band members required a pass from the Indian Agent to leave their reserve. The pass system was a departmental policy instituted to prevent Indians from joining the 1885 North-West Rebellion, but the policy continued well into the 1940s. Indians caught off-reserve without their papers were subject to arrest by the police.[19] Since the Agent also had to power to refuse entry of visitors or any other outsiders, exercised at his own discretion, there was little point in packing up the family and moving to a better reserve, only to be turned away.

In the 1970s, Cardinal seemed to be pleading for course correction to address the distorted power dynamics on reserves under the *Indian Act* elections.

"We can set up in our laws a system of responsible local government that distributes power fairly between the chief, the council and the people on the reserve. We can set up legislation that guides, that guarantees, that protects the basic rights of the individual."[20]

Otherwise, he warned, they would end up with "a national system of village-level tyrants."[21]

Was anyone at Indian Affairs listening? Apparently not. In Manitoba, "partnership" on economic development between the Manitoba Indian Brotherhood (MIB) and Indian Affairs had turned into a farce. MIB president Dave Courchene was thoroughly fed up. Between the frustration of failed development projects and the pressure on band councils to deliver more IA-managed services, Courchene realized with great bitterness, "We are administering our own people's misery."[22]

Working on the inside

After nine years as president of the Indian Association of Alberta, Cardinal finally wearied of the never-ending conflict with Indian Affairs, and often with other Indian organizations and band councils. He decided in 1977 that if he couldn't effect change from outside IA, he'd try to do it from the inside. Cardinal became the first Status Indian to be appointed to the post of regional director general of Indian Affairs in Alberta. (Phil Fontaine followed suit shortly after, and moved to the Yukon in 1978 to become the regional director general there.)

There is an old saying that the best way to silence a radical is to turn him into a bureaucrat. Cardinal took up his new job in Edmonton in April 1977. In November, he informed Indian Affairs minister Hugh Faulkner that he suspected there was a kickback scheme going on involving economic development money that might implicate senior bureaucrats in IA in Alberta.[23] Faulkner responded by immediately firing Cardinal. So much for silencing the radical. The staffers Cardinal had brought into IA with him on contract were let go, too.[24] The firings resulted in about fifty Indians occupying the IA's Edmonton office,[25] and the adverse publicity forced Faulkner's hand. He turned to the department's favourite fixer, Jack Beaver, who had just retired as president of the Churchill Falls power company and had a bit of time on his hands.

At issue was a $10 million loan from Alberta's allocation of the Indian Affairs economic development fund. Given that Cardinal had just moved from president of the Indian Association of Alberta to a senior management position in the Alberta IA offices, he appeared to have already had some suspicions about inappropriately cozy relationships between some chiefs and IA bureaucrats.[26] Cardinal's allegations of financial mismanagement triggered an immediate backlash from his former colleagues at the association, who denounced him as being abrasive and arbitrary.[27] They were unhappy with Cardinal, who had been trying to rein in the growing abuses on reserves by documenting problems such as non-repayable "loans" to band officials, and warning chiefs that he might go to the police.²⁸ Following Cardinal's firing, IA denied there was any wrongdoing, maybe just a little sloppiness in the paperwork while Indians were learning the ropes about development loans. Beaver disagreed. After a three-month investigation, he called in the RCMP.²⁹

In an interim report released by IA minister Hugh Faulkner at a news conference in mid-February 1978, Beaver called the controls in place after loans were made as "completely inadequate and should be unacceptable to any responsible person in any form of economic development."³⁰

Beaver told The Canadian Press that he was continuing to work with the RCMP. "There is significant data to indicate poor judgement and management of several, if not the majority of, projects involved."³¹

Faulkner pointed out that there was a world of difference between misuse of funds and poor judgement, but promised that financial controls at the Alberta regional Indian Affairs office would be straightened out quickly.³² The "straightening out," it seems, took the form of tidying up the whole mess by retroactively approving suspect transactions.³³ The investigation promptly ended with no charges being laid.

It's not hard to figure out what kind of message such "tidying" sent to Indian Affairs bureaucrats, the Indian political organizations funded by IA, and the chiefs and councils that handled the money flowing to reserves from IA. If someone as respected as Harold Cardinal could be run out of town for attempting to address the odour of corruption surrounding large piles of poorly controlled money, what was the point of complaining about suspected financial mismanagement on reserves? It signalled to the growing number of "village tyrants" that they were unlikely to face any penalties from IA or the justice system for their bad behaviour either.

Harold Cardinal, at the age of thirty-three, walked away from a decade in Indian politics in disgust. Jack Beaver, however, was appointed Special Adviser to the Indian Affairs minister on April 1, 1978.³⁴

Beaver barely had time to tidy up his files on the Alberta IA investigation before Faulkner had another job for him back in Ottawa. Beaver was to undertake a comprehensive review of the same troubled IA socio-economic development program, but on a national scale. He would be working with the National Indian Brotherhood, with an eye on how best to transfer control of the economic development funds to Indian organizations.³⁵ That suited the NIB president, thirty-four-year-old Cree Noel Starblanket, because the NIB felt that it should be in control of the millions being spent on development projects on reserves.

The new National Indian Socio-Economic Development Committee was jointly sponsored by IA and the NIB, and was headed by Beaver, who had a three-year mandate to develop a holistic approach to Indian economic development that included sensitivity to cultural and community needs. The committee's board met for the first time in December 1978. Beaver was fired three months later.

Beaver had been promised independence, but the NIB wanted his work to be under its own economic development sub-committee. Beaver refused, and in March 1979, the NIB executive called on its provincial and territorial counterparts to boycott Beaver's consultations, and requested that all band councils in the country submit resolutions confirming that they would not deal with him either.[36]

Beaver was not deterred by such a public show of political shunning. Besides, the horse was already out of the barn and across the pasture. Being independently wealthy, Beaver had not waited on funding from the new committee to get started on his consultations. He'd spent much of the summer and fall of 1978 holding more than seventy meetings with Indian people and their organizations, and another seventy with non-Indigenous people involved in socio-economic development. He already had most of his work completed when he was fired.[37]

Why did the NIB want Beaver out? It might have had something to do with his examination of the flow of funds from IA to Indian people and an evaluation of band governance. He was prying the lid off a box in which its inhabitants had started getting comfortable with the easy way money could flow in the dark when there was no one watching too closely. And Beaver was also looking again at that pesky question about the legitimacy of Indian political organizations to speak for ordinary Indians.

The NIB was ready this time. Chiefs and regional organizations had been chafing for a while about having to work politically through the provincial Indian organizations, and complained their voices were not being heard. While Beaver and Starblanket were still battling it out over Beaver's control of the development committee, Starblanket called for an "All Chiefs Conference" to be held in April 1979. It would be the first of its kind in Canadian history.[38] It was also the first step in NIB becoming the Assembly of First Nations. If the chiefs were the legitimately elected voices of their people, then an organization representing the chiefs could legitimately claim to be "the one and only voice of Indian people in Canada."

After Beaver was fired, he decided to finish the job he'd taken on and "exit with voice." He produced a final report called "To have what is one's own," generally referred to as the Beaver Report, and submitted it to Starblanket and the newest Indian Affairs minister Jake Epp in October 1979.

Perhaps because Beaver had already taken a deep dive into the messy complexities of the tangled relationship in Alberta between IA and Indian organizations, he took a hard line on how both sides were making a mess of economic development programs. IA bureaucrats wanted control of its programs and how they would be delivered. NIB, aware that its existence depended on IA funding, wanted to demonstrate its independence by fighting IA every step of the way. The result was that, even where they had common goals, they couldn't get out of their own way.[39]

For Beaver, the way to untie this Gordian knot was to cut IA and Indian organizations out of the process and to give Indian bands the authority and responsibility of developing their own policies for development specific to their community, with their own definition of what constitutes "development."[40]

But first, Beaver outlined the problems on reserves, with IA policy and with Indian organizations.

On reserves: "Indian people have lost control over their lives. They have lost their traditional capacities for healing, caring, learning and providing food and shelter. Instead, increasingly large numbers of Indian people are heavily dependent on welfare; large numbers of children are neglected and relegated to the care of Children's Aid Societies; and large numbers of adults are dependent on alcohol… The tragedy is that there is no evidence of improvement in this intolerable condition in spite of increasing Government expenditures."[41]

On IA policy: "Indian Affairs has taken on exclusive control over the definition and the purported satisfaction of almost all the basic human needs (healing, teaching, provision of food and shelter, burying the dead) to the point that it prevents or inhibits the natural competence of people to provide for themselves." This radical monopoly of a captive clientele, said Beaver, revealed itself in the attitude of government officials "that Indian people are somehow not competent enough to decide for themselves."[42]

On Indian organizations: The NIB legitimately defines itself as a political entity, said Beaver, (although not the legitimate "sole voice" of Indian people) but its constant posturing "practically guarantees the collapse of all joint efforts [and] it has impeded, and in many cases prevented absolutely, the search for innovative and pragmatic solutions to the real problems on reserves."[43]

Beaver also provided possible solutions. He had long been pushing for Indian self-government, depending on how ready various bands were to undertake such responsibilities. He called for a transformational change in band government, from being agents of IA to being political organizations, with issues decided for and by Indian people, and endowed with the power and responsibility to do so.

Beaver's recommendation for Indian Affairs was to get out of the way, stop meddling in everything and limit itself to a supporting role in band development.[44] And what of his suggestion for Indian political organizations like the NIB and its provincial and territorial counterparts? Change the associations, he urged, to better reflect the interests of its members, and look to its constituency for funding instead of IA.

Forgotten in all the pushing and pulling between IA, Indian political organizations and band councils were ordinary people on reserves. Even Beaver overlooked them. The focus was on empowering the collective, and nobody was talking about empowering the individuals within the collective or trying to figure out how an impoverished constituency was supposed to find the money to fund political organizations.

Jean Allard's plan to use his position in the Manitoba government to make "substantial changes to the lives of impoverished Indians on northern reserves" got off to a strong start in 1971, but collapsed under the weight of a government agenda moving in a different direction. In frustration, he quit the NDP party the following year to sit as an Independent,[45] leaving him plenty of time to brood about poverty and powerlessness on reserves.

When the dust settled at the end of the 1970s, Harold Cardinal had left Indian politics behind him and become a director of an oil and gas company.[46] Jack Beaver put a great deal of distance between himself and the messiness of Indian politics—half a world, in fact. He became a vice-president of Atomic Energy of Canada in 1979, in charge of the construction of a CANDU nuclear power plant in South Korea.[47]

So much had changed over a decade from the "great thunderclap of '69" when Cardinal had led the successful challenge against the Trudeau government's plan to eliminate the *Indian Act* and the treaties, and to shut down the Indian Affairs department. The Act was still a bone of contention and the treaties still had no constitutional protection. The big change was the flourishing of Indian political organizations funded by the government and the increased politicization of band governance. Life on many reserves was not getting better. It was getting worse.

Harold Cardinal didn't stay away from Indian politics for long. In 1980, Pierre Trudeau had begun the process of repatriating the constitution, and as soon as it became apparent that there was an opportunity for treaty rights to be enshrined in the constitution, Cardinal returned to the fray. He was elected chief of the Sucker Creek band in 1982, and he added his efforts to constitutional reform as vice-chief for the Western Region of the Assembly of First Nations.[48]

The plan to include the right to self-government in the constitution was stirring up a lot of controversy in Ottawa between cabinet ministers, Indian Affairs and the National Indian Brotherhood.

The federal government's objective was to roll out Indian band government legislation in 1982 that would enable bands to begin a more organized move to self-governance after the constitution was repatriated, and it included significant money for economic development. A report from the Indian Affairs department on band governance that same year noted that the *Indian Act* was an impediment to strengthening band governance:

"The terms of the Act are such that Bands can be little more than administrative arms of the Federal Department of Indian and Northern Affairs, administering programs which react to poverty on Indian reserves rather than to respond to traditional Indian socio-economic and political standards."[49]

There was a very real fear, however, that if the legislation was not handled properly, it might feel like a repeat of the 1969 White Paper, and nobody wanted that. The Standing Committee of Indian Affairs and Northern Development was to address only governance at the band level, and avoid straying into regional and national Indian government discussions, as that would raise constitutional concerns.⁵⁰ There would be official consultations so that Indian organizations would be sure to feel like they were participating in the constitutional issues affecting them, and the Canadian public would see for themselves that this time Indians were being properly consulted.

This move for visible consultations was happening under an IA department that viewed itself in 1982 as "the official representative of Indian and Inuit peoples,"⁵¹ where the department "assumes an active role as policy maker, arbiter of land claims, protector of Indian and Inuit interests and advocates on their behalf vis-á-vis federal and provincial governments."⁵² At this point, IA's client base consisted of the 71 percent of the 317,000 Status or Registered Indians who lived on reserves, and 23,626 Inuit, about half of whom lived above the tree line.⁵³

The sticking point on the tactics of consultations was how to fund NIB to take on most of the workload, while at the same time dancing a two-step around the issue of NIB's questionable legitimacy to speak for all Indians.

IA had three options in front of it. One was to give the NIB a pile of money so they could get on with the consultations. It would have the benefit of not disrupting the status quo, and would avoid the potentially unwieldy problem of having to deal with a range of different Indian groups with different opinions. Or the NIB could be given the funding on the condition that they had to consult with other Indian groups. Or, the government could fund other groups to speak for themselves, but this would be an open admission that the government knew very well that the NIB did not speak for all Indians.⁵⁴

The government actually considered bringing in Jack Beaver to sort out the various confusions and entanglements. He was back in Canada, but had his hands full running the commission in charge of supplying electric power across the country, north of the 60th parallel.⁵⁵ Besides, Beaver's clash with the NIB might have still been too fresh a wound for that to have worked.

The NIB formalized its shift to becoming a chiefs' organization in 1985 by adopting a new constitution and changing its name to the Assembly of First Nations (AFN), while retaining the NIB as its corporate entity. The reorganization did not include cutting the umbilical cord with Indian Affairs. The chiefs could have settled the question about AFN/NIB legitimacy by deciding to fund the Assembly themselves or through band member contributions. Of course, it is unlikely that the roughly 600 chiefs could have come up with anywhere near enough money to replace IA funding.

The IA policy of limiting bands to twenty-five-cents per capita for political organizing was long gone, but it was still IA money going to the band governments and still IA calling the shots. Besides, during a critical time in negotiating a self-governance framework, why would the federal government want to reduce its leverage by giving up its "ownership" of all the Indigenous political organizations? Of course, the federal government would have to tread carefully because the AFN/NIB had learned a thing or two about how to play the political game, fight for Aboriginal rights, and influence public opinion through the media.

The finalized *Constitution Act* of 1982 included section 35, which defined Aboriginal people as Indian, Métis and Inuit, who would collectively fall under the umbrella of Indian Affairs jurisdiction. It also recognized the existence of aboriginal and treaty rights.

However, section 35 nearly didn't make it into the Act at all after Justice Minister Jean Chrétien stuck his oar in. Following the so-called "meeting of the long knives" in 1981, where the nine anglophone provinces worked out an arrangement, Chrétien had agreed with the premiers of Alberta and Saskatchewan that Aboriginal treaty rights be dropped from the draft constitution for later discussions. It immediately triggered a national outcry by Indian leaders.

George Manuel, president of the Union of BC Indian Chiefs (and the first president of the National Indian Brotherhood), organized two trains leaving from Vancouver on November 24, 1980, with one going the north route through Edmonton, the other south through Calgary. The trains met in Winnipeg, and the estimated 1,000 passengers went on to Ottawa, adding more supporters on their way to storm Parliament Hill.[56]

"Along the way," recalled George's son Arthur, "they raised such consciousness amongst Indigenous people that the train was literally stopped in northern parts of Ontario so people could give them moose stew and bannock as Indigenous people started to become aware that the constitutional framework was vitally important to them."[57]

The "Constitution Express" train demonstration also got the attention of the Canadian public, and section 35 was put right back into the draft text of the Constitution. The inclusion of section 35 was, however, the equivalent of an empty box. The rights, including self-governance, were yet to be determined. Were rights inherent or were they dispensed by the federal and provincial governments? There were many questions yet to be answered, but Cardinal was not at the table for this debate. Once the *Constitution Act* passed, he left politics again. Cardinal and his wife packed up their six kids and moved to Saskatoon so Cardinal could go to university. He was going to become a lawyer specializing in treaty issues.

Four First Ministers Conferences on Aboriginal matters, with the Prime Minister, premiers, territorial government leaders, and the four Aboriginal Representative Organizations (AROs), were held from 1983 to 1987 to try to figure out what would go into the section 35 empty box. The AROs included the Assembly of First Nations (formerly the NIB), the Métis National Council (formed in 1983), Inuit Tapirisat of Canada, and the Congress of Aboriginal Peoples (formerly the Native Council of Canada). The Native Women's Association of Canada (NWAC) was not invited to participate.[58] The meetings failed to produce any kind of resolution on how Aboriginal rights were to be defined.

Meanwhile, conditions on reserves continued to worsen, even as more and more money was spent, primarily to address social and economic dysfunction. In 1984, suicide rates, particularly for younger people, were six times the national rate,[59] and incarceration rates, particularly for Indigenous men, were seven times the national rate.[60]

As the poverty and suffering on reserves grew, so did Indian Affairs. A good government department is typically defined as one that is delivering more and more programs, and Jean Chrétien was cheering on his department in what he considered its "glory days."[61] He considered the department's rapid expansion as a boon to his political reputation and for his popularity with bureaucrats.

"In a period of expansion," said Chrétien, "ministers are judged by how much money they can spend and how well they can extract money from the system for their projects. Spending was easy, because there was no end to the useful and imaginative initiatives bubbling up in the department."[62]

By 1984, the department, which had started out with a budget for delivering Indigenous programs and services of about $131 million in 1967 (with two co-delivery partners), had seen its expenditures soar to $2.42 billion (with eleven co-delivery partners) over just seventeen years.[63] Apparently, there was still no end to the "useful and imaginative initiatives," as Jean Chrétien had called them, bubbling up at IA. Perhaps there's a better description of this state of affairs. As Indian Affairs grew, so did the poverty and suffering on reserves.

Endnotes to Chapter 7

1. Indian Chiefs of Alberta, "Citizens Plus," *aboriginal policy studies*, Vol. 1, No. 2 (2011): 228.
2. Minister of Crown-Indigenous Relations, https://en.wikipedia.org/wiki/Minister_of_Crown%E2%80%93Indigenous_Relations#Cabinet_ministers.
3. Canadian Bar Association Civil Liberties Section, 1956, "The Legal Status and Civil Rights of the Canadian Indians."
4. Indian Band Government Legislation (Report), 1982, Indian Affairs and Northern Development, 89, http://publications.gc.ca/collections/collection_2017/aanc-inac/R32-304-1982-eng.pdf.
5. Lynda Kuhn Boudreau, 1981, "Economic Development Strategies and the Micmac of Nova Scotia," M.A. Thesis, McGill University, 44.
6. Ibid., 44.
7. Harold Cardinal, 1969 (1999 reprint), *The Unjust Society*, Hurtig Publishing, 101.
8. Harold Cardinal, 1977, *The Rebirth of Canada's Indians*, Hurtig Publishers, 27.
9. Cardinal, 1969, 100.
10. Christopher Curtis, June 13, 2018, "Kahnawake election uncontested, but Mohawk politics 'never boring,'" *Montreal Gazette*, https://montrealgazette.com/news/local-news/politics-kahnawake.
11. "First Nations Elections: The Choice is Inherently Theirs," 2010, Report to the Standing Senate Committee on Aboriginal Peoples, 17.
12. Frances Abele, 2007, "Like an Ill-Fitting Boot: Government, Governance and Management Systems in the Contemporary Indian Act," National Centre on First Nations Governance, 10.
13. First Nations Elections, 2010, 24.
14. Cardinal, 1977, 30.
15. Jean Allard, interview with author, 1999.
16. Jean Allard, 2002, "Big Bear's Treaty: The road to freedom," *Inroads*, Issue 11, 118.
17. Ibid.
18. Mistahimaskwa (Big Bear), https://library.usask.ca/northwest/background/bear.htm.
19. Kathryn Warden, 1993, "Indian Act: Permit to control a culture," *The Star Phoenix*, Vol. 11, Issue 6, http://www.ammsa.com/publications/windspeaker/indian-act-permit-control-culture.
20. Ibid., 38.
21. Ibid., 37.
22. James Burke, 1976, *Paper Tomahawks: From red tape to red power*, Queenston House Publishing, 73.
23. Canadian Press, "Cardinal allegations disputed," *The Medicine Hat News*, November 29, 1977, 8.
24. Cher Bloom, 2002, "Margaret Vickers: The Hand of Change," *First Nations Drum*, http://www.firstnationsdrum.com/2002/09/margaret-vickers-the-hand-of-change/.
25. Suzanne Zwarun, "The not-so-happy warrior," *Maclean's*, December 12, 1977, http://archive.macleans.ca/article/1977/12/12/the-not-so-happy-warrior.
26. Ibid.
27. Editorial: "Was Cardinal misjudged?" *The Lethbridge Herald*, February 18, 1978.
28. Allard, 2002, 133.
29. Editorial: *The Lethbridge Herald*, 1978.

30 Canadian Press, 1978, "Indian affairs finances to be cleared up by June," *The Lethbridge Herald*, February 18, 1978, 32.

31 Ibid., 32.

32 Ibid.

33 Allard, 2002, 133.

34 Jack Beaver, 1979, "To have what is one's own," Report, The National Indian Socio-Economic Development Committee, 15.

35 Report, 1978, INAC National Executive Planning Committee Meeting, Regina, Saskatchewan, November 15–17, 1978, 5.

36 Beaver, 1979, 18.

37 Ibid., 15.

38 Michael Posluns, 2007, *Speaking with Authority: The Emergence of the Vocabulary of First Nations' Self-Government*, Routledge, 198.

39 Beaver, 1979, 33.

40 Ibid., iii.

41 Ibid., 23.

42 Ibid., 26.

43 Ibid., 33.

44 Ibid., 73.

45 "Allard Leaves NDP—Says Leftist Radicals Hold Govt. Control," *Winnipeg Free Press*, Saturday, April 8, 1972.

46 Catherine Clennet, 2005, "Profile of Harold Cardinal," *Hidden in Plain Sight: Contributions of Aboriginal Peoples to Canadian Identity and Culture, Volume 1*, David R. Newhouse, Cora J. Voyageur, and Dan Beavon, eds., University of Toronto Press, 35–36.

47 Dr. Jack Beaver, Obituary, *Queen's Alumni Review*, January-February 1990, http://images.ourontario.ca/Cobourg/48315/data.

48 "Harold Cardinal," *The Canadian Encyclopedia*, https://www.thecanadianencyclopedia.ca/en/article/harold-cardinal.

49 Indian Band Government Legislation (Report), 1982, Indian Affairs and Northern Development, page 3 of composite document, http://publications.gc.ca/collections/collection_2017/aanc-inac/R32-304-1982-eng.pdf.

50 Ibid., page 5 of composite document.

51 Ibid., Consultation and Participation of Native People: Policy, page 22 of composite document.

52 Ibid.

53 Ibid., Section G: Demographics, page 39 of composite document.

54 Contribution Agreements: A Partial History of "Devolution" June 2012, p 26–27, http://www.thunderchild.ca/upload/documents/Why%20There%20Are%20Contributions%20Agreements[1].pdf

55 Obituary: "Dr. Jack Beaver was CEO of NCPC," *Queen's Alumni Review*, January-February 1990, 35.

56 Arthur Manuel, and Ronald Derrickson, 2015, *Unsettling Canada: A National Wake-Up Call*, Between the Lines.

57 Arthur Manuel and Ronald Derrickson, 2017, *The Reconciliation Manifesto: Recovering the Land,*

Rebuilding the Economy, James Lorimer and Company, 96.

58 The Native Women's Association of Canada was excluded from the First Ministers meetings until 1993. Premiers' Conferences 1887–2002, Canadian Intergovernmental Conference Secretariat, 38, https://www.scics.ca/wp-content/uploads/2016/10/premiers_report_e.pdf.

59 Laurence J. Kirmayer et al, 1994, *Suicide in Canadian Aboriginal Populations: Emerging Trends in Research and Intervention*, prepared for the Royal Commission on Aboriginal Peoples, 1, http://data2.archives.ca/rcap/pdf/rcap-93.pdf.

60 Erik Nielsen, Deputy Prime Minister, Memorandum to Cabinet: Report of the Ministerial Task Force on Native Programs, April 12, 1985, 11.

61 Jean Chrétien, 1985, *Straight from the Heart*, Key Porter Books, 72.

62 Ibid.

63 Ibid.

8

THE BUFFALO JUMP POLICY OF '85

Prime Minister Brian Mulroney was about to put a stop to the out-of-control spending on Indian programs and services. The day after his Conservative government was sworn into office in the fall of 1984,[1] the PM ordered his deputy PM Erik Nielsen to begin a hush-hush task force review of "Indian and native programs."[2] The task force considered that "neither the deplorable social and economic circumstances for native people, nor the rapid escalation of costs associated with native programs, are acceptable."[3]

The 1985 Task Force report bore remarkable similarities to the 1969 White Paper, as if the federal government had never really abandoned its termination policies. Maybe it hadn't. According to a memo sent April 1, 1970 to Trudeau and Indian Affairs minister Jean Chrétien by one of IA's assistant deputy ministers on preserving the principles of the White Paper, "We can still believe with just as much strength and sincerity that the policies we propose are the right ones...." However, he added that "we should adopt somewhat different tactics in relation to policy, but that we should not depart from its essential content."[4]

Mulroney was not advancing a Trudeau policy so much as attempting to rein in the out-of-control spending the new Conservative government had inherited. One part of the deficit reduction plan was focussed on Indian Affairs. But once again, consultations with ordinary Indigenous people were nowhere in sight. Nielsen's bureaucrats did, however, consult "program managers, economic development co-ordinators, deputy heads, and the Private Sector Advisory Committee to the Task Force," along with "limited consultations with selected client groups" and with senior deputies from several provincial governments.[5] The idea was to keep a lid on what the task force was doing as it prepared its report to Cabinet, and Nielsen's team went to considerable lengths to ensure secrecy.

What the task force was most concerned about was the continuing upward spiral of costs for programs and services delivered by IA and its co-delivery partners, which had reached $2.42 billion in 1983–85. Those costs were projected to hit more than $5 billion in five years, and that did not include the estimated $500 million backlog in housing and potential for about $8 billion in land claims settlements over the next decade or so.[6] The main problem was that "anything having to do with natives, especially Indians and Inuit,"[7] was assumed to be a federal matter, and within the federal government, the responsibility of IA. Over time, IA had evolved into a hybrid of a federal department and a provincial government, but without the depth of capacity to meet such a wide range of needs.

The plan was to divest Ottawa of as much responsibility for Indians as possible, with the federal government legally obliged to cover only 25 percent of what IA was spending. Another 40 percent of programs and services were considered to properly be the responsibility of the provinces and municipalities, including responsibility for band governments. The remaining 35 percent was considered discretionary social spending. The objective was to offload as much as possible as quickly as possible, and then redistribute Indian Affairs' remaining program responsibilities to other federal departments. The department would then be dismantled.[8]

The task force team anticipated that Indian organizations would vociferously oppose the task force plan. One tactic to quiet dissent was to have the Justice Minister review the practice of funding only select Aboriginal groups (AROs) to see if the practice contravened the Charter of Rights. Another was to take the consultation funding for the self-government negotiations going to AROs and give it directly to band governments. Both moves would weaken the clout of political organizations that were becoming more adept at using the media to move public opinion.[9]

In particular, the strategy for rolling out the new policy for IA relied on continuing to keep Indian leadership in the dark. With the federal budget scheduled to be released on May 20, 1985 and a First Ministers Conference with Aboriginal leaders slated for the following week, the task force advised "withholding news of specific native programming until June" as part of the budget discussions so that the conference could proceed "without the added complication of an adverse native reaction to the program changes."[10]

Because of the demand for secrecy, it is highly unlikely that any bureaucrats ever intended that the informal name they had given to the 395-page termination plan — The Buffalo Jump of the 1980s — would ever be made public.[11] They were mistaken.

"The entire review was conducted behind a dense wall of secrecy," said Menno Boldt, author of a number of books on Indigenous issues, "thereby creating a good deal of curiosity and speculations about political intrigue. It was predictable that when a summary of one of these secret reviews, a sixty-one-page document entitled *Memorandum to Cabinet: Report of the Ministerial Task Force on Native Programs*, was leaked to the media, it would achieve instant 'celebrity status' and become the focus of intense (media, political, and academic) scrutiny."[12]

Indeed, it triggered immediate howls of outrage in the Indigenous political community, just as the White Paper had done.

The informal Buffalo Jump title, whether intended as a joke or not, was a dead giveaway. A buffalo jump is a cliff over which bison would fall to their deaths after being herded into narrowing drive lanes and then spooked from behind so that the herd stampeded forward and pushed each other over the edge. Any injured animals that survived the fall could be easily dispatched at the bottom of the cliff.

What exactly did the Mulroney government have in mind? It seemed that the task force agreed that the past twenty-five years of IA devolution policy had left an unfortunate legacy on many reserves: "participation rates in employment are low and unemployment remains consistently high. Suicide, particularly for younger people, is six times the comparable national rate.... Incarceration rates are high—seven times the national rate."[13] However, the task force was advising dumping the whole mess onto reserve residents to fix themselves, and with less money.[14] "Experience has shown," it noted, "that these problems cannot be solved by the application of more money."[15]

Under this new policy, Canada's 579 band governments,[16] squeezed for money by funding caps and a ban on deficit financing—while still facing all the same social and economic problems—could be pushed towards self-governance agreements and maybe not notice the danger ahead. If band governments took the jump, they would be required to give up their Aboriginal rights in exchange for multi-year block funding, and turned into ethnic municipalities at the bottom of the governance hierarchy. As more bands took on "self-governance," it would be easier to start stampeding the others over the cliff.

It's no wonder the Mulroney government wanted to keep a lid on its new policy. The Indian Affairs minister of the day was David Crombie, formerly Toronto's "tiny perfect mayor," and he was poorly equipped to handle the blowback from a report for which he had no responsibility. The leaked details of the Nielsen report were damning, and Crombie and the Prime Minister quickly scrambled to assure everyone that the report was just a report and not government policy.[17]

Crombie, in the House of Commons, dismissed the report as "the entrails of policies which have been found in the wastebaskets of the bureaucracy."[18] However, it seemed that Mulroney was still intending to advance the Buffalo Jump policy, but do it quietly. Mulroney promised to maintain government spending, but the government continued its efforts to downsize Indian Affairs, and continued the devolution efforts begun during the Trudeau years.

Behind the "self-government" drive was the goal of extinguishing federal responsibilities for Indians—a policy of termination. Unlike the Trudeau era prior to the repatriation of the Constitution, the federal government could no longer unilaterally nullify treaties or eliminate Aboriginal rights. Those rights were now enshrined in the Constitution. Since it was the chiefs who had the legal authority to sign agreements with IA, it would be necessary to "persuade" band chiefs to voluntarily sign away their peoples' rights.

The means for doing so was two-fold: squeeze bands financially until the suffering of the people compelled chiefs to sign away their peoples' rights, while extending the promise of five-year block funding and relief from the controls of the *Indian Act.*

However, much of the Mulroney agenda on Indigenous issues was sidelined by a hostile relationship with Indigenous people (excepting the Métis political organizations, which were secretly pursuing their own Métis Nation agenda). In the summer of 1990, the animosity between the federal government and First Nations came to a head in a violent, armed stand-off on Mohawk land near Oka, Quebec that lasted nearly eighty days. That confrontation led to Mulroney shifting gears and setting up the Royal Commission on Aboriginal Peoples in 1991.

And then Mulroney was out and the new government of Jean Chrétien was in. Chrétien decided he would take a different tack on Indigenous issues.

The Manitoba self-government experiment

In 1994, the newest Department of Indian Affairs and Northern Development minister Ron Irwin signed the ambitious Manitoba Framework Agreement with Phil Fontaine, who had returned to Manitoba to head the Assembly of Manitoba Chiefs (AMC), formerly the Manitoba Indian Brotherhood. The Framework Agreement set out the process to "dismantle DIAND operations, develop Manitoba First Nations government institutions, and restore to Manitoba First Nations governments the jurisdictions currently held by DIAND and other federal departments."[19] The Framework had two goals: to establish First Nations governance in accordance with the inherent right to self-governance, and to develop band governments legally empowered to exercise their authority.[20] As Manitoba's First Nations took over governance authority, the Indian Affairs regional departmental structures in Manitoba would be dismantled. It was the most ambitious self-government initiative undertaken in Canada.[21]

If it looked like it might be just another White Paper/Buffalo Jump gambit, that's not how the AMC saw the $60 million agreement. It was determined to base the new governance method on a consensus around what the people wanted. Success depended on the individual communities buying into the results. The AMC hired dozens of staff, set up a variety of committees, and got right to work. How hard could it be to take over IA administration jobs? There was surely nothing difficult about dismantling the IA regional office, and then moving in and taking over what was there.[22]

Community consultations were more of challenge, but they were crucial to the Framework's success.

"Outcomes cannot be imposed," stated the Memorandum of Understanding for the Framework Agreement. "Moreover, consultation and communications throughout the Project must be focused on, and delivered primarily by, individual First Nations communities and tribal councils in order to ensure the widest possible support and maximum absorption of information and decision-making."[23]

It turned out that there weren't very many people AMC could hire who could go out to the province's sixty-two reserves to talk about self-governance and what it might mean to communities. AMC had to start by educating and training community co-ordinators on such topics as the Constitution, citizenship, judicial systems, accountability and governance structures. They would then be able to talk with ordinary people on reserves about different ideas they might have for governance. The coordinators would then bring the results of their discussions back to Framework officials, who would attempt to make sense of all the information coming in to develop a governance model.

In rural areas, coordinators ran into problems with outdated band lists and the fact that many band members were transient. Reaching out to urban Status Indians was enough of a complication that they were dropped from the consultations.

It was a slow process, in part because many ordinary FN people were so used to governance being decided in government offices somewhere else and then imposed on them that they hadn't given much thought to the issues. Nonetheless, it soon became apparent in interviews with community Elders that there was a strong leaning towards governance based on traditional culture and values. But how many people even knew what that meant anymore? Traditional governance had ended a century before with the signing of the treaties.

The coordinators themselves had to be brought up to speed first before they could go back out into the field to share what they'd learned about traditional ways with ordinary people on reserves.[24] It was a learning opportunity for everyone, but the seeds of traditional self-governance were taking hold. Governance through humility, honesty and balance held great appeal. What the people were considering, whether they realized it or not, was governance based on self-determination, which is loosely defined as "the right and ability of a people or a group of people to choose their own destiny without external compulsion."[25]

The AMC team was confident that all was going according to plan and that the possibility of developing a traditional governance model that could function in the modern world was beginning to take form. True, according to the initiative's work plan, they were running behind schedule because of all the training and education needed just to get started, and because some communities were taking their time with their deliberations. Not all chiefs were on board, either. Some saw a return to traditional governance as a direct threat to the power they wielded under the Indian Affairs system.[26]

Due to the substantial amount of money involved in the Framework initiative, the agreement called for regular reviews by IA. By 1999, the AMC had already spent $27 million on research and consultations over five years, and suddenly, IA froze their funding.

When IA wouldn't bend, the AMC authorized three chiefs to head directly to Ottawa to appeal to the Standing Senate Committee on Aboriginal Peoples.

"The federal government," explained one of the chiefs to the senate committee, "has been under a lot of pressure to make sense of this $27 million which was spent but, to my mind, there is no better way to spend $27 million than on building the foundation of a new government. When this process is done, in all honesty, we will be able to say we have a government by the people for the people."[27]

And further, consultations were making progress and funding should be reinstated.

"We consult with our home communities and ask how we can look after ourselves so that we can go forward. Our people back home have been waiting for this for a long time. When we go to meetings and talk to the elders, we talk about this new self-government initiative. They shake their heads and say, 'What took you so long?' They have always known that this was the way."[28]

Unfortunately, the presentation to the Senate proved fruitless; so three Grand Chiefs were dispatched to Ottawa to negotiate directly with Indian Affairs. Part of the problem was the changeover in leaders. The principals who signed the agreement were no longer involved. Phil Fontaine had departed the AMC to run for national chief of the Assembly of First Nations (he won), and of course there was yet another new IA minister, Jane Stewart.

The Grand Chiefs did get the funding for the Framework Initiative reinstated, but at a cost that compromised the entire effort. The minister would allow the initiative to continue only if the AMC immediately ceased community consultations. They weren't necessary because Indian Affairs had already decided that "self-government" would be modelled on municipal-style governance. The initiative continued, as there was still work to be done in the area of devolution of responsibilities for education, child and family services, and fiscal relations.[29] But the heart and soul of the project—genuine self-determination—had been cut out.

Perhaps the AMC had been naïve to believe they were truly going to be allowed traditional self-governance on First Nations terms. It seemed clear in retrospect that IA was only going to countenance modern governance models of its choosing. While the people did get an education on governance, both traditional and modern, that they hadn't had before, the effort ultimately exhausted their good will and interest.[30] The project sagged under the great weight of people's frustration and disappointment, and finally ended in 2007.[31]

The Framework Initiative ended ignominiously, without any reports to detail the work that was accomplished, and with an internal IA audit into what happened to the $55 million or so that was spent with so little to show for it. The audit led to "two senior department officials being marched out of their offices."[32]

The people were not going to decide their own governance after all. It was far from the first time First Nations people had been teased with the promise of finally being heard, only to be ignored. And every time it happened, the futility of even bothering to try to take control of their lives anymore resulted in more apathy, despair and hopelessness.

Endnotes to Chapter 8

1. Jack Stillborn, 1986, *Government Restraint: An Issue of the Eighties*, Parliamentary Research Branch, Library of Parliament, published April 17, 1986, revised April 20, 1990, 5.

2. Erik Nielsen, 1985, Memorandum to Cabinet: Report of the Ministerial Task Force on Native Programs. Deputy PM Erik Nielsen was mandated to secretly review five spending areas in government, one of which was "Indian and native programs." https://www.scribd.com/document/330654416/Memo-to-Cabinet-on-Native-Programs-Buffalo-Jump-of-1980-s-April-12-1985.

3. Ibid., 11.

4. David Munro, ADM Indian Affairs, in a memo dated April 1, 1970, as quoted in "Prime Minister Harper Launches First Nations 'Termination Plan,'" by Russell Diabo, *Global Research*, January 10, 2013 https://www.globalresearch.ca/canada-prime-minister-harper-launches-first-nations-termination-plan/5318362.

5. Nielsen, 1985, 11.

6. Ibid.

7. Ibid., 13.

8. Ibid., 3.

9. Ibid., 21, 35.

10. Ibid., 56.

11. Ibid., 9.

12. Menno Boldt, 1993, *Surviving as Indians: The Challenge of Self-Government*, University of Toronto Press, 295.

13. Nielsen, 1985, 11.

14. Ibid., 57.

15. Ibid., 1.

16. Ibid., 9.

17. Gina Cosentino, and Paul L.A.H. Chartrand, 2007, "Dream Catching Mulroney Style: Aboriginal Policy and Politics in the Era of Brian Mulroney," in *Transforming the Nation: Canada and Brian Mulroney*, editor Raymond B. Blake, McGill-Queen's University Press.

18. Boldt, 1993, 296.

19. Jill Wherrett, 1999, *Aboriginal Self-Government*, a report prepared for the Political and Social Affairs Division, Government of Canada, http://publications.gc.ca/Collection-R/LoPBdP/CIR/962-e.htm.

20. Harvey McCue, 1999, *Self-Government Agreements and Jurisdiction in Education*, a report prepared for the Assembly of First Nations, 10.

21. Jennie Wastesicoot, 2004, "A Cultural Framework for Cree Self-Government: Retracing Our Steps Back," M.A. Thesis, University of Manitoba, 75.

22. Ibid, 77.

23. Assembly of Manitoba Chiefs, 1994, *The Dismantling of the Department of Indian Affairs and Northern Development, the Restoration of Jurisdiction to First Nations People in Manitoba and Recognition of First Nations Governments in Manitoba, Framework Agreement Workplan, Memorandum of Understanding*, as quoted in Wastesicoot, 2004, 76.

24. Wastesicoot, 2004, 79.

25. Frank Cassidy, 1990, "Self-Determination, Sovereignty and Self-Government," *Aboriginal Self-*

Determination: Proceedings of a Conference held September 30 - October 3, 1990, ed. Frank Cassidy, The Institute for Research on Public Policy, 1.

26 Mia Rabson, "Abandoned grand plan cost $55M - Nothing to show for run at native self-government," *Winnipeg Free Press*, February 12, 2008.

27 Michael Lawrenchuk, 1999, Evidence, Proceedings of the Standing Senate Committee on Aboriginal Peoples, Issue No. 25, April 13, 1999.

28 Ibid.

29 Wastesicoot, 2004, 81.

30 Ibid., 85.

31 Rabson, 2008.

32 Aboriginal Affairs' internal watchdog target of investigation, *APTN National News*, October 31, 2012, http://aptnnews.ca/2012/10/31/aboriginal-affairs-internal-watchdog-target-of-investigation/.

9
IF THE PEOPLE HAD DECIDED

The Kennedy family has had a lasting impact on American politics, but they also left their mark in Mi'kmaq culture. Yes, we're talking about John and Jackie, Robert and Ethel, mother Rose, and the rest of the famous Massachusetts clan, although their glory days have faded. According to Mi'kmaq cultural researcher Lynda Kuhn Boudreau, in the 1980s it was still possible to hear someone on a Nova Scotia First Nation being called "a Kennedy." It wasn't a compliment. Local families featuring a strong matriarch and politically ambitious children with a taste for luxury and power were "Kennedys." So was someone who was enjoying the power of patronage that came from being kin to the chief or councillors, thus having access to the best jobs and best houses. It was less about knocking a caricature of the American "royal family" than it was a condemnation of band members for being too materialistic.[1]

When Indian Affairs was ratcheting up its economic development policies in the 1970s based on its top-down inversion of the Red Paper, the results in Mi'kmaq communities were close to total failure. It didn't seem to matter how well-crafted were the plans worked out in the offices in Ottawa (or in Amherst), they just didn't seem to work on the reserves. After years of failure, it seemed logical to ask about what was going wrong. Why didn't IA's development plans "take"?

The simple answer is that the people didn't want to be Kennedys, or anything like ambitious people constantly striving for economic status. Yet the development policies that Indian Affairs bureaucrats were mandated to enact were based, more or less, on the assumption that all people wanted to be the Kennedys, given half a chance. It was almost entirely at odds with what the Mi'kmaq people would have welcomed, if they had been allowed to decide.

The Mi'kmaq communities in Nova Scotia were centralized in the 1950s for the convenience of Indian Affairs, with one reserve at Eskasoni on Cape Breton and the other on the mainland at Shubenacadie. The people were promised new houses and jobs at sawmills that would be built. To help people "decide" to move, IA officials burned schools to the ground and set farms on fire, and threatened to end medical care for families showing resistance.[2]

The centralization program destroyed the "delicate economic equilibrium" that had sustained the Mi'kmaq communities since the 1880s.[3] The men had been employed in the coal mines, the lumber and pulp industry or the Sydney steel plant or supplemented welfare payments with fishing and farming. That ended with the relocation to the two reserves, where they found poor-quality housing and a paucity of decent land to resume farming. And there were no jobs because the promised mills were never built.[4] While rations and social assistance had played a role in the earlier communities, it became the primary source of income support, especially on Eskasoni.

As with many reserves, the Eskasoni and Shubenacadie communities faced overcrowding, high unemployment and tensions created by relocation and the disruption of familiar community dynamics. The Cape Breton reserve, in part due to its relative isolation, retained a stronger attachment to a traditional approach to the social and political structures. Many of the mainland Mi'kmaq chose to live off the Shubenacadie reserve. Most Cape Breton Mi'kmaq continued living on the Eskasoni reserve, but there were the usual problems of poor education, high suicide rates, poverty, depression and drug abuse. However, the separation from mainstream society helped them preserve their language, and enjoy the benefits of living close to family and friends, with pride in being Mi'kmaq.[5]

It's not that the Mi'kmaq people were unable to change or adapt to new ways. They could and did, if that was what they wanted. They were exposed to the Roman Catholic faith by the early French fishers, traders and missionaries who arrived on the shores of Acadia. In 1610, Grand Chief Henri Membertou became intrigued by the similarities between the rituals and symbolism of the Catholics and of the Mi'kmaq traditional spirituality. He was a man of considerable standing in the Mi'kmaq community, in part because he was taller than other Mi'kmaq men and sported a long beard, and because he was old enough to recall having met Jacques Cartier when he came ashore in 1534. He was about 100 years old when he and his family became the first Mi'kmaq baptized into the Catholic faith, and on his deathbed, he made his family promise to continue as Catholics.[6] The community embraced Ste. Anne as their patron saint, the mother of the Virgin Mary, who they considered an Elder and Grandmother. People still make the annual pilgrimage to Chapel Island (Potlotek) in late July for the Feast of Ste. Anne.[7]

If many people were going to stubbornly remain on the reserves (and they were), the Mi'kmaq communities in the 1970s certainly seemed ripe for economic development programs. Community leaders wanted small projects that originated from reserve residents, employing maybe two, but no more than ten, and preferably linked to traditional jobs in fishing and forestry.[8] In other words, employment that was familiar to people, even if it was seasonal or sporadic.

Indian Affairs, however, was organizing its policies around wage-labour and capital investment. The senior management designing IA policy were simply reflecting the long-held belief within mainstream Canadian society that the value of a human being was measured by his or her economic status and ability to contribute to the Gross Domestic Product (GDP) as "economic man" and "economic woman." Yes, this ideal required a great many people to become wage slaves, where they endured employment that brought them little joy, until they "got their numbers" and could became "pension slaves" and retire with a decent pension. There is a price to be paid for becoming part of the rat race.

The Mi'kmaq can be excused for not really wanting to buy into that particular lifestyle, even if the Indian Affairs department had been actively pushing assimilation for many years by trying to get Indigenous people to join the rat race. It turns out that many Mi'kmaq could see no appeal in working their lives away in the role of "economic man" or "economic woman." Theirs was a simpler view, where you worked for as much as you needed and after that you were free to enjoy other aspects of life.

However, such an attitude has always been anathema to the capitalist system. As economist John Kenneth Galbraith described it in 1967, "The system requires that people work without any limiting horizon to procure more goods. Were they to cease to work after acquiring a certain sufficiency, there would be limits on the expansion of the system. Growth could not then remain the goal. Advertising and its related arts thus help develop the kind of man the goals of the industrial system require—one that reliably spends his income and works reliably because he is always in need of more."[9]

In traditional Mi'kmaq culture, there was no value in acquiring more than was needed for one's family, other than for the prestige of offering a surplus to the Chief to distribute to the rest of the band.

Cultural researcher Boudreau noted, "Once sufficient energies had been expended to ensure a stable food supply, sufficient clothing and a warm place to live, an 'economic ceiling' was reached which allowed individuals to devote their time to social, educational and spiritual matters."[10]

The Mi'kmaq people were exercising the inherent right of humans to decide for themselves how to spend their time. If it meant living a welfare-based lifestyle, so be it. Boudreau described the value of the family-based community:

"Every individual grows up with the comfort and security of knowing that he or she will be provided for, primarily by the extended family unit, but also by fellow Band members if called upon… This facet of [Mi'kmaq] culture enables individuals to subsist on a welfare economy as the family, not the individual, survives on the welfare budget. This situation indicates the viability of the family, not the individual, as the central economic unit on reserves.[11]

If the family was the central economic unit, it would make sense to develop economic policies to suit families. A small business in a small community that had to pay regular wages to employees might not survive for long. But, as in many small rural communities across Canada, whether on or off a reserve, an enterprise where family members contributed their time and energy—sometimes paid, sometimes not—is for the benefit of the whole family. It means Granddad can snooze behind the counter between customers in the convenience store, while a fourteen-year-old daughter pumps gas. Or the other way around, if that's what the family decides. It would also mean the freedom to close up shop in August so the whole family could join the other half of the community picking blueberries in Maine.[12] Or let the cousins take over a garage bay for their snowmobile repair business at no charge until they had a bit of extra cash to pay rent. They're family, too.

This was not, of course, the capitalist, wage-based type of enterprises IA had in mind. Where were the professionals to write up the management plan, keep the accounts up to date and file financial reports? How could IA possibly justify using public funds to subsidize such a haphazard operation? Ultimately, the refusal by IA to support economic efforts that could work and the insistence on imposing development projects that wouldn't work—or worked exactly as long as the government subsidy lasted—led to a general failure all around.

It wasn't just the fact that development projects were designed, implemented and monitored by people from outside the community. It was the overall assumption by Indian Affairs that development policies for mainstream society would work the same on reserves.[13]

This disparity in expectations was pointed out in the 1996 report from the Royal Commission on Aboriginal Peoples: "While new initiatives were undertaken, the federal approach continued to be premised on the idea that development of Aboriginal communities should proceed in a manner similar to that in the mainstream; that is, if given a kick start, Aboriginal communities would develop business and economic infrastructure resembling the rest of Canada."[14]

A new kind of employment

Was it really so difficult to find a compromise, a way to marry wage-based employment with the preferred lifestyle of people living in remote communities and reserves? That was exactly what Jean Allard was trying to do in Manitoba in 1970. As a Member of the provincial Legislature and legislative assistant to Premier Ed Schreyer, Allard had been given special responsibility in the new NDP government for developing innovative job programs for people in northern Manitoba, about 90 percent of them Indigenous.[15]

Schreyer wanted to avoid imposing a quota system on northern companies, many of them forestry and mining companies, to force them to hire more Indigenous people. "I hope we will never have to resort to that, but a quota system is still better than what we have where out of 100 new jobs two or three, if that, will wind up with northerners."[16]

In 1968, a mining company discovered copper and zinc deposits in the northern wilderness, about 1,000 kilometres northwest of Winnipeg. The new operation, called the Ruttan Mine, was expected to produce ore over a twenty-year lifespan. Accessing a stable workforce in remote locations had always been a challenge for mining operations. The companies had long since shifted from work camps filled with single immigrant men to constructing proper towns with good housing and amenities, intended to attract and keep the quality of workers they wanted. It was considered part of the cost of doing business. In the Ruttan Mine case, the company deemed it essential that the town site be developed as quickly as feasible "in order that the percentage of married men be as high as possible."[17]

Married men were more desirable employees. When they moved to the company town with their families, they were much more likely to settle in and stay put than single men who were not encumbered by mortgages, children in school or a spouse with her own job. The Schreyer government was looking for "innovative practices to alleviate widespread and worsening unemployment, underemployment and welfare dependency in much of the remote north."[18] There was a problem, however, with enticing Indigenous families to relocate to mining towns. They did not want to move from their communities.

Allard was pushing the idea that there was a better alternative for the company than building a typical Canadian town and filling it with married men and their families from the south. What if men from the northern reserves were allowed to fly into the mine camp on rotating shifts? It would allow the men to work, get paid upon leaving, and return to their families with money to spend. Families could stay in their communities and the men would have work as they needed it. The companies would avoid the time and expense of building a whole town from scratch. Dormitories near the mine would do the job.[19]

A gathering of northern companies in mining, forestry and fishing met in Winnipeg in August 1971 to discuss exactly these kinds of innovative ideas with Allard, Schreyer and other government officials. The gathering included "decision-making" executives of northern resource companies, local presidents and some international officers of major unions, representatives from Crown corporations with business in the North, along with representatives from the Manitoba Indian Brotherhood and the Manitoba Métis Federation.[20]

There was a need, Schreyer told them, to try out new ideas, such as the idea proposed by Allard, that would include the kind of transportation facilities it would take "for a systematic commuter system so that native workers would not be uprooted from their communities, while earning an income."[21]

A media release four days later announced that a commuting employment experiment for Indigenous workers was starting at another northern mining operation, and it would serve the Ruttan Mine, too. A work schedule of two weeks on and two weeks off had already been established, with commuting flight service arranged between selected remote communities.[22]

Allard was pleased with the results. It seemed like a workable balance between the desire by Indigenous men to remain close to their families and community, while also earning good money working at the mine.

Except that is not what happened.

The NDP government, with the zeal of the first socialist government to hold power in Manitoba testing its ideological wings, suddenly switched gears. There would be no commuter plan. And the mining company wouldn't need to build a new town for the mine workforce. Instead, the government itself would build the town. Leaf Rapids, as it was called, would be a government town, and it would be a bold social experiment in taking an idealized southern town for 3,500 people and transplanting it into the remote North.[23] The public investment that had been planned for a substantial commuter transportation system for Indigenous people was now to be invested in building roads, houses and a shopping mall. The mining company cut its support for the commuter program down to just fifty jobs.[24]

The government encouraged Indigenous people to move with their families into the new homes built on tree-lined streets that were given Cree names. In other words, they were supposed to emulate the modern, mobile nuclear family. They would be self-sufficient and have no need of deep community roots or a network of family supports. A winter festival in Leaf Rapids with muskrat-skinning and flour-hauling competitions could not disguise the fact that this was just another effort at pulling Indigenous people into the wage-based consumer economy. It was still the rat race.

The Manitoba government invested $30 million into what its critics called "pie-in-the-sky little-boy socialism."[25] The construction of the "instant town" happened at lightning speed. The roads were built starting in September 1971, and by December, eight families had moved in.[26]

Allard was furious. He had spent two years cajoling and arm-twisting stakeholders and fellow legislators, only to see his plans for developing a regular income stream that would suit the lifestyle of Indigenous people thwarted. Allard was not afraid to push hard for what he wanted to accomplish and use sharp elbows if necessary, but in the process, he exhausted the political goodwill of the NDP caucus. He abruptly and bitterly quit the NDP in April 1972 and sat as an Independent.[27] In retrospect, it was unrealistic for Allard to have expected the company behind Ruttan Mines to go all-in on an untested employment model, especially when the company never intended to fly in more than half its workers. A town site had always been on the table.

Allard could at least console himself that during his tenure as a legislator he had achieved the long-sought goal of honouring his great-great uncle, Louis Riel, with a sculpture on the grounds of the Manitoba Legislature.[28] The stylized figure of a tall, tortured martyr was, to say the least, controversial. It was not all that dissimilar from Allard himself.

It turned out that political parties and bureaucracies have a way of bushwhacking big ideas and shredding the dreams of idealists. It was more or less what happened to the Manitoba Framework Initiative in the 1990s, too. What seemed to be a clear effort by the Assembly of Manitoba Chiefs to arrive at a model of genuine self-governance was derailed by a bureaucracy determined to pursue its own plan.

If the Manitoba First Nations people had been allowed to decide for themselves what kind of self-governance they wanted, what might it have looked like? Researcher Jennie Wastesicoot asked the same question in 2000, and set about interviewing Elders who were known in their communities for their traditional knowledge and understanding of traditional Cree governance.

A long time ago in self-government, an Elder told her, "everyone was given a voice to speak. At meetings the men spoke and the women spoke. Even the young people had a say. Everyone was listened to. Their needs were heard. That is what happened a long time ago."[29]

Another Elder shared the same idea about the importance of people being heard when there were decisions to be made that affected everyone.

"The ones who spoke were not really old men but were of age. They spoke of how they wanted everything to work. They talked about how they did not want anyone to control the way we live."[30]

According to Wastesicoot, Cree self-government would depend on returning to the traditional ways, where the governing philosophy is based on love, respect, sharing and humility, and the traditional governance positions are reinstated. The Caller gives the roll call at council meetings and organizes ceremonies that are important to a shared community experience. A second Caller brings people to meet with the Headman to address issues, and makes community announcements to keep everyone informed. The Council is made up of representatives of women, youth and elders, with positions for Warriors and Helpers. The Warriors are responsible for keeping peace in the community and maintaining law and order. The Helpers do just that—help community members as needed. The governance system also has Societies to deal with the law, environment and hunting issues.

Traditional governance, Cree-style, contained many of the same elements of modern government, with a leader (Headman), protocol officer (Caller), chief executive officer (second Caller), law and order (Warriors), social services (Helpers), and various civil society groups (Societies). At the root, however, would be spirituality.[31]

"If the Cree Nation is to succeed," said Wastesicoot, "they must restore their traditional governing system first by reclaiming their spirituality. Second, they must rekindle their kinship ties and thirdly, they must pick up their traditional spiritual practices and start conducting the ceremonies they need to bring balance and harmony back to their Nation… The Cree Elders cannot stress enough how critical it is for them to bring balance and harmony back to their communities."[32]

The ideal of traditional governance remained out of reach even though, by the late 1990s, many reserve communities across the country were desperately in need of balance and harmony. The village-level tyrants were running amok.

Endnotes to Chapter 9

1. Lynda Kuhn Boudreau, 1981, "Economic Development Strategies and the Micmac of Nova Scotia," M.A. Thesis, McGill University, 65.
2. Michelle Coffin, 2003, "United They Stood, Divided They Didn't Fall: Culture and Politics in Mi'kmaq Nova Scotia, 1969–1988," M.A. Thesis, Saint Mary's University, 37.
3. Ibid., 144.
4. Lisa Paterson, 1985, "Indian Affairs and the Nova Scotia Centralization Policy," M.A. Thesis, Dalhousie University, 105.
5. Anne-Christine Hornborg, 2008, *Mi'kmaq Landscapes: From animism to Sacred Ecology*, Ashgate Publishing, 11.
6. Henri Membertou, Biography, http://www.biographi.ca/en/bio/membertou_1E.html.
7. Potlotek, http://mikmaqrights.com/our-community/communities/potlotek/.
8. Coffin, 2003, 145.
9. John Kenneth Galbraith, 1967, *The New Industrial Society*, Houghton Mifflin, 200.
10. Boudreau, 1981, 56.
11. Ibid., 64.
12. Ibid., 71.
13. Jacqueline T. Romanow, 1999, "Government Policy and the Economic Underdevelopment of First Nations Communities in Manitoba," M.A. Thesis, University of Winnipeg, 80.
14. RCAP Report, 1996, *Restructuring the Relationship: Part 2*, 790.
15. Egon Frech, "Allard leaves NDP," *Winnipeg Free Press,* April 8, 1972, 10.
16. Media Release, "New Work Concepts Needed For North," Manitoba Government, August 27, 1971.
17. Robert Robson, 1988, "Manitoba's Resource Towns: The Twentieth Century Frontier," *Manitoba History*, No. 16, August 1988.
18. Media Release, 1971.
19. Jean Allard, 1999, interview with author.
20. Media Release, 1971.
21. Ibid.
22. Ibid.
23. Sarah Ramsden, 2012, "Developing a Better Model: Aboriginal Employment and the Resource Community of Leaf Rapids, Manitoba (1971–1977)," *Manitoba History*, No. 64, Spring 2012.
24. Media Release, "Joint Job Program for North Planned," Manitoba Government, May 12, 1972.
25. Ramsden, 2012, 8.
26. *Leaf Rapids: A Local History, 1970–1989*, 1989, Leaf Rapids Education Centre, p 7–12 http://manitobia.ca/resources/books/local_histories/399.pdf.
27. Frech, 1972, 10.
28. Catherine L. Mattes, 1998, Whose Hero? Images of Louis Riel in Contemporary Art and Métis Nationhood, Thesis, Concordia University, 19.
29. Jennie Wastesicoot, 2004, "A Cultural Framework for Cree Self-Government: Retracing Our Steps Back," M.A. Thesis, University of Manitoba, 92.
30. Ibid., 94.

31 Ibid., 128.
32 Ibid., 131.

10
UNLEASHING THE FURY OF MOTHERS

It used to be Indian Agents who came to the reserves and took the children away, and in doing so, removed the heart of the community. The grandmothers remembered when the agents took them away from their mothers when they were small and took them to residential schools. And when they grew up, their children were taken away to schools, too. But now it was their own people who were seizing the children. Not to take them to residential schools, but as a means to exact revenge against mothers and fathers who challenged the power and authority of the chief and council on reserves. It was, at last, too much.

Leona Freed was no shrinking violet in the face of abuse of power by band employees. She was the daughter of Rufus Prince, who became chief of the Ojibway Long Plain reserve in southern Manitoba after returning from army service in Italy in the Second World War. He was a founding director of the Manitoba Indian Brotherhood,[1] and fought a 1964 hunting-rights case to the Supreme Court of Canada.[2]

Freed had avoided the residential school system because her Saulteaux mother moved Freed and her little sisters off the reserve to prevent that from happening. But Freed, along with her husband and children, were unable to escape becoming a target when she became a thorn in the side of the band chief on the reserve near Portage la Prairie where she lived with her family.

Some of Manitoba's sixty-two reserves had created their own version of the "Kennedys," and Freed was concerned about what she saw as systemic financial abuse.

"The elite clan is the chief and council and their families. They own property off-reserve that is their own personal property, take exotic vacations and get new vehicles regularly. Everything has to go through chief and council, so they only fund themselves and their friends."[3]

That might sound like resentment from a woman bagging onions for a living, except that the chief and council did have control over the funding, and anybody who dared question what seemed like lavish spending could face retribution. Even when welfare cheques from the band officer were bouncing, people like Freed couldn't get answers. The chief and council controlled who got houses, who got welfare and who had their electricity cut off. The Indian Agents who used to have dictatorial control over every aspect of life on reserves had been replaced, in some communities, by dictatorial chiefs and councils. When Freed tried to find out where the band's money was going, she faced a backlash.

"It wasn't just me," she said. "It happened to other families, too. They would have their dogs killed, car tires slashed and be labelled as Satanists."[4]

Freed further angered the band council when she wrote a letter to the federal Minister of Health in 1998 to demand immediate action on the health hazard caused by a broken sewage pipe on the reserve. The Health department forwarded her letter to the chief and councillors, who promptly threatened to sue her.

The issue of the confidential letter from Freed being provided to the band chief was raised in the House of Commons.[5] It wasn't the first time that complaints about band issues made to government authorities had been referred directly back to the people who were the focus of the complaint. Indian Affairs minister Jane Stewart was on the hot seat in Parliament in 1997 after a confidential letter sent to her by Tsuu T'ina band member Bruce Starlight, outlining concerns members in his community had about financial mismanagement on the reserve near Calgary, ended up in the hands of the band chief. The chief then launched legal action against Starlight for defamation of character.

Stewart confirmed that the letter had the minister's stamp on it, indicating it had reached her office, but she couldn't explain how it had ended up in the chief's hands.

"I can confirm that it didn't come from me and it didn't come through official channels in my department, but there will be an internal investigation to, if we can, identify how indeed and if indeed, this letter came from our department."[6]

A year later, an internal investigation by a different government department concluded that it could not disclose who sent the letter to the chief and no further action would be taken. IA did, however, say it would cover Starlight's legal costs. That seemed fair, since it was IA funds being used by the band chief to sue Starlight.[7]

The leaking of the confidential letter to the IA minister and the failure to hold anyone accountable was a signal to ordinary Indigenous people that the insiders were taking care of each other, and the chief's lawsuit against Starlight was an intimidation tactic meant to muzzle any opposition. It was also a tactic that would go unchallenged by Indian Affairs.

In response, the Indigenous publication *Windspeaker* announced that it would break with the standard journalism practice of requiring people to reveal their names in published letters to the editor and that it would now print some anonymous letters. The lesson learned from the Starlight affair, said the publication staff, was that "you've got to protect yourself, because no one else will."[8]

The publication also accused Indian Affairs of losing all credibility by denying protection to Starlight, a whistleblower, saying, "By not protecting its source, Indian Affairs stripped the average Joe of the only leverage average Joes have to effect change in Aboriginal communities... Efforts to strengthen Aboriginal governance and develop a 'stable, predictable and accountable' fiscal relationship with Aboriginal governments and organizations had been dealt a levelling blow."[9]

The "outing" of whistleblowers appeared to be less an orchestrated campaign to silence troublemakers than an effort to paper over the obvious problems created when large amounts of money were dispersed with little accountability required from those who had control over it.

Freed collected what documentation she could on suspicious band spending on her home reserve and took it to the RCMP. The band authorities hit back hard. The local tribal council Family Services seized her teenage daughter, claiming that Freed had been beating the girl, and removed her to a reserve rumoured to have a problem with pedophiles. Freed was terrified for her daughter's safety, and knew there was no one she could go to who would have the authority (or willingness) to intervene, not even the RCMP.[10]

The Manitoba government had been devolving responsibility for child welfare services to the reserves through regional tribal agencies since the 1980s. The Indigenous Child and Family Services agencies, managed by directors appointed by band councils, worked well in some communities, but not so well in others. There was an accountability gap because the chiefs' political organizations insisted that they had an inherent right to run their own agencies, while provincial officials were taking the hands-off approach to oversight lest they be accused of paternalism.

The only tool Freed had left was the threat of public shaming of officials. She went directly to the media-savvy CEO of the Winnipeg Child and Family Services and to the provincial minister of Family Services. Freed's daughter was quickly and quietly returned to her when it became clear there was no abuse. The girl confessed that she had been pressured by a Family Services staffer from Freed's reserve to make a false statement claiming her mother was beating her.[11]

Freed had every reason to be furious, but she knew she and her daughter had been lucky. What about all the other women who were raising the alarm about similar abuses by band councils on their reserves? How many of them would have the guts to press a provincial cabinet minister for help if their children were taken from them as retribution?

When control of band membership was handed off by IA to band councils in 1985, it gave councils exclusive authority over who could live on reserves. The threat to band members of being struck from the band list and evicted from the reserve was yet another weapon that could be used to keep them from speaking out. But First Nations women on reserves saw a new threat in the federal government's push for self-governance as proposed in the "Gathering Strength" policy, which was a response to the Royal Commission on Aboriginal Peoples (RCAP) initiated by Brian Mulroney and completed in 1996.

The Chrétien government had been under criticism for its silence on RCAP, the most expensive inquiry in Canadian history at that time. The action plan announced by Indian Affairs minister-of-the-day Jane Stewart in 1998 was intended to answer that criticism. The plan offered an apology for the abuse of children in the Indian Residential Schools system and $325 million for a healing fund. It was also about rebuilding the relationship between the government and Aboriginal leaders, and the IA minister had consulted about this directly with the heads of the five designated Aboriginal Representative Organizations (AROs): the Assembly of First Nations, the Métis National Council, the Congress of Aboriginal Peoples, the Inuit Tapirisat of Canada, and the Native Women's Association of Canada.[12]

"We want to achieve measureable results," said Stewart, "by supporting self-reliance at the individual and community level. We will work with Aboriginal people to support healthy, sustainable communities by improving health and public safety, investing in people and strengthening economic development."[13]

Those were fine words, but they were rendered meaningless by what seemed to be the deliberate blindness of IA and the AROs to complaints of corruption and abuse of power on reserves. There was no specific incident that triggered the uprising of First Nations women in 1998, but rather a growing fury at the mistreatment of people on reserves and the seemingly unchecked powers of the "village tyrants." They found a voice through a handful of women like Freed and Rita Galloway from Saskatchewan who were publicly challenging band authorities. The women were inundated with calls and letters from band members from reserves across the country—both men and women—who were outraged by what they saw as the blatant and criminal misuse of money intended for reserve programs and services.

Freed, Galloway and other women who would not be silenced any longer channelled their outrage into creating the First Nations Accountability Coalition. They had no money to organize, so they emptied their wallets and let it be known that they would hold meetings across the country in the name of protecting the futures of their children.

Gail Sparrow, the former chief of the Musqueam band in BC, supported the women. "Like the phoenix rising from the ashes, we're spreading our wings and the men are all flapping around and they don't know what to do to us."[14]

The Coalition found help from an unexpected source. For the first time in Canadian political history, the upstart Reform Party of Canada held official opposition status in the House of Commons. MP Myron Thompson, "the barrel-chested giant in a huge Stetson"[15] from the Wild Rose riding in central Alberta, was appointed Indian Affairs critic. He had lots to criticize.

Media stories about brazen misspending by chiefs and councils and tribal organizations were in the public spotlight, and they were garnering international attention. According to the *New York Times*, "the message of tribal corruption has been most vividly illustrated by reports of junkets to sunny climes. In Toronto, government support for an Indian addiction center, Pedahbun Lodge, was cut after it was disclosed that $110,000 in treatment money was used last year to send employees to California. In Alberta, unfavorable publicity forced the Samson Cree tribal government to cancel a 12-day trip to Hawaii for 55 members. But, according to auditors, $200-a-day stipends paid to each trip participant were never returned."[16]

Such stories were hard to ignore when the reserves that were home to the big spenders on luxury cruises and world travel were also home to some of the worst living conditions in the country. One such reserve was in Myron Thompson's riding. The oil-rich Stoney First Nation had been a hotbed of allegations of financial mismanagement, with enough evidence of criminal activity that more than forty allegations of wrongdoing were turned over to the RCMP.[17]

For her part, IA minister Stewart was quick to assure critics that band chiefs and councils were making progress toward self-governance, and that it would be paternalistic to interfere in band matters.

Meanwhile, Thompson decided he needed to do something about all the complaints he was receiving:

"Immediately after word got out that I was responsible for accountability on the reserves I was literally bombarded by grassroots natives from all across Canada. The files I received number in the hundreds, while well over 200 cases of mismanagement had been reported by the media."[18]

Since the First Nations Accountability Coalition women were already organizing meetings across the West in 1998, the Reform Party decided to lend a hand, which Leona Freed greatly appreciated.

"We were all volunteers," she said. "I paid for my own office expenses out of my pocket. The Reform Party provided a little money to pay for halls and food for meetings. And the party covered my travel costs using their MPs' Air Miles."[19]

The coalition held thirteen meetings in seven provinces, drawing people from about 200 reserves. Freed sat, she said, with hundreds of women and listened to their anger, their pain and the hopelessness generated by futile efforts to make themselves heard. As she comforted them when they cried, Freed grew more and more angry. Ordinary Indians had absolutely no one to go to for help, and that had to change. The women marched, demonstrated, and held sit-ins at government and band offices. Indian Affairs and the Assembly of First Nations dismissed the women as troublemakers, and explained away the growing litany of high-profile abuses as "growing pains" that would be ironed out as chiefs and councils grew into the responsibilities of self-governance. Critics, on the other hand, called it blatant whitewashing to prevent a backlash against the self-government policies being pushed by Indian Affairs.[20]

The conditions on reserves were not some "Lord of the Flies" scenario where the colonial "adult" supervision of Indian Affairs bureaucrats had been withdrawn, leaving reserve residents to fight it out among themselves to see who would be in control. This was a deep entanglement that grew out of the White Paper of 1969, resulting in a triad of Indian Affairs, the Aboriginal Representative Organizations (AROs), and chiefs and councils as the power brokers. The three factions pushed and pulled against each other for political and financial control. Ordinary Indians had no role to play. They were relevant only insofar as their continued suffering provided the justification for programs that kept the money flowing for the benefit of IA and its agents.

Some First Nations leaders were unapologetic participants in oppressing their own people. A chief testified before a judge investigating multiple youth suicides on the ostensibly wealthy Stoney First Nation in Alberta in 1998 that he opposed economic development on the reserve as a matter of policy. Stoney people were much easier to control, he said, when they were kept poor and dependent.[21]

But didn't band members have the power of the vote to get rid of chiefs that wanted to keep them under their boot? Sure, there were elections every two years, but reserve communities had never institutionalized elections in a way that made them a legitimate part of the community. According to the Institute on Governance, governing institutions must have legitimacy for them to be successful, and there must be a good cultural match for the way that particular society is being governed. Traditional consensus governance had no corollary to adversarial elections. The result of the externally imposed election system was that "many Indigenous citizens have no authentic connection to the systems and structures they live under."[22]

In a democratic society like Canada, it is assumed that mechanisms will be in place to ensure that elections will be free and fair, but elections on reserves have no such requirement. The incumbent chief and council are in charge of the election process, which gives them a considerable advantage in elections that can be hard-fought and vicious battles where the winner takes all. It is not about who represents the will of the people; it is too often about who gets the big prize.

As one chief from a New Brunswick reserve put it, "With elections every two years, there is a constant division of families, and emotions tend to run deep. When you are talking about people's livelihoods, matters of the election are of the highest importance. This is why we have such high voter turnouts on the reserve at about 95 per cent. There is a tendency for people to strike out at each other and do things to hurt one another for the most celebrated positions of power—chief and council. After an election, a community might begin to heal, but that healing is never complete because before you know it, there is another election."[23]

Despite media stories across the country about claims of vote-buying, voter intimidation, chiefs who had declared themselves chief-for-life, and other election irregularities on reserves, Indian Affairs took the same stance as on allegations of band corruption. After years of dictating band affairs, IA decided to defer to chiefs and councils. Noted a former IA senior manager, "Even though the *Indian Act* allowed the minister to intervene, most incumbents rubber-stamped whatever system of 'election' a band wanted, under the pretense that these were traditional band customs."[24] IA ministers took the position that it would be "totally inappropriate" to interfere with band elections.

The Senate Standing Committee on Aboriginal Peoples was set to resume its hearings on self-governance in March 1999. Freed hadn't even considered an appearance at the hearing until she got a phone call from Jean Allard. He'd heard Freed give a radio interview, and encouraged her to take her message directly to the Senate. She had no idea how to go about doing that. People can't just show up at hearings; they have to be invited. Freed got on the phone and talked about the issues at stake until the Senate issued her an invitation.[25]

Leona Freed and Myron Thompson had a plan. Freed would make a presentation before the Senate committee, detailing band administration and election corruption, advocating for a modernized treaty annuity, and calling for the creation of an Aboriginal ombudsman. Thompson would put forward a private member's bill, the *First Nations Ombudsman Act*.

Freed was not a sophisticated political activist. She was the mother of six and grandmother of seven, was married to a tow-truck driver, and bagged onions at a market garden company for a living. The Accountability Coalition had no money to pay for political advisers or professional writers to help them produce a polished presentation. What they had were women fuelled by the fierce passion of mothers protecting their children, and they would be silent no longer.

"At the outset, honourable senators," Freed began her presentation to the senators, "I want to apologize if I offend anyone because the choice of words in our brief is quite strong. However, it comes from the heart and I am speaking on behalf of many band members."[26]

Rita Galloway was speaking for Saskatchewan; Freed was speaking on behalf of band members in Manitoba, Ontario, British Columbia, New Brunswick and Alberta.

"Our aboriginal people in these five provinces are not ready for self-government," said Freed. "In order for a First Nation to be self-sufficient, successful and self-governing, there must be accountability, democracy and equality. These three factors are non-existent.

"What does exist in the majority of our First Nations is that the chiefs and their families, relatives and friends benefit from nepotism, employment opportunities, education, housing off and on the reserve, properties being purchased off the reserve including some outside of the province, exotic vacations and trips as well as gambling sprees to the United States. We also have self-appointed chiefs, silent chiefs, illiterate chiefs, bought-and-paid-for chiefs and band hereditary/custom chiefs which means 'chief for life.' In the latter instance, they are not elected. We cannot vote for our leader. The chief and his family make all the rules and there is no democracy."[27]

Freed turned her sights on the Indian Affairs department, with the accusation that it "condones the criminal activities of chiefs and councils of Canada's First Nations. There has been absolutely no punishment administered to these people."[28]

First Nations political organizations fared no better.

"The accountability coalition members in the provinces I represent here today do not recognize the Assembly of First Nations as our aboriginal leaders. We did not vote them in, nor did we have a say in the elections or the voting. They call themselves 'aboriginal leaders' but true aboriginal leaders would not ignore the cries and pleas of their people. A true aboriginal leader would come to the aid of the people in their time of need, and put an end to all the needless suffering."[29]

Freed called for the end of all band funding flowing through the hands of chiefs and councils, with funds flowing directly to individuals to empower them to take charge of their lives. And finally, she called for a native ombudsman "who would activate accountability of band funds on the First Nations; guide and aid band members to self-sufficiency and eventually towards self-government; act as dispute mediator."[30] More than anything, the coalition members wanted somebody to *listen* and to act on their concerns.

What caught most of the media attention, however, was Freed's declaration that too many bands were not ready for self-governance.

The Indian Affairs minister responded by saying that the last thing the government wanted to do was impose self-government on bands that weren't ready, and suggested that there could be improvements to accountability.

"Maybe it is an ombudsman," said Stewart. "Maybe it is an auditor-general. Those kinds of institutions are very much the focus."[31]

The next day in the House of Commons, Thompson stood to introduce Bill C-222, the *First Nations Ombudsman Act*: "an Act to establish the office of First Nations Ombudsman to investigate complaints relating to administrative and communication problems between members of First Nations communities and their First Nation and between First Nations, allegations of improper financial administration and allegations of electoral irregularities."[32]

Freed and Galloway were watching from the Visitors' Gallery in the House of Commons. Ordinary Indigenous people were once again getting their concerns heard on Parliament Hill, but it was fully thirty years after the Cardinal/Trudeau showdown in 1969.

Endnotes to Chapter 10

1. J.M. Bumstead, 1999, *Dictionary of Manitoba Biography*, Winnipeg: University of Manitoba Press.
2. Prince and Myron *v.* The Queen, [1964] S.C.R. 81, Supreme Court of Canada, https://scc-csc.lexum.com/scc-csc/scc-csc/en/item/6590/index.do.
3. Leona Freed, interview with author, July 1999.
4. Ibid.
5. Mike Scott, MP, speaking in 36th Parliament, 1st Session, Hansard, No. 128, September 29, 1998.
6. Paul Melting Tallow, 1998, "Leaked letter leads to libel lawsuit," *Windspeaker*, Vol. 15, Issue 11.
7. Paul Melting Tallow, 1998, "No answers, no culprits in leaked letter investigation," *Alberta Sweetgrass*, Vol. 15, Issue 4.
8. *Windspeaker* Staff, 1998, "Protect the Whistle Blower," *Windspeaker*, Vol. 15, Issue 11.
9. Ibid.
10. Leona Freed, interview with author, July 1999.
11. Ibid.
12. Jane Stewart, Address by the Honourable Jane Stewart, Minister of Indian Affairs and Northern Development, on the occasion of the unveiling of *Gathering Strength—Canada's Aboriginal Action Plan*, Ottawa, January 7, 1998, 12.
13. Jane Stewart, 1998 as quoted in "Federal government makes untimely response to RCAP," *Saskatchewan Indian*, Vol. 29, No. 1, 25.
14. Dianne Rinehart, "Indian women say fraud, nepotism rife on reserves," *Vancouver Sun*, April 13, 1999.
15. Roy MacGregor, "The man from Wild Rose hasn't felt this alive for nearly half a century," *The Globe and Mail*, June 11, 2004.
16. James Brooke, "Canada's Tribal Women Fight (Mostly Male) Graft," *New York Times*, January 1, 2001, http://www.nytimes.com/2001/01/01/world/canada-s-tribal-women-fight-mostly-male-graft.html.
17. Myron Thompson, speaking on First Nations Ombudsman Act, Second Reading of Bill C-222, House of Commons, November 4, 1999, https://openparliament.ca/debates/1999/11/4/myron-thompson-2/only/.
18. Myron Thompson, speaking on The First Nations Ombudsman Act, House of Commons, November 4, 1999, https://openparliament.ca/debates/1999/11/4/myron-thompson-2/only/.
19. Leona Freed, interview with author, August 2017.
20. Rinehart, 1999.
21. Thompson, 1999.
22. Marcia Nickerson, 2017, "Characteristics of a Nation-to-Nation Relationship," Institute on Governance, 16.
23. *First Nations Elections: The Choice is Inherently Theirs*, Report of the Standing Senate Committee on Aboriginal Peoples, 2010, 22.
24. Harry Swain, 2010, *Oka: A Political Crisis and Its Legacy*, Douglas & McIntyre, 28.
25. Freed, 2017.
26. Leona Freed, 1999, Evidence, Proceedings of the Standing Senate Committee on Aboriginal Peoples, Room 160-S, Tuesday, March 2, 1999.

27 Ibid.
28 Ibid.
29 Ibid.
30 Ibid.
31 Sheldon Alberts, "Self-government is self-destruction, native group says," *National Post*, March 3, 1999.
32 Bill C-222, *First Nations Ombudsman Act*, 1999, http://www.parl.ca/LegisInfo/BillDetails.aspx?billId=9554&Language=E.

11

CALM AT THE EDGE OF THE STORM

The shores of Lac Ste. Anne in Alberta are shallow and reedy, but the area where pilgrims gather provides an easy slope for wading out into the healing water. The lake, about seventy-five kilometres west of Edmonton, has been the destination of Roman Catholic Indigenous pilgrims since 1889.

About 40,000 people gathered there over several days in late July 1999. The Lac Ste. Anne gathering is the largest Indigenous pilgrimage in North America, drawing families towing pop-up tent trailers, state-of-the-art Winnebagos, fifth-wheelers, battered pickup trucks with campers on the back, and those prepared to pitch tents in the large cattle pasture by the lake. Like the Mi'kmaq of the Maritimes, the pilgrims honoured the grandmother of Jesus, the mother of Mary, who was said to have been seen walking across the water.

Among the throng were Leona Freed, Jean Allard and Harold Cardinal. Allard and Cardinal were both raised as Catholics. Freed was there to talk to people about accountability. She knew that the chances of the *First Nations Ombudsman Act* becoming law were slim. Most private member's bills got lost inside the legislative machinery, never to be seen again. But the bill was something real that offered hope for change, which was more than she and the other women in the First Nations Accountability Coalition had thought possible when they started out.

The Lac Ste. Anne gathering offered a window into a different Indigenous reality. Under the sea of blue plastic tarps serving as canopies over lawn chairs gathered around a Coleman stove or "porches" where people could sit and visit, were Indigenous people from all across the Prairies, from the North and from central United States. They were not the impoverished and hopeless Indigenous people portrayed in so many media stories. Nor were they the panhandlers seen on city street corners or the tragically broken men and women regularly rescued by social workers from freezing to death in the wintry back alleys of the cities. They were also not the people involved in Indigenous politics. They stayed well away from that toxic nonsense and got on with the same things everyone else does—raising their kids, enjoying their grandchildren, worrying about whether the teens were mature enough to start dating and whether Mom's cancer would stay in remission, and looking for peace and solace.

The People of Always

The people gathered on the edge of the lake could be described as the modern face of the "People of Always." The historic term was actually "Men of Always," which seems to have originated in the rather fanciful writings of François-René Chateaubriand, a minor member of the French aristocracy who set sail for North America in 1791 to escape the French Revolution. He claims to have travelled from Albany to Niagara Falls, where he broke his arm and lived with the Iroquois for a month while it healed. The Iroquois, he said, called themselves the "Men of Always" or the Ongoueonoue.[1]

A professor of geology used the term in a speech before the Historical and Scientific Society of Manitoba in 1922, but there is not much evidence of its widespread use.[2] It is, nonetheless, an apt term to describe a culture that has endured for a very long time—the "People of Always."

Tribal communities, with their own particular territories and customs that suited their physical and cultural needs, have walked the landscape of what became Canada for many thousands of years. All of Canada, prior to 14,000 years ago, was covered by ice sheets up to three kilometres thick in some places. All the living things on the land either perished or were driven south ahead of the vast ice sheets that spread south and west from the Hudson Bay—crushing and grinding everything in their path under their own enormous weight—west to the Rocky Mountains and south to Wisconsin. The exceptions were the dry interior regions of Alaska and Yukon that remained relatively ice-free, where mammoths, horses, camels and giant short-faced bears flourished in vibrant communities. With so much water lying frozen on the land, the global sea level had dropped an incredible 120 metres (400 feet), which laid bare a land bridge between Siberia and Alaska across which animals and people migrated from west to east, although some animals went in the opposite direction. As the ice masses began melting back about 12,000 years ago, the land opened up and animals like bison, horses and bears began reclaiming parts of their former range. With them, from the north, came the ancestors of the tribes that established themselves across the landscape.[3]

Of course, this is the story of modern archeology. For people whose memories were passed on through stories from generation to generation, the oral stories of those from ten generations back might well have seemed like deep history. Yet if the people had lived on the landscape for, say, 6,000 years, it would count as about 250 generations. Would stories passed down through such a long time not have seemed like "always"?

The people gathered on the shore of Lac Ste. Anne in 1999 could well have been the "People of Always." It was a serene gathering. There was occasional gridlock in the parking area, mainly because no one appeared to be organizing anything, and drivers just figured it out among themselves. It had the feel of a familiar traditional event where many people knew each other and how it was more or less organized. Even the higgledy-piggledy arrangement of the campers, trailers and tents seemed to work, somehow.

Jean Allard had spent some years brooding about the plight of Indigenous people, and he had come to Lac Ste. Anne to talk to the people there about an idea he was mulling over. He had had lots of time to think on the long nights in the summer of 1994 when he chained himself to the statue representing the tortured and troubled Louis Riel on the grounds of the Manitoba Legislature. Other Métis leaders wanted a proper buttoned-up suit-and-bow-tie statue of Riel. Allard disagreed, in part because he was a prime mover in getting the original Riel statue there in the first place, and more than one person had remarked on how much the stylized Riel looked like Allard. But it was also about duking it out via statues to see which Métis group would dominate in Manitoba—between Allard, the past president of the Union nationale métisse Saint-Joseph du Manitoba (founded in 1887) and Yvon Dumont, the president of the Manitoba Métis Federation (founded in 1969). After twelve days chained to the statue, Allard gave in when the work crew showed up to move the statue from the Legislature to the grounds of St. Boniface College, where Allard and Riel had both once been students of the Jesuits. The MMF had won.

It was this ideological battle with the MMF about what it meant to be Métis that got Allard thinking. He figured government funding of the MMF had turned the leaders into beggars, constantly seeking more and more money to deliver what he considered to be "apartheid" programs. He knew that the MMF had been started by the Manitoba government with the sole purpose of delivering services to poor, rural Métis.

In 1959, the Manitoba Department of Agriculture and Immigration commissioned a study to identify Aboriginal people, the better to target government aid to the impoverished. The terms of the study made it clear that only the Métis "living like Indians" were to be included. The government was only interested in the Métis, "living in shanties on the edge of reserves, or in small remote communities where they eked out a living trapping, fishing, or selling wood. They were interested only in the Métis who were illiterate and living in poverty."[4] That accounted for about 20 percent of the Métis in the province.

The majority of modern-day Métis, who counted themselves as descendants of the Scottish and French families of the Red River Settlement, were generally urban, middle-class or living comfortably without the need for government assistance. Many of the country-born children of Protestant Hudson's Bay Company men and their Cree, Saulteaux or Assiniboine wives were sent to the Orkney Islands or to Scotland for their education, which meant the Anglo-Métis tended to be more prosperous than the families of the Catholic French fur traders and bison hunters and their country wives. When the province of Manitoba was created in 1870, the population was about evenly split, with about 4,500 "half-breeds," as the Scottish Métis were called at the time, and about 5,500 French Métis.[5] (There were also more than 500 "settled Indians" and about 400 British and Canadian people in the Red River Settlement.[6]) Many of the Métis moved to rural communities or joined other Métis communities on the edge of reserves in a substantial diaspora. Others stayed in Winnipeg, where Métis names such as Isbister, Norquay, Grant, Riel, McKay and many more grace streets, schools and public buildings.

But in 1969, the Manitoba government was looking for an organization to run programs for the poor Métis identified in the 1959 report. Allard, newly elected to government that year, was also a past president of L'Union nationale. He said his organization was insulted when asked to run the programs; they would not demean their brothers and sisters by treating them like second-class citizens who were too incompetent to manage for themselves. He saw it as a trap. The Métis would get some money. The bureaucrats would have lots of work to do overseeing the Métis-run programs. Of course, said Allard, it meant that the programs couldn't be too successful. If poor Métis no longer needed help, the programs would no longer be needed, and neither would the bureaucrats.[7]

The Manitoba Métis Federation in 1969 represented just the twenty people who had created the organization, but to be considered legitimate, it needed to have some semblance of representing the Métis people. With $20,000 from the Schreyer government and another $45,000 from the federal Secretary of State, the MMF set up a Winnipeg office and five regional offices in rural Métis communities, with elections in each regional centre.

The MMF leaders went to Ottawa in 1971 to meet with Robert Stanbury, the man doling out core funding on behalf of the Secretary of State. They could accept taking government money for running programs, but figured relying on the largesse of government to run their basic operations was dangerous. Nonetheless, they left Ottawa with $125,000 in core funding. Stanbury had insisted. It was, said one of the leaders, "the worst thing that could happen to Métis people. All it's going to do is lead to fighting."[8]

Allard considered the dependency on government funding of the Métis political organizations, especially after the Métis were officially designated as Aboriginal in the *Constitution Act* of 1982, as no different from the Indian organizations. It struck him, as he sat chained to Riel's statue, that the issue was ever and always about the money and who controlled it. The people who had no control were the ordinary Indigenous people. So, what if they did control the money? What would happen then?

Allard thought about an expanded family allowance to put more money into the hands of ordinary Indigenous people, but that seemed complicated and unwieldy. He had been going through documents about his grandparents' farm in St. François Xavier on the Assiniboine River that showed they had paid one dollar per acre in the 1870s for their land. Five acres of land would have cost five dollars, which was exactly the amount of the annuity being paid to every man, woman and child in bands that signed on to Treaty One. He figured that the same land, in 1999, would be worth $1,000 an acre. If the annuity were increased to $5,000 per person, it would put money directly into the hands of families, and with that money, they could gain some measure of personal power to balance the power of the band government.[9] The annuity was the single provision in the treaties from the 1850s onward that provided some measure of individual empowerment within the collective of the band. By government policy, it was paid directly to people — IA officials were literally handing five-dollar bills to eligible recipients — and it never went through the hands of the band council.

The treaty annuity would apply only to Treaty Indians, of course, but the more Allard played the idea around in his mind, the more logical and simple it seemed.

Allard had been shopping the idea of what he called a "modernized treaty annuity" in political circles in 1998, including at a gathering of federal Liberals in Winnipeg. Bill Balan, regional executive director of Canadian Heritage for the Prairies and Northwest Territories, listened to his pitch and suggested Allard write a book about it. He would, said Allard, but he needed funding. Balan just happened to have funding available under Heritage's Aboriginal programs, and in short order, Allard had $24,000 and a book to write.

He was working on the first draft of "Big Bear's Treaty: The Road to Freedom," which is what took him to Lac Ste. Anne in the summer of 1999. He wanted to meet with ordinary Indians and talk to them about what a modernized annuity would mean to them.

When asked about the $5 annuity they were getting, people laughed and rolled their eyes.

"The cost of buying food in the North is very high," said Violet Camsell-Blondin, a Dene from the Dogrib Rae band north of Great Slave Lake in the Northwest Territories. "The value of five dollars doesn't go far. Just one loaf of bread costs four or five dollars."[10]

Blondin said her family got $35 in annuities, which they put into a savings account as a symbolic gesture.

"The money doesn't mean what it meant in the early 1900s. It's a joke."

Ben Merasty from Brochet in the far northwest corner of Manitoba near the borders of Saskatchewan and Nunavut said, "I agree that $5 isn't right, but I don't know if $5,000 is the right amount. If you were to increase the annuity, I think generally people in Canada would have to be convinced that this is the right thing to do. But it would be one way for fighting for the true value of what treaty money means."[11]

However, Eileen Maytwayashing from the Lake Manitoba reserve in south-central Manitoba had been talking to others over lunch, and was rather pessimistic. She concluded that modernizing annuities would only work if the people had someone to champion the idea for them.

"Nobody recognizes us," she said. "The people who speak about our funding, nobody hears us. Everybody is deaf."[12]

It is hard to bring about change when those who have the power to bring about that change cannot or will not hear. Leona Freed, who was walking among the tents and campers on the sunny July afternoon, was still on a bit of an emotional high from the ombudsman bill passing first reading in Parliament, but her anger had not really dissipated.

A month earlier, eight band chiefs under the Swampy Cree tribal council in northern Manitoba had threatened to sue Freed for her statements before the Senate about band corruption. A spokesperson for the tribal council said serving notice of a lawsuit was the chiefs' way of showing they were accountable. Freed dismissed the threat as an intimidation tactic, and said that the suit would not proceed because a court case would mean the bands would have to open up their books to prove that they weren't corrupt, and they weren't going to want to do that.[13]

The *Winnipeg Free Press* editorialists struck back in response to the chiefs.

"If they are democratic and accountable, then Ms Freed's remarks have no application to them, as their members will be perfectly well aware. If the Swampy Cree chiefs agree with Ms Freed that some bands are unaccountable and dictatorial, then they should join with her in urging them to shape up. They should not be using their privileged access to government funds in order to hire a lawyer and try to silence the crusaders."[14]

Freed already knew about Allard's idea for modernizing treaty annuities. When he had urged her to make an appearance before the Senate committee earlier in March, he had asked her to include treaty annuities in her presentation. It would be the first public pitch for the idea. Freed did include it, but it was lost in all the noise her presentation had generated about band corruption.

"The treaty money," said Freed, as she sat at a rough wooden picnic table at Lac Ste. Anne, "would be money that doesn't go through Indian leaders' fingers. A family of four could have $20,000 distributed in twelve equal payments. That is far more than welfare. People would be able to build their own homes. They could live anywhere." Freed had often pointed out that band membership lists that triggered per capita funding from Indian Affairs were routinely inflated, with significant disparities between who actually said they lived on the reserve according to the Canadian Census and the much larger number claimed by the band council. Indian Affairs officials waved away her concerns, and a spokesperson said, "We rely on First Nations government to inform us of population changes," and that census figures couldn't be relied on because not every reserve household filled out the census.[15]

It was exactly that kind of thinking that nurtured the growth of "a national system of village-level tyrants,"[16] as predicted by Harold Cardinal in 1977. After finishing his undergraduate law degree at the University of Saskatchewan, Cardinal went on to complete his Master of Law at Harvard University, with his thesis focussed on the underlying principles of Treaty 8.[17] He was working on his PhD in law at the University of British Columbia when he took time to attend the Lac Ste. Anne gathering. There, he met up with Jean Allard.

They were two men who had seen a great deal over the years. Allard had become cynical and contemptuous of the politicians and Indigenous political leaders who continued what he considered a cruel charade that used the pain and suffering of ordinary Indigenous people as leverage to keep the money flowing. He was not at all surprised that the RCMP investigation into band corruption on the Stoney reserve in Alberta wrapped up with no charges being laid. Allard considered reserves to be lawless societies.[18] Chiefs and councils were allowed to write their own rules. If the council's loose rules didn't explicitly forbid the chief from using band funds to take his entire extended family on a Caribbean cruise, it was unlikely to be successfully prosecuted in a court of law. And Indian Affairs seemed unwilling to hold band governments accountable.

Leona Freed joined the two men in their discussions. Harold Cardinal was a thoughtful man of few words. He listened and said little. But what Cardinal said that day struck both Allard and Freed as a powerful statement of the key reason why the ideals of the Red Paper had never been realized.

"Non-accountability," Cardinal said, "is the reward Indian Affairs gives to chiefs and councils for their compliance.[19]

For Allard, that simple statement crystallized all that was wrong with the system of Indian Affairs and Indigenous leadership.

"What has transpired over the past thirty years," he said at the time, "is that the poorest and most powerless bear on their shoulders the weight of the entire Indian Affairs bureaucracy, Indian political organizations and the army of consultants they both employ. Their problems cannot be fixed because their very neediness is absolutely essential to sustaining the whole system. There is no escape."[20]

Sustaining the continued growth of Indian Affairs required band councils to go along with the programs and services the department developed, whether it served the real needs of band members or not. IA had the wherewithal to punish uncooperative chiefs and councillors by, for instance, going slow on processing funding applications, and reward those who played along by not looking too closely at how they managed band funds and band powers. It was, in Allard's view, inevitable that corruption would take hold in the absence of accountability, not only to band members but to IA as well.

"There have been many exceptions at the reserve level, as people fought the corrupting effect of the bait offered by the system. But slowly, inevitably, greed and personal ambition took hold. People with good hearts and good character, concerned with the welfare of the people, were weeded out. That left in charge the people whose first priority was to serve the system, the source of their power and money."[21]

The Canadian public was becoming increasingly angry and frustrated in the late 1990s with the seeming inability of the federal government and Indigenous leaders to fix the problems facing Indigenous communities, despite continually increasing spending. The media focussed on multiple band-level scandals and accusations of corruption, while the international community shone an embarrassing spotlight on the Third World living conditions on many of Canada's reserves.

Some opinion writers argued that doing away with Indian Affairs, the *Indian Act* and reserves (as in the 1969 White Paper) would be doing First Nations people a favour. An editorial in *The Globe and Mail* argued that turning the top-down power structure of IA on its head would give ordinary Indigenous people power and authority over their lives and their band governments.

"One way to change this perverted power relationship quickly and decisively would be for Ottawa to give its contribution directly, on an equal per capita basis, to individual aboriginals. Then let the band councils tax their citizens for the amounts they judge necessary for the provision of public service."[22]

In many respects, this was a cry of frustration over a system that seemed intractable and unfixable, and anything had to be better than the status quo. However, even if that was what ordinary Indigenous people wanted — and there was no means in place for determining that — the Indian Affairs department had been undertaking new obligations on behalf of the Crown. It had entered into more than a dozen modern treaties on behalf of the Crown since 1975, covering nearly 40 percent of Canada, mainly in Quebec and the North. Those treaties came with obligations that IA was duty-bound to deliver. With treaties covering some 90 percent of the country, the department wasn't going anywhere. It was, in fact, in negotiations over another twenty or so self-government agreements and protocols as the 20th century came to a close.

The women of the First Nations Accountability Coalition weren't demanding a complete overhaul of the Indian Affairs system. There were asking for a federal ombudsman — just one single person — to whom ordinary Indigenous people could take their issues and concerns.

Endnotes to Chapter 11

1. François-René Chateaubriand, 1826, *Travels in America* (Eng. Trans.), Vol. 2, 93.
2. R.C. Wallace, as quoted in "A Provincial Museum," *Winnipeg Free Press*, December 15, 1922, 17.
3. James A. Burns, Curator Emeritus, Quaternary Paleontology, Royal Alberta Museum, interview with author, November 2017.
4. Sheila Jones Morrison, 1995, *Rotten to the Core*, 101060, 46.
5. Darren O'Toole, 2012, "The Red River Jig Around the Convention of 'Indian' Title: The Métis and Half-Breed *Dos à Dos*," *Manitoba History*, No. 69, 17.
6. John Elwood Ridd, 1934, "The Red River Insurrection, 1869–1870," M.A. Thesis, University of Manitoba, 2.
7. Jones Morrison, 47.
8. Ibid.
9. Jean Allard, based on extensive interviews with the author, 1999.
10. Violet Camsell-Blondin, interview with author, July 1999.
11. Ben Merasty, interview with author, July 1999.
12. Eileen Maytwayashing, interview with author, July 1999.
13. Bill Redekop, "Native whistle blower faces suit," *Winnipeg Free Press*, June 21, 1999.
14. Editorial: "Earning respect," *Winnipeg Free Press*, June 22, 1999.
15. Bill Redekop, "RCMP investigating Indian band's population list," *Winnipeg Free Press*, July 14, 1999.
16. Harold Cardinal, 1977, *The Rebirth of Canada's Indians*, Hurtig Publishers, 37.
17. David R., Newhouse, Cora J. Voyageur, and Dan Beavon, eds., 2005, *Hidden in Plain Sight: Contributions of Aboriginal Peoples to Canadian Identity and Culture,* University of Toronto Press, 36.
18. Jean Allard, 2002, "Big Bear's Treaty: The Road to Freedom," *Inroads*, Vol. 11, 146.
19. Jean Allard, on his discussion with Harold Cardinal, July 1999, in the unpublished manuscript "Big Bear's Treaty: The Road to Freedom," 63.
20. Allard, 2002, 136.
21. Ibid., 131.
22. Editorial: "Power to the aboriginal people," *The Globe and Mail*, April 27, 1999.

12
TESTING A REVOLUTIONARY IDEA

Leona Freed was back in Ottawa in November 1999 for the second reading of Bill C-222, the *First Nations Ombudsman Act*. Reform MP Myron Thompson delivered his pitch to fellow parliamentarians, but the debate Freed was listening to on the floor of the House of Commons was not encouraging.

The Liberal perspective was encapsulated in the argument of MP Steve Mahoney, who said it was up to First Nations to ask for an ombudsman if they wanted one, not the opposition Reform Party. Further, the solution to any problems was the pursuit of self-governance, as led by the Indian Affairs minister, which would bring self-esteem and democracy to reserves.[1]

The Bloc Québecois immediately made it clear that it would vote against the bill because there were no problems that required an ombudsman; even suggesting that an ombudsman was needed was deemed a form of paternalism.[2]

Certainly Indian Affairs and politicians looking for something positive to say about Canada's reserves could point to successful bands like the Osoyoos First Nation in British Columbia, with its winery and eighteen-hole golf course in the Okanagan valley, or the new Casino Rama on the Rama First Nation near Orillia, Ontario, or the thriving businesses in Saskatchewan's Lac La Ronge First Nation selling mushrooms and wild rice to international markets. Unfortunately, such success stories were notable for being the exceptions, not the rule.

Some federal MPs might have decided that there weren't any real problems on reserves, but Freed knew differently. She and the Accountability Coalition had collected the stories they heard from band members about corruption and election fraud on their reserves, and put it together in a 200-page report that she had delivered to the Senate.

"I told them the elections were rigged," Freed told a *New York Times* reporter. "The chiefs pay for the voting. They bribe the people. They intimidate the people. The same crooks get in, year in, year out… The chiefs were so mad."[3]

The chiefs were very angry with Freed and the other noisy women who persisted. Even with international publicity about allegations of band corruption and the number of investigations initiated by the RCMP, politicians in Ottawa seemed almost eager for any excuse to justify doing nothing to address the problems head on. The Assembly of First Nations, representing the chiefs, continued to dismiss complaints by the First Nations Accountability Coalition, accusing them of fuelling anti-Indian sentiment. A spokesperson for the AFN said they wanted the Coalition to "refrain from using innuendo and unsubstantiated allegations, and stop wallowing in a negative attitude."[4]

Freed, in turn, dismissed the AFN as too busy going after more money to worry about the lives of ordinary Indians, and suggested that perhaps chiefs were unnecessary, too.

"We need to eliminate welfare for all status Indians. We've got to get out from under the chiefs' thumbs. Welfare dollars are being used to control us. The ones fighting us now are not just government, but our own aboriginal leaders. I'm going to start saying that we don't need chiefs."[5]

The following spring in April 2000, the Ombudsman bill was up for the third and final reading, after which MPs would be voting. It wasn't often that a private member's bill made it to the third reading, and Freed was back in Ottawa for the vote.

Myron Thompson acknowledged the supporters of the Ombudsman bill who were watching proceedings from the Visitors' Gallery, and Freed specifically.

"I would like to salute Leona Freed and her colleagues with the First Nations Accountability Coalition. In one year this group has brought aboriginal accountability to the forefront and has worked tirelessly to correct this inequity. Leona held meetings for grassroots people last summer. The purpose was to hear concerns about living conditions on and off reserve. The grievances were many and were extensively documented. Many had proof of mismanagement of tax dollars, illegal and corrupt activities and electoral irregularities, just to name a few.

"In the words of Leona, unless the 'grassroots natives' concerns are addressed and thoroughly investigated, a new relationship with band members cannot exist and self-government will not succeed. Leona, I salute you."[6]

She received a standing ovation. It was the high point of a tense day. Passing the bill was not going to be a miracle cure for what ailed Indian communities, but it would mean that the politicians—the people who had the power to change laws and policies affecting Indian lives—were actually listening to what ordinary First Nations people had to say.

During the substantial debate that followed that afternoon, the Bloc again opposed the bill, and the Liberals reiterated the party's belief "that First Nations can be trusted, that they are responsible and that they deserve to run their own lives. Our preference is for partnerships not paternalism, and for co-operation not control."[7]

Thompson then made a final impassioned plea for members to pass the bill that evening.

"I encourage honourable members to support these people and I encourage them to remember that the basis of all of this is a plea for accountability. A no vote means no to accountability."[8]

The vote split along party lines, with the Canadian Alliance (Reform) voting for it, and the Liberals and Bloc voting against it. The bill went down to defeat. For Freed and the other ordinary Indians who had fought so hard to be heard, it was a crushing disappointment.

When the Liberal government insisted that "they" were responsible and "they" deserved to run their own lives, who were the "they" they were talking about? The people whose pleas for help that had just been dismissed? When the Liberals said they preferred partnerships, who were the partners they wanted to work with? The answer is easy. "They" were the same chiefs and councils the Coalition had been accusing of corruption. And the partners were the Aboriginal Representative Organizations, as always.

Despite the retribution that the women like Leona Freed had endured by standing up to Aboriginal leaders, despite the demonstrations, marches and RCMP investigations, and despite the clear evidence that there were angry, upset First Nations people across the country, those with power apparently could hear only the soothing reassurances from Indian Affairs and its chosen AROs. Steps were being taken, they said, to address accountability issues, audit procedures were improving, and besides, the complaints were just a few problems blown out of proportion. There was no need for an ombudsman.

Why did a large majority of parliamentarians vote down the ombudsman bill? Politicians are not particularly brave people. They are motivated by the primary objective of getting elected, and the secondary objective of staying elected. If a political stance threatens those objectives, why would they risk their finite amount of political capital?

Politicians were not deaf or blind to the deluge of media stories about band corruption and election fraud playing out across the country, whether on CBC, in *The Globe and Mail*, the *New York Times*, or on local talk radio. Their political calculations, however, would measure the disadvantages of going up against the Assembly of First Nations publicly and against Indian Affairs senior bureaucrats behind the scenes.

The AFN had learned to play political hardball, and its leaders knew that most non-Indigenous Canadians knew little of what was going on in Indigenous politics, except what they, too, might hear in the media. The general public, confused about contentious fights over land claims, Indigenous rights and other issues they didn't understand, would just stop listening or throw up their hands in disgust, and move on to issues that they could understand.

Politicians were no different. If anything, they were justifiably afraid of the AFN. They knew that if the AFN went after them, they would have no means of defending themselves that the public would understand. Politicians also had good reason to be afraid of Indian Affairs. The department seemed immune to criticism, sloughing off efforts by minister after minister to "fix" the department.

The Reform Party was always an unlikely ally of angry First Nations women, but the crusade by Freed and the Accountability Coalition fit with the party's strong belief in government accountability for how taxpayers' dollars are spent. And the party hadn't been around Ottawa long enough to learn the hard lesson about going up against the immutability of Indian Affairs.

Politicians should never be mistaken for Don Quixote; if an issue does not serve the primary or secondary objective, what would be the point of tilting at windmills?

Jean Allard was a politician, but he was not immune to playing a Métis Don Quixote. He was still promoting the idea of individual empowerment through a modernized annuity in the fall of 1999, and still working on the manuscript for "Big Bear's Treaty." But he'd run out of money to finish it. He decided to send the nearly finished draft, typos and all, to selected politicians and other public figures to see how people would react to his idea of increasing annuities from $5 to $5,000 based on increased land values. He wanted to get a discussion going, and maybe shake a few dollars loose to finish the book. The response to the draft of the book came quickly.

Allan Blakeney, the former NDP premier who had been a force in Saskatchewan since serving in Tommy Douglas's cabinet in 1960, promptly wrote back in November 1999 that he considered the book to be a solid piece of work.

"The idea of paying out a substantially greater amount as treaty money going directly to individual registered Indians with a reduction of the amount that goes to bands is an ingenious idea."[9]

He added, "It is important that after the individual treaty payments are made, there be enough money left to fund health services, education services, and welfare services, but I suspect that there would be a substantial amount left after treaty payments are made, even if the payments are of the general level that you have suggested."[10]

Blakeney's main concern was about paying an increased annuity to off-reserve Indians, since he figured the federal government would resist the idea of ongoing substantial payments at a time when it was clear the government wished to reduce its financial commitment to Aboriginal people.

Frank Price had lots to say about Allard's book. Price had served as a business adviser to the Manitoba Indian Brotherhood when Dave Courchene was president, and later an adviser to Indian Affairs regional directors.

"The proposed change in the delivery of treaty money, as an alternative method of distributing funds in meeting treaty obligations and those services that have developed beyond the treaties, is in my opinion an exciting departure from the autocratic control currently vested in Band Councils.

"The opportunity to require that councils secure the support, financially as well as politically, of those they would hope to represent would bring true accountability for the use of those funds. Democracy in the truest sense would be possible."[11]

Price liked the idea of each family unit having a monthly income, which would reduce the need for welfare and other services directed at addressing poverty.

He did, however, wonder about the learning curve needed to figure out how to handle income after so many years of welfare dependency. It might not go well, and it might result in stories of mismanagement and waste.

But, he said, "One of the rights that we all enjoy in a free society is the right to be wrong as well as to be right. There is no perfect solution."[12]

Tom Flanagan, an Alberta professor who has been a long-time advocate of individual Aboriginal rights (as opposed to collective rights), shared his two-cents' worth with Allard.

"Your portrait of the reserve system is devastating. It makes me wonder how long we will go on pumping more money into such a rotten system, thereby making it worse rather than better."[13]

Bob Connelly, who had served in many positions in Indian Affairs, including as Manitoba regional director and Director of Specific Claims, made his opinion quite clear. He offered Allard his congratulations and declared "Big Bear's Treaty" "the best diagnosis ever done of Indian Affairs. I feel it has supplanted Jack Beaver's report in that regard."[14]

Supplanting Beaver's report from 1979 when he "exited with voice" was praise indeed.

"Until very recently," said Connelly, "the main thrust of federal policy was to break up the extended family, the clan structure, to detribalize and assimilate Indian populations… The Indian people's refusal to be assimilated is a triumph of the human spirit; it is to be celebrated, not deplored."[15]

Gordon Gibson had his own particular interest in Indigenous politics. He had served for five years as an assistant to Northern Affairs minister Arthur Laing, who was Jean Chrétien's immediate predecessor as minister of Indian Affairs. Gibson then became s a special assistant to Prime Minister Pierre Trudeau during the brouhaha over the 1969 White Paper. He had also sat as a Liberal in the British Columbia legislature in the 1970s, and occasionally appeared on the CBC-TV At Issue panel on *The National*.

Gibson and Allard met in Vancouver in the summer of 1999, and they talked about the idea of modernizing treaty annuities.

"Because he could give his ideas the credibility that came from personal experience," Gibson said of Allard, "I expressed hope that he would write a book. He said he had already started, and I got a look at the first draft a few months later."[16]

Gibson liked Allard's manuscript. "He is a clear and original thinker, and he has personally lived with the people and events that have shaped the past fifty years of Indian policy. A Métis himself, he has been with, but not of, the Indian Industry as it has evolved. He has been close enough to know where the bodies are buried, but has avoided personal burial in the stultifying conventional ideas dominating Indian affairs."[17]

It was exactly the kind of response Allard had hoped for. The next challenge was to finish the manuscript and get the book out into the public domain. That didn't happen quite as planned. After about a year with no further progress, Gibson had a proposal.

Gibson was a Senior Fellow in Canadian Studies at the right-wing Fraser Institute, and he knew John Richards, a professor of public policy at Simon Fraser University and the co-editor of the policy journal *Inroads*. Gibson thought it important that Allard's treaty annuity idea get out into the public domain; he was worrying that it might not get finished and published. Gibson and Richards proposed to Allard that an extensive excerpt of the manuscript be published in the *Inroads* journal. That would ensure the idea was out there where others could develop it. Or challenge it, as the case may be. The idea of modernized annuities was a debate worth having.

Allard agreed. Gibson and Richards polished and edited excerpts from "Big Bear's Treaty" and devoted sixty pages of the May 2002 *Inroads* to it. Sure, it might be read only by policy wonks and academics, but it was officially on the record, and that was a win.

In an op-ed piece that was published in *The Globe and Mail* in July 2002, Allard spoke to a wider audience:

"Big Bear fought for a meaningful annual payment of 'treaty money'—payable to all individual Indians. Individual treaty money is the only treaty benefit that has, over the past 130 years, not been modernized. It was $5 annually in 1871; it remains $5 today."[18]

For many Canadians, this might well have been the first time that they heard about treaty annuities, what they were intended for, and the absurdity of still paying out the same amount of money as when the treaties were signed.

"The principle is simple," explained Allard. "Paying significant treaty money directly to individual Indians empowers individual Indians. And it honours Canada's obligations under the treaties."[19]

The *Winnipeg Sun* followed that up with an editorial titled "A legacy for Jean," but it was a legacy for the prime minister, not Allard. The editorialists suggested that Jean Chrétien should return to his political roots from the time he was Indian Affairs minister—not to produce another political disaster like the White Paper—but to act on Allard's idea of modernized annuities.

"So Allard says if Chrétien is searching for his legacy, he should update the treaty money and put it in the hands of each individual Indian... This is the kind of idea that Chrétien could quickly adopt to bring his political career full circle and end the cycle of misery and poverty amongst natives."[20]

But that obviously wasn't going to happen, not if Liberal policy on First Nations issues was that there weren't any real problems, and if there were, they would be solved by self-government.

Endnotes to Chapter 12

1. Steve Mahoney, House of Commons Debate, *Hansard*, Vol. 136, November 4, 1999, 1162.
2. Ghislain Fournier, House of Commons Debate, *Hansard*, Vol. 136, November 4, 1999, 1164.
3. James Brooke, "Canada's Tribal Women Fight (Mostly Male) Graft," *New York Times*, January 1, 2001, http://www.nytimes.com/2001/01/01/world/canada-s-tribal-women-fight-mostly-male-graft.html.
4. Len Kruzenga, "Two views, one meeting, says AFN," *Windspeaker*, Vol. 17, No. 6, 1999: 14.
5. Cory Howard, "Chief Injustice," *Homemaker's Digest*, April 2000, 48.
6. Myron Thompson, House of Commons Debates, *Hansard*, Vol. 136, No. 078, Tuesday, April 4, 2000, 5658.
7. John O'Reilly, House of Commons Debates, *Hansard*, Vol. 136, No. 078, Tuesday, April 4, 2000, 5690.
8. Thompson, *Hansard*, 2000, 5695.
9. Allan Blakeney, correspondence with Jean Allard, November 17, 1999.
10. Ibid.
11. Frank Price, comments with regard to "Big Bear's People," correspondence with Jean Allard, c1999.
12. Ibid.
13. Tom Flanagan, correspondence with Jean Allard, November 12, 1999.
14. Bob Connelly, Letter to the Editor: Allard's Big Bear's treaty, *Inroads*, Vol. 12 (2002): 9.
15. Ibid.
16. Gordon Gibson, 2002, Foreword, "Big Bear's Treaty; The Road to Freedom," Jean Allard, with Sheilla Jones, *Inroads*, Vol. 11, 110.
17. Ibid.
18. Jean Allard, "Indian Governance: The white man's burden," *The Globe and Mail*, July 16, 2002.
19. Ibid.
20. Editorial: "A legacy for Jean," *Winnipeg Sun*, July 24, 2002.

13
ESCAPING THE REACH OF IA

The defeat of the *First Nations Ombudsman Act* bill was a serious setback for people wanting to see some evidence that anybody with power and authority was willing to listen to the voices of ordinary Indians. While people like Myron Thompson were willing to listen and to act, the majority of politicians appeared more disposed to believe the assurances of Indian Affairs and its agents. The Parliament of Canada is the highest seat of democratic power for the country. If its members were unmoved by the plight of angry, desperate First Nations mothers, what hope was there for change for the better?

It was the end of the fight for Leona Freed, who said activism in Indigenous politics "got you bullets with your name on them."[1] After five years of listening to horror stories of abuses on reserves, facing threats of lawsuits from angry chiefs and comforting despairing women who wanted help that Freed had no power to provide, she couldn't take it anymore. She was tired of banging her head against the proverbial brick wall.

"Nobody was listening to us. No one heard our cries for help. Nothing was changing."[2]

Indian Affairs, seeing an opportunity to silence a very noisy critic by pulling her inside the bureaucracy, offered Freed a $65,000 contract to produce a report on election fraud on reserves. Freed knew what she was doing when she took the deal.

"As soon as I took the money, I knew I was compromised and that I would lose my credibility as a fighter for ordinary Indians. But it was an enormous relief to get out of politics."[3]

Freed would, at least, "exit with voice," just as Jack Beaver had done thirty years earlier. She held hearings across the country and submitted her report to Indian Affairs. The report she submitted, "Corrupt Elections in First Nations Communities," was chewed up by the machinery of Indian Affairs without leaving a trace. Recall that old saying: You don't change Indian Affairs. Indian Affairs changes you.

Despite the defeat of the Ombudsman bill, there were some small signs that indicated possibilities for change in Indigenous politics. One was Prime Minister Chrétien's appointment of Robert Nault in 1999 as the newest IA minister. The square-jawed politician from northwestern Ontario was a good choice. He was a down-to-earth, practical man, elected an MP in 1988, and he had more than fifty First Nations communities in his riding.

Perhaps Chrétien's confidence in Nault had something to do with the similarities between them, according to *Maclean's* magazine writer John Geddes.

"Like the boss, he's a scrapper who revels in his image as a no-nonsense pragmatist. And like Chrétien in an earlier era, he's making a bid to solidify his big-league political credentials in one of Ottawa's toughest jobs, minister of Indian affairs."[4]

Nault claimed that he was "the only Indian Affairs minister in history who lobbied for the job," and that his work as an MP in his riding gave him a good education on Indigenous issues.

"I came into the department knowing a lot about the policies and programs. I had lived them every time I went to a community."[5]

Chrétien was well aware of the growing heap of junked policy proposals and IA research papers on eliminating or amending the *Indian Act*, but he was prepared to give Nault a shot at it. After nearly two years of incessant outcry in the media about corruption and election fraud on reserves, it was obvious from a political perspective that something had to be done. Unlike the harshly condemned Buffalo Jump policy from the Mulroney years that had been shrouded in secrecy, Nault would have in-depth consultations with, well, anybody who was interested. Indian Affairs set about organizing consultations across the country as part of its new First Nations Governance Initiative, with a big pot of money to pay groups to make presentations. However, not many people were interested. At some Manitoba meetings, nobody showed up but the IA employees.[6] This was hardly surprising, given that First Nations people in the province were still bitter about the aborted Manitoba Framework Initiative on self-government. The extensive consultation with ordinary FN people just a few years earlier had lit a spark of hope for real self-determination, which, from an Indigenous perspective, had been so thoroughly doused with cold water by Indian Affairs that no embers remained. Why would anyone waste their time on more useless IA consultations that would end with IA again imposing its pre-determined outcome?

Nonetheless, about 500 people did eventually participate in about sixty meetings across the country,[7] which allowed Nault to assert that the newly proposed *First Nations Governance Act* of 2002 was the result of extensive consultations. The legislation proposed major amendments to the *Indian Act* that would require bands to develop and adopt codes covering elections, financial accountability, and band administration. It even had a provision for several ombudsmen. It affected all FN bands except those who had already signed self-government agreements — the Nisga'a and Sechelt in British Columbia, the Cree of northern Quebec, and a number of Yukon First Nations groups.[8]

Nault described the act as a bridge between the status quo and self-government, which was the policy direction for IA ever since the White Paper. But, once again, conflict immediately emerged over how to define "self-government." IA was still pushing for the same municipal-style band governance it demanded of the Manitoba Framework Initiative, which would leave reserves subordinated to the powers of the provincial and federal levels of government. For the Assembly of First Nations, bands had the inherent right to self-government and self-determination as guaranteed under the *Constitution Act* of 1982, and did not need any permission or buy-in from other government levels.

A growing distinction was emerging between three different forms of self-governance. IA was pushing municipal-style self-government. The AFN was naturally focussing on self-government that would see the political power of First Nations (and the funding that went with it) anchored in the chief and council system, from which the AFN derived its own legitimacy. The right to self-determination supported by many ordinary FN people was another kettle of fish altogether. It offered, in theory, individual and collective rights of the kind more closely resembling traditional governance, which did not include elected chiefs and councils.[9] However, the Manitoba Framework Initiative's truncated attempt to identify how traditional government might work revealed that the concept was not yet well thought-out in the modern context, and the desire for governance based on love, respect and harmony tended to sound more like the basis for a '60s hippie commune than a workable form of governance.

Nault was inclined to be blunt rather than tactful in his dealings with Indigenous leaders, and he locked horns with the AFN more than a few times while trying to persuade the Indigenous politicians to work with him to negotiate changes to the *Indian Act*. Nault and the AFN worked out an agreement on how the negotiations would work, only to have a large group of chiefs at a national meeting vote, behind closed doors, to nullify the agreement. The chiefs demanded the AFN boycott consultations, rather than assist in amending the colonial act.[10] Nault was obviously frustrated, and word leaked out from "senior government sources" that the AFN was now considered "irrelevant" and "dysfunctional."[11] IA officials hastily disavowed the remarks.

The Assembly of First Nations was having its own internal struggles with the chiefs it represented. The bands across the country came in all shapes and sizes, and with different priorities. Trying to shoehorn all those different voices into the "one voice" claimed by the AFN was chafing. When it came to electing the AFN executive and national chief, the chief heading a band with 20,000 members in Ontario had one vote, as did a chief in BC with 200 band members. Since the majority of the reserves were in the West, the western priorities, particularly treaties, regularly took precedence over the agendas of the eastern bands. To quell internal dissent, AFN politicians had little choice but to go along with what the majority of chiefs demanded.

The hardening of AFN's opposition to Nault's governance bill and the denunciations by the National Chief Matthew Coon Come were dismissed by Nault.

"He's a lobbyist," Nault told *Maclean's* in an interview in the summer of 2002. "His role is to lobby on behalf of the chiefs, and there are a number of chiefs who prefer the status quo."[12]

Nault might not have liked the intransigence of the AFN, but there was a limit on what he could do to force the AFN to the table without there being some kind of backlash from the public. Indian Affairs did, however, slash AFN's funding nearly in half, from about $20 million in 2001 to $12 million.[13] Since the public had little idea of funding arrangements with the Aboriginal Representative Organizations, there was little the AFN could do but fume. The AFN was also said to have refused $2 million from the substantial pot of money allocated to fund First Nations groups participating in IA's consultations, which did not sit well with some chiefs who wanted access to those funds.[14]

The Native Women's Association of Canada, one of the five AROs, was not as well protected. It was supposed to speak for all Indigenous women in the consultations. However, in the fall of 2001, NWAC made the mistake of publicly siding with the AFN, which IA interpreted as meaning the women's group was boycotting the consultations, too.

Indian Affairs promptly took NWAC's consultation allocation of $225,000 and gave it all to the newly created National Aboriginal Women's Association (NAWA). The NAWA president, Pamela Paul, who was the former executive director of the NWAC, defended the move by saying that someone had to represent the voices of women if the Native Women's Association of Canada would not.[15]

At a hearing of the parliamentary Standing Committee on Aboriginal Affairs on the *First Nations Governance Act* in March 2002, NDP MP Pat Martin challenged NAWA's legitimacy when Paul spoke before the committee.

"You can't blame people," said Martin, "for assuming you were created, you were manufactured, just to collaborate with the minister on this initiative… How can you blame people for thinking you were set up as some sort of a puppet organization?"[16]

It was, said Martin, as if the government was saying that if this organization won't co-operate with us, we'll find one that will.[17]

The conflict between Nault and the political organizations was laying bare the legitimacy question that had simmered under the surface of Indigenous politics since first raised by Jack Beaver in 1973.[18] At that time, Beaver had identified the two key conditions for measuring the legitimacy of an organization as the voice for the constituency it claimed to speak for. First, people in that constituency required a means to withdraw their support. Second, legitimacy could not be based on the government funding a group and then designating it as the sole voice for a particular constituency.

Under the "Beaver Legitimacy Test," band chiefs could certainly withdraw their support from the AFN, and often threatened to. The AFN, however, claimed to be the sole voice, not just of the chiefs, but of all First Nations people in Canada. However, only band chiefs could withdraw their support; the rest of the FN population had no means to do so. Thus, AFN failed the legitimacy test. As for the women's organizations, the mere fact that Indian Affairs could pull the funding for the Native Women's Association of Canada (NWAC), hand it to the newly created National Aboriginal Women's Association (NAWA) and declare it the new "sole voice" meant the two women's groups failed the legitimacy test as well.

Ordinary FN people might appreciate the valuable work done by groups like the AFN to raise awareness of Indigenous issues in government and in the public, but they generally held a jaundiced view of the organization and considered it little more than a chiefs' lobby group.

Cree writer Jordan Wheeler said at the time, "The AFN has lost its ability to make any direct impact on the lives of your average native. They've never been a real government anyway—just a fancy office to give career politicians a place to go beyond the band office."[19]

Besides that, Wheeler added, the AFN seemed to conveniently forget that chiefs were never part of the traditional system of governance but rather a creation of Indian Affairs.[20]

As had always been the case in whichever new policy was put forward by Indian Affairs, whether in Trudeau's White Paper, Mulroney's Buffalo Jump, or Jane Stewart's more recent Gathering Strength, Nault's new governance act did not address self-determination. There was no mechanism available for bands that wanted to return to a more traditional form of governance. As a result, there was no consideration given to restoring the power balance on reserves, either by empowering individuals through modernized annuity payments or by empowering band families to reject inept or corrupt band governments by "voting with their feet" to find a band more to their liking.

"Change is in the air," promised Nault. "Change that encompasses an integrated set of priorities to build communities and economies. Change that puts the tools for an improved quality of life into the hands of the communities."[21]

But Nault's "change" was looking remarkably similar, in the end, to the policy changes that had been proposed before. It was clearly pushing First Nations communities into municipal-style governance structures, and Nault confirmed that the department had no intention of revisiting its policy requiring bands to sign away their peoples' Aboriginal title and rights.[22] At the same time, Nault's new governance act formalized the long-standing power of the Indian Affairs minister to intrude into band affairs and elections at will.

Maybe such ministerial power was intended to provide a check on the kinds of excesses that band governments had proved themselves only too willing to indulge in, but it also further reinforced the fact that band governments were accountable to Indian Affairs, not to ordinary band members.

The *First Nations Governance Act* was being touted in the media as Chrétien's legacy legislation, especially with his retirement now a sure thing.[23] However, Parliament recessed for the summer in June 2003 with a multitude of amendments to the bill yet to be addressed ahead of second reading.

Jean Allard's push for modernizing treaty annuities as a means of empowering ordinary First Nations people had been attracting some significant interest from politicians and Indigenous activists who saw the idea as a revolutionary approach. It focussed on redirecting a portion of the money the Canadian public was already allocating to Indian Affairs into the hands of individual FN people to spend as they chose — buying a home, going to university, starting a business, paying membership dues to their own advocacy organizations to legitimately speak for them, or however they wanted. And it was readily justifiable, since it was nothing more than increasing the five-dollar annuity that Indian Affairs was still paying every year to Treaty people who showed up at Treaty Days events across the country to collect it. And Allard was wisely pitching it as revenue-neutral. He figured it didn't need to cost Canadians any more than they were already paying to support Indian Affairs.

Professionals who were directly concerned with the poverty of Indigenous people, whether on or off the reserve, were paying attention because it was a very long time since anyone had brought such an innovative idea to the table. Among them was Wayne Helgason, the executive director of the Social Planning Council of Winnipeg. The Planning Council, with its roots in the infamous Winnipeg General Strike in 1919,[24] was first and foremost a powerful voice for identifying community needs, especially those of the destitute, impoverished and imprisoned.

Given that Winnipeg was a city with the largest per capita population of First Nations people calling it home,[25] Helgason could immediately see the benefit of a modernized annuity.

"Just look at what would happen in Winnipeg," said Helagason. "Nearly 80 percent of kids living in poverty in this city are from Aboriginal families. In one fell swoop, we could lift almost all of them out of poverty and welfare dependency. This would have an amazing effect, not just on the Aboriginal community, but for the whole of Winnipeg."[26]

The impact on western cities like Regina, Saskatoon and Edmonton would be much the same. But what about eastern urban centres like Brantford, Montreal and Halifax?

Indian Affairs was paying its piddling $4 or $5 annuity only to the members of the bands whose chiefs had signed treaties between 1850 and 1923. Bands in southern Ontario and to the east either did not sign treaties or their treaties did not contain an annuity provision. Would the annuity be modernized to include all Status Indians? Who would be eligible? How would the annuity be delivered? What programs or services from Indian Affairs would have to be cut to pay for the increased annuity?

There were a great many questions but few answers. That's when the Treaty Annuity Working Group (TAWG) was born, created by Helgason and Allard as a special committee of the Social Planning Council. The small committee included a number of former politicians from across the political spectrum, including former Conservative Finance minister Clayton Manness and NDP Agriculture minister Sam Uskiw, and former Winnipeg city councillor and president of L'Union national métisse Saint-Joseph du Manitoba Guy Savoie.

Helgason was himself a Status Indian with Liberal leanings, the son of an Icelandic father and Saulteaux mother. He had studied psychology, attended Harvard University and lectured at the University of Toronto on policy issues. And he was a three-term president of the National Friendship Centres. He was also president of the Aboriginal Council of Winnipeg, which had taken over the grand, old Canadian Pacific Railroad station in the city's downtown and turned its marble floors and soaring columns into a community campus where kids from reserves could upgrade their education and prepare for university or college.

A big, amiable man, Helgason worked for a time early in his career as a social worker for the Children's Aid Society in Winnipeg. It provided him with some hard lessons about extreme poverty, its impact on families, and the obstinacy of a bureaucracy serving its own interests. He figured a modernized annuity would help keep Aboriginal people from becoming entangled in the "helping" bureaucracy.

"Child welfare is about economics. Neglect is economics. If you don't have enough money, if you don't have the ability to hire a babysitter, and there's not enough money for food, the outcomes are frustration, maybe inappropriate arrangements for supervision. About 70 percent of kids are taken into care because of economic constraints. That's where treaty money could make a big difference."[27]

Helgason said that the child welfare industry had been built on the need to incarcerate children. The system made it far easier to apprehend children than to help a household through a troubled night. He could get $200 for an initial clothing allowance within an hour if he seized a kid, but if what the family really needed was a homemaker so the kids could stay in their home for the night, it would mean filling out lots of forms, and a three-day wait. Sometimes, it just made more sense to keep the family intact and the kids out of the system, but that option was often not available.

"Actually," Helgason admitted, "one time I apprehended a Cabbage Patch doll. There was a birth certificate. I swear to God I put the name of the Cabbage

Patch doll on the form, took the address, and got this doll an initial clothing cheque for $200. What the family really needed was groceries. No one ever knew. I just cancelled the apprehension afterwards and said 'returned home.' The Cabbage Patch doll is doing just fine."[28]

What Helgason recognized was a perverse system that was supposed to be helping children in need but was instead using those same children to justify the need for the system's institutions and the jobs that went with them. He could see the similarities to the institutional needs of Indian Affairs.

The Treaty Annuity Working Group was a decidedly eclectic group, but it had big ideas. The committee met in the fall of 2002 to figure out how best to examine all the questions surrounding a modernized treaty annuity and set priorities.[29]

The first priority was making sure that the modernized annuity was on Jean Chrétien's radar. The prime minister was the one person who had the clout to institute such a revolutionary change at Indian Affairs. But the group felt he would need to be sold on what the change in treaty annuities would mean, and assurance that it would have the kind of positive impact Allard and others hoped for — the kind that would provide Chrétien with the legacy he wanted. However, getting Chrétien's attention was not easy, in part because he had already given Nault a long leash on instituting reform through the new governance act, and it was still working its way through the legislative process.

Chrétien had also been distracted for some time by the power plays going on behind the scenes in the Liberal party, with Finance minister Paul Martin nipping impatiently at his heels in his desire to take over the leadership of the party, and hence, the prime ministership. Their feuding had been going on for more than a decade, and it finally exploded into the open in June when Chrétien abruptly dropped Martin from his cabinet. It did not go down well with Martin's supporters, and the normally supportive media started to use terms like "dead man walking" to describe Chrétien.[30] The media also started quoting Chretien verbatim in print, rather than smoothing out his sometimes mangled English so that his comments would sound better. It was a small cruelty on the part of the media, but it also signalled that Chretien had lost a certain level of respect in political circles. Martin was suddenly a backbencher, but his demotion gave him the time to campaign for a party leadership review with the objective of forcing Chrétien out.

As the Treaty Annuity Working Group was being set up, NDP MLA Sam Uskiw had already taken the initiative of sending letters to both Chrétien and Nault in the summer of 2002, urging them to consider the proposal for updating treaties as a mechanism for individual empowerment of First Nations/Treaty people. Chrétien didn't answer but Nault replied in September. His response was not really surprising. He stated that the department supported increasing economic self-reliance of First Nations but that Indian Affairs was prioritizing strengthening band governance through Bill C-61, the first version of the *First Nations Governance Act* that later became Bill C-7.

Uskiw responded to Nault. "If, as you say, you and I share the same goals as those spelled out in Bill C-61, then the Allard proposal must be seen as being worthy of close analysis and evaluation. To ignore its positive features and fail to act would be doubly counter-productive; it would constitute a missed opportunity to correct a century-old problem of inequality, and doom the Indian people to more of the same in the future. On the other hand, an updated annuity would, in my opinion, restore pride in the treaty itself. It would remove the sense of grievance that plagues Indian/non-Indian relationships and return to the native people control over their lives."[31]

What Uskiw was talking about was a potential basis for reconciliation.

TAWG also wanted to get people talking about treaty annuities. A national workshop that would bring together "stakeholders" would help publicize the issue. The C.D. Howe Institute had already proposed a round-table discussion for early 2003 that would be hosted by president Jack Mintz, with a number of policy people leading the discussion on the fiscal reforms necessary to pay for the annuity. It was not, however, the kind of crowd that Allard thought should be initially involved in sorting out the treaty annuity issues, so he turned it down.

The TAWG board figured its own two-day national workshop in June 2003 was the best route to go, but how would it be paid for? Since the Social Planning Council had charitable status, it was eligible for funding from various philanthropic organizations. The workshop was pulled together in short order, with the modest but welcome sum of $16,000 in combined funding from the Winnipeg Foundation, the Sill Foundation, Ed Schreyer's Canadian Shield Foundation, and a few small personal donations. It wasn't a lot of money, but as Leona Freed had shown, a few committed people could accomplish a great deal with just a few dollars.

The people invited to the workshop, called Modernizing Treaty Annuities: Implications and Consequences, included policy wonks like Gordon Gibson and academic John Richards, but mainly it was Indigenous people involved in gang prevention activities, social workers, university students, a former Indian Affairs manager and a news editor from the Aboriginal Peoples' Television Network. TAWG made an explicit decision not to invite the leaders of Indigenous political groups or chiefs and councils. This was an opportunity to listen to the voices of the people who rarely got to speak and be heard.

As the final planning got underway in May 2003 for the workshop scheduled for later in June, Allard got a surprise invitation. Kevin Lynch, the Deputy Minister of Finance, wanted to talk to him about treaty annuities. This was great news. A busy person like Lynch wouldn't take time for such a meeting unless he already thought the annuity idea had something of value. John Richards, who had been working behind the scenes to promote modernized annuities since the excerpt from Allard's "Big Bear's Treaty" was published in *Inroads*, had gotten some senior people in Finance interested. As one official close to Paul Martin when he was still Finance minister noted, Martin was very focussed on First Nations issues and both he and Lynch were looking at fundamental reforms.

TAWG had no expectation, based on the earlier response from Nault, that Indian Affairs was suddenly going to leap on the idea of modernizing annuities, but maybe the chances of actually implementing change were better coming from a government department not directly threatened by the shift in power that the annuity change was designed to bring about. A department such as Finance. Was this a way to work around the legendary immutability of Indian Affairs?

Allard met with Lynch in Winnipeg in early June. The Finance deputy minister liked what he heard enough that he flew Allard to Ottawa to speak with other government bureaucrats. But that's where it ended. It could have been that modernizing treaty annuities was too revolutionary, or maybe the annuity idea just got lost in the maelstrom of Ottawa politics. Chrétien announced he was going to retire, setting off a race for the party leadership. Finance minister John Manley, Martin's replacement at Finance, threw his hat in the ring. Inside the bubble of Ottawa politics, the party was largely consumed by an anticipated purge of Chrétien loyalists if Martin became leader, which was considered highly likely as he had a huge lead over any other contenders. The drama in Ottawa left little time for issues like treaty annuities.

Meanwhile, the treaty annuity workshop proceeded as planned at the Aboriginal Centre in Winnipeg, with delegates hashing out the benefits and complications that a modernized annuity might bring to Indians living on reserves and off reserves, and the impacts it could have on communities, provinces and the country as a whole.

A big question was how it would be paid for. The price tag for a $5,000 modernized annuity would be substantial. If it were paid only to Treaty Indians (about 400,000 in 2002), it would mean reallocating about $2 billion from the Indian Affairs budget to pay for it. If a policy decision was made to include all Status Indians (about 600,000 in 2002), it would be about $3 billion. The general consensus at the end of discussions was that there was considerable value to ordinary Indian people in being freed from welfare dependency, with the annuity strengthening the family because all its members—children included—contributed to the family's well-being. Those benefits outweighed the complexity of sorting out questions of what would be re-allocated from the Indian Affairs budget.

It was obvious that the idea of modernizing annuities needed far more research and study. It was a new idea that needed to be explored, and so far, all that had been spent on it were the donations to fund the TAWG workshop and Allard's grant from Canadian Heritage to write "Big Bear's Treaty," totalling all of $40,000.

As the TAWG report, Modernizing Treaty Annuities: Implications and Consequences,[32] pointed out, modernizing treaty annuities did not rest solely on there being a political climate suitable for instituting such a significant change. It was justiciable, which meant there were grounds for a court challenge, where a judge, or perhaps the Supreme Court of Canada, would decide whether there were legal grounds for the annuity to be increased, and how much that increase would be.

The challenge for TAWG was persuading politicians that putting their support behind a government policy change served their interests more than leaving it to the courts to decide for them.

When parliament resumed in September 2003, the *First Nations Governance Act* seemed to have disappeared. Had Nault given up in the face of considerable public opposition fuelled, in part, by the AFN boycott? He had. The requirement for band codes to run fair elections, requirements for accountability to band members, ombudsmen to address grievances—all disappeared under yet another IA policy failure. The possibility of a Chrétien legacy based on significantly changing First Nations governance was gone, too.

The TAWG committee wasn't sure if the opportunity to influence Chretien was now lost, or whether a lame-duck prime minister might be more amenable to hearing about treaty annuities. He was essentially being forced out by Martin's people in December when the Liberal Party held its leadership vote, but perhaps he, too, might want to "exit with voice." And what a roar it would be if he chose to upend Indian Affair's monopoly with a bold and provocative last-minute policy change. Sure, a Martin administration could reverse anything Chrétien announced in his waning days, but once a modernized annuity was offered to Treaty people, it would be very difficult to rescind. TAWG decided to take the chance, and sent the outgoing prime minister a draft of the final report of the workshop, along with a pitch to modernize annuities.

Their timing was off. Paul Martin won the leadership of the Liberal Party by a landslide and became Prime Minister on December 12, 2003. The purge of Chrétien supporters happened quickly, just as feared. In the time lag, the TAWG report ended up on Martin's desk instead of Chrétien's. Martin forwarded TAWG's letter to his new Indian Affairs minister, Andy Mitchell, who had replaced Nault in the December purge. Mitchell replied to TAWG in March 2004.

"I recognize the hope that an increase in annuities to individuals would reform the system, redistribute power and wealth, and empower individuals to achieve their economic independence. However, I believe enhancing treaty annuities would not result in a meaningful or sustained positive economic or political change for individual community members."[33] Mitchell curiously went on to say, "Treaty annuities are not viewed as part of a general livelihood right but rather as a fulfilment of a specific obligation identified in the treaty relationship. In addition, there are no provisions in the treaties for an increase in the amount of the treaties."[34]

The new minister was quite mistaken.

Endnotes to Chapter 13

1 Leona Freed, interview with author, August, 2017.
2 Ibid.
3 Ibid.
4 John Geddes, "Tough guy," *Maclean's*, July 1, 2002, 40.
5 Ibid.
6 Stéphanie Boisard, 2003, "Conflicting Discourses in Canadian Aboriginal Politics,: A Case Study in the First Nations Governance Initiative," M.A. Thesis, University of Saskatchewan, 55.
7 Legislative History, Bill C-7: *The First Nations Governance Act*, October 10, 2003, lop.parl.ca/About/Parliament/LegislativeSummaries/bills_ls.asp?ls=c7&Parl=37&Ses=2.
8 Ibid., Endnote 2.
9 Boisard, 57.
10 Paul Barnsley, "Chiefs reject executive-negotiated governance plan," *Windspeaker*, Vol. 19, No. 9, 2002, 6, http://ammsa.com/publications/windspeaker/chiefs-reject-executive-negotiated-governance-plan.
11 Ibid.
12 Geddes, 2002, 42.
13 Paul Barnsley, "AFN reeling, budget cut by half," *Windspeaker*, Vol. 19, No. 4, 2001, 1.
14 Ibid.
15 Paul Barnsley, "DIAND consultations fail to impress women's group," *Windspeaker*, Vol. 11, No. 9, 2002, 2.
16 Pat Martin, Evidence: Standing Committee on Aboriginal Affairs, Northern Development and Natural Resources, 37th Parliament, 1st Session, Thursday, March 14, 2002.
17 Ibid.
18 Jack Beaver, 1973, in a report to ADM Robert Connelly, Indian Affairs and Northern Development, given by Connelly to Jean Allard, part of which is referenced in "Big Bear's Treaty: The Road to Freedom," 2000, unpublished manuscript, 43–45.
19 Jordan Wheeler, "AFN election doesn't matter," *Winnipeg Free Press*, July 14, 2003.
20 Ibid.
21 Indian and Northern Affairs Canada and Canadian Polar Commission, 2002–2003 Estimates, Part III, Plans and Priorities, 1.
22 Arthur Manuel, 2017, *The Reconciliation Manifesto: Recovering the land, rebuilding the economy*, James Lorimer and Company, 141.
23 Frank Cassidy, "The First Nations Governance Act: A Legacy of Loss," *Options Politiques*, April 2003.
24 Jared Story, "Nearly a century of planning," *Winnipeg Free Press*, May 13, 2014, https://www.winnipegfreepress.com/our-communities/times/Nearly-a-century-of-planning-259099611.html.
25 Statistics Canada, Aboriginal peoples in Canada: Key results from the 2016 Census, https://www150.statcan.gc.ca/n1/daily-quotidien/171025/dq171025a-eng.htm.
26 Wayne Helgason, interview with author, 2003.
27 Wayne Helgason, interview with author, 1999.
28 Ibid.

29 Disclosure: the author served as a facilitator and researcher for TAWG.
30 "Jean Chrétien v Paul Martin: now it's really war," *The Economist*, June 6, 2002, http://www.economist.com/node/1169236.
31 Sam Uskiw, correspondence with The Honourable Robert D. Nault, Minister of Indian Affairs and Northern Development, November 12, 2002.
32 Modernizing Treaty Annuities: Implications and Consequences, 2004, Treaty Annuity Working Group, Social Planning Council of Winnipeg, http://archive.li/6LAkY.
33 Andy Mitchell, Minister of Indian Affairs and Northern Development, in correspondence with Wayne Helgason and Jean Allard, Social Planning Council of Winnipeg, March 26, 2004.
34 Ibid.

14
THE NEW PM TAKES CHARGE

Paul Martin, now prime minister, was still searching for a revolutionary idea or some kind of fundamental reform on First Nations issues. His "Kelowna Accord," as it came to be called, emerged from a series of round-tables between selected representatives of the federal, provincial and territorial governments and the five Aboriginal Representative Organizations (AROs).

What set this new round of negotiations and consultations apart from all the others that had gone before was that, this time, it was not the Indian Affairs minister running the show. It was the prime minister. Surely this time, there would be success instead of failure.

It is unlikely that many (or any) of the Indigenous politicians attending the first roundtable in April 2004 would have recognized the irony that day of Martin's invitation to "sit down on the same side of the table, as partners."[1] They would have had to know about that time when, about six months before the 1969 White Paper "thunderclap" that changed the course of Indigenous politics in Canada, Dave Courchene invited Indian Affairs minister Jean Chrétien to sit with the Indian chiefs on their side of the table to signify the start of a new relationship as partners.[2] That hadn't worked out so well.

The roundtables under Martin's new plan were certainly keeping the AROs busy. The first session was attended by 65 ARO representatives.[3] The rest of the 147 participants were government people, with another twenty-five representatives from a variety of other Aboriginal organizations. Because the prime minster was in charge, all the big guns were coming out, including cabinet members, parliamentary secretaries and senators.[4]

Who wasn't represented at the roundtables were ordinary Indigenous people. Their voices would not be heard. And neither would the voices of ordinary non-Indigenous people.

The first roundtable was followed by seven "sectoral tables," with more than 750 people invited who were experts in health care, education and job training, housing, economic opportunities, accountability and negotiation skills.

The representatives for the five AROs were there, too, along with government bureaucrats from the various federal departments, especially the IA co-delivery partners who were directly affected by the topics under discussion. Each of the thematic discussions included breakout sessions for First Nations, Inuit and Métis special interests.[5]

The consultations wrapped up in a policy retreat in May 2005 with the Cabinet Committee on Aboriginal Affairs and the leaders of the five AROs. To recap, the five AROs were (and still are):

- Assembly of First Nations, representing the chiefs of Canada's roughly 630 First Nations,
- Métis National Council, representing the presidents of the five Métis provincial organizations,
- Inuit Tapiriit Kanatami, representing the four presidents of the Inuit corporations created as part of Northern self-government negotiations (the presidents are elected by their corporate boards),
- Congress of Aboriginal Peoples, representing the presidents of nine affiliated provincial and territorial organizations,
- Native Women's Association of Canada, representing the presidents of thirteen Aboriginal women's organizations across Canada (the National Aboriginal Women's Association got dropped in the aftermath of the failure of Bob Nault's governance act).

The AROs were funded by Indian Affairs and its co-delivery partners such as Canadian Heritage, but it was all public funding; the AROs had no resources of their own, nor were they financed by the constituencies they were assigned by IA to speak for. In the Kelowna discussions, it appeared that the AROs and the government bureaucrats had finally found a tune they could all dance to.

Certainly the roundtable process with the AROs was paying off for the Martin government, and doing so in a way that the messy consultations undertaken as part of the First Nations Governance Initiative had not for Bob Nault. There were no boycotts or outraged news conferences, and no insults flying back and forth between the IA minister and the ARO leaders. Rather, the federal government was sitting down on the same side of the table as the five Indigenous political organizations that it funded, and everyone was playing nice.

The reward for each ARO was a special accord of its own. These weren't just "thank you for your compliance" accords; these were really nice ones, signed by either the Government of Canada, or Her Majesty the Queen in Right of Canada.

With their special accords in hand, each ARO had a job to do. The AFN was to get right to work on reconciling First Nations rights from section 35, the "empty box" of rights in the *Constitution Act* of 1982; the Métis National Council could look at taking over more programs and services for Métis people from the "Ontario westward" provinces; the ITK could work on negotiating a Canada-Inuit Action Plan; and the Congress of Aboriginal Peoples and Native Women's Association—always junior players at these events—could work at figuring out how to advance their roles in development of relevant federal policies.[6] Naturally, each of these accords came with additional money attached.

Then came the big meeting in Kelowna in November 2005 and the public "reveal" of the report, First Ministers and National Aboriginal Leaders: Strengthening the Relationship and Closing the Gap. The money needed to support the Kelowna expectations was just over $5 billion spread out over five years. The plan included $1.8 billion for education; $1.6 billion for housing and clean water; $1.3 billion for health services; $200 million for economic development; and $170 million for the AROs to help them work with the federal government on land claim and self-government policies.[7]

Martin earned the kudos he received for achieving the Kelowna Accord. It may well have galled Chrétien that during his seven years as Indian Affairs minister and ten years as PM, he was never able to achieve that kind of unanimity with Indigenous political leaders. And it probably irked him even more that it was his long-time archrival who had succeeded where he had failed.

A couple of policy wonks writing for *Policy Options* thought there were valuable lessons to be learned from the process Martin used in arriving at the Kelowna Accord. In particular, they pointed out that Martin allowed the five AROs to take the lead in discussions and thereby "own" the solutions, and that Martin recognized that the provincial, territorial and Indigenous governments were best suited to implement and spend the money allocated in the accord. The role of the federal government was to provide the money to fulfill the ambitious agenda.[8]

The process was not perfect, noted the authors, "but by allowing indigenous groups to set the priorities and drive the process, the federal government achieved something that is rare in Aboriginal policy: a sense among indigenous leaders that meaningful consultation had occurred."[9]

Did Paul Martin's success in arriving at an accord with the leaders of the AROs mean that all that had been missing for the past forty years was the Martin approach, plus a commitment to $5 billion in new spending? It obviously made a big difference that the prime mover in the process was the prime minister, who was the most powerful politician in the land, even if he was leading a minority government. And working solely with the AROs had paid off. The efficiency of dealing with organizations designated to be the sole voice for a constituency—while sustaining the pretense that people with contrary opinions, agendas and values didn't exist—was a tangible fulfillment of the purpose for which the AROs had been set up back in the '70s.

Aside from the unanimity between the PM and the leaders of the AROs, had anything else changed? Indian Affairs was just the same—although the number of co-delivery partners was growing—and it would be in charge of delivering the elements of the Kelowna Accord. The AROs were still the same organizations, funded by the government, and still with the cloud of questionable legitimacy hanging over their heads. And there was still no requirement that band council elections be free and fair. In other words, the system in place before the accord was the exact same system as after the accord, except for the promise of new spending. And, as always, ordinary Indigenous people had no say in what was being decided for them. And non-Indigenous people had no say in what was happening, either.

Sure, the Kelowna Accord process seemed like a success, but ordinary Indigenous people had to take it on faith that the accord would actually result in something beneficial to their lives and not turn out to be nothing more than wind and rabbit tracks. Unfortunately, the Accord never even got out for a test drive. Paul Martin's Liberals were hit with the sponsorship scandal from the Chrétien era and the Liberals lost the 2006 election to Stephen Harper's Conservatives.

The Conservatives didn't outright kill the Kelowna Accord; funding for the accord simply wasn't included in the first budget. It soon became clear that the Harper government was not interested in fundamental changes on Indigenous issues. It seemed that the new prime minister had no interest in revolutionary ideas.

Endnotes to Chapter 14

1 Roundtable Report, Government of Canada, April 19, 2004, ii, 28, http://publications.gc.ca/collections/collection_2016/aanc-inac/R5-122-2004-eng.pdf.

2 Dave Courchene, Report of the Indian Act Consultation Meeting, Winnipeg, December 18–20, 1968, Department of Indian Affairs and Northern Development, 3.

3 Lisa L. Patterson, 2006, *Aboriginal Roundtable to Kelowna Accord: Aboriginal Policy Negotiations, 2004–2005*, Library of Parliament, 2, lop.parl.ca/content/lop/researchpublications/prb0604-e.pdf.

4 Ibid.

5 Ibid., 4.

6 Ibid., 6.

7 Ibid., 9–11.

8 Christopher Alcantara, and Zac Spicer, 2015, Learning from the Kelowna Accord, *Policy Options*, policyoptions.irpp.org/magazines/clearing-the-air/alcantara-spicer/.

9 Ibid.

15
A NEW PICTURE OF ANNUITIES

Jean Allard's push for a modernized treaty annuity lost steam with the election of the Harper Conservatives, but that didn't mean there was no one looking into the significance of annuity enhancement and whether there was a legal basis to support it. After all, half of Canada's landmass was covered by pre-1975 treaties that almost all included annuity payments. The significance of annuities mattered, and in ways that the Treaty Annuity Working Group (TAWG) could not have foreseen when the committee wrapped up its efforts in 2005.

When Allard and Harold Cardinal met at Lac Ste. Anne in the summer of 1999, Cardinal had already spent a number of years interviewing Elders from the Prairies who could recall the stories told to them by their Elders about the meaning of the treaties. He and Edmonton historian Walter Hildebrandt asked about the importance of livelihood assistance for chiefs and headmen when they were signing the treaties.

"Scholars," they said, "have clearly documented that First Nations negotiated for and worked to establish a variety of economic promises/clauses that they believed would ensure their right to a livelihood. First Nations understood that the right to make a living was a fundamental part of what was agreed to in the treaties."[1]

The Indigenous leaders knew their traditional means of livelihood were changing with the arrival of settlers and the disappearance of the bison herds on the Prairies. Up to that point, Indigenous people had successfully sustained themselves for several millennia through hunting, fishing, trapping and trading, and utilizing the resources of the land for medicine, food and other necessities. Recall that the Slavey band in northern Alberta continued to live the nomadic, traditional way until the 1950s.[2] (Slavey Chief Harry Chonkolay was Canada's last traditional hereditary chief when he died in 1998. He was buried in the same Treaty suit he received in 1938 from the federal government, the same suit he wore to the 1970 showdown with the Pierre Trudeau cabinet in Ottawa.[3])

Treaty-making has a deep history in Canada, and has its foundation in the *Royal Proclamation* of 1763. It was instituted by the British Crown as a means of heading off further uprisings and Indian wars following the British defeat of the French in North America. It banned any private person from buying (or taking) traditional Indian lands. That land would first need to be purchased from Indians by the Crown at a public meeting, after which the Crown could sell it to settlers or others.[4] After the American Revolution, the United States no longer adhered to the *Proclamation* but the British colony of Canada did.

The requirement to purchase Indian lands soon became a strain on the Indian Department, which was funded out of the Britain's military budget. After the War of 1812 and the assumption of peace thereafter, London was urging negotiators to reduce expenses.[5] One method was to offer annuities to Indigenous communities selling their land, rather than a substantial, upfront payment. Annual presents were already a tradition between Indigenous communities and the Crown to sustain alliances and ensure loyalty in times of conflict. It wasn't too great a leap to move to annuities.

The first annuity payments were made in three treaties with the Mississaugas on Lake Ontario in 1818.

"After the land had been purchased from the Indians for a small annuity it could then be sold to new settlers, whose interest payments on their purchases could cover the cost of the Indian annuity. In this fashion the British taxpayer would be relieved of the burden of buying Indian land, for the costs were, in effect, borne by the colonists....Agents seeking lands from Indians could argue that by selling land they would receive an annual income which would assist them forever. It was a powerful inducement..."[6]

In 1850, however, the annuity in Robinson Superior and Robinson Huron treaties changed from a fixed, lump-sum payment to a payment subject to change over time. The whole impetus for the treaties covering lands from the Quebec border west to Fort William, Ontario was to clear the way for mine development following significant discoveries of copper and other minerals north of the lakes. The Anishinaabe chiefs and headmen for the bands bargained hard during the treaty-making process, and ensured that the livelihood of their people was secured by two key provisions: the "full and free privilege" to follow their usual vocations of hunting, fishing and trapping throughout the ceded lands[7] (with some limitations), and an annuity for every band member in perpetuity.

However, the Anishinaabe negotiators, familiar with the higher annuities being paid in the United States,[8] wanted an annuity of about $30 per person. It put government commissioner William Robinson on the spot. He was under pressure by the Crown to conclude the treaties but not at the price of such a substantial annuity. Although it appears Robinson was not authorized to do so, his way out was to include an "escalator clause" in the treaties,[9] whereby the annuity payment would increase as the value of the ceded lands increased due to development and settlement.[10] The chiefs and headmen accepted a lower initial annuity of $4,000 to be divided among all band members, with the promise of it increasing in the future.[11]

The lump-sum annuity worked out to about $5 a person. At the time of treaty-writing in 1850, an annuity of $5 meant that the income for a family of five was about one-third to one-half of the wages for an unskilled labourer earning about $60 a year in Toronto or Montreal.[12]

It was a livelihood assistance that families could build on, if they wished, through wage-labour, farming and other enterprises they might already be involved in, such as producing maple syrup, building birchbark canoes and supplying fuel wood to steamers plying the waters of the Huron and Superior lakes.[13] Or they could continue to hunt, fish or trap on traditional lands not occupied by settlers or businesses.[14] However, as the Huron and Superior band populations grew, the lump-sum annuity had to be divided among more and more people. By 1875, the annuities had fallen to between 92 and 99 cents per person, or about $5 per family per year.[15]

The eleven Numbered Treaties, signed between 1871 and 1921,[16] also included the livelihood provisions of the Robinson treaties. They did not, however, contain the "escalator clause" language.

There was considerable pressure on the government negotiators to keep the costs of annuities down. Commissioner Wemyss Simpson, who represented the Crown in negotiations of the Numbered Treaties underway west of Fort William, defended the $3 annuity offered for every man, woman and child for Treaty 1, arguing that Indians could buy goods second-hand.

"The sum of three dollars does not appear to be large enough to enable an Indian to provide himself with many of his winter necessaries, but as he receives the same amount for his wife or wives, and for each of his children, the aggregate sum is usually sufficient to procure many comforts for this family."[17]

Treaties 1 and 2 were amended in 1875 to increase the annuity to $5 per person, after the chiefs refused the annuity payments for four years in protest when they found out about higher annuities offered in Treaty 3.[18] At $5, a family of five would have $25 in annuity money, which was more than enough for a hunter to equip himself for a year. The Hudson's Bay Company had been outfitting Indian hunters and trappers in the western interior of Canada for nearly two centuries, and $25 was enough for the ammunition, nets, lines, traps, knives and other goods, with some left over for tea and tobacco,[19] and maybe furniture and other "comforts" for the family. In the early 1880s, an annuity of $5 each for a family of five "was equivalent to about one month's wages as either an Aboriginal farm labourer or a saw-mill worker."[20] The annuity was, in the terminology of that era, specifically for a man and his wife (or wives) and his children.

According to Erik Anderson, a senior researcher with the Strategic Research and Analysis Directorate at Indigenous Affairs, "It is clear from historical evidence that at different times, both Aboriginal and government representatives at the treaty discussions intended and perceived the annuity to be a significant economic benefit....The expectation from both parties was that the annuity would assist in transitioning from a hunting and trapping economy to one based on agriculture, or supplement the continuation of a traditional hunting and fur trade economy."[21]

If, over time, the annuities had been regularly increased as land values increased, the annuity payment would have continued to serve its role as a meaningful livelihood support for families. But that's not what happened.

Anderson believes the evidence is clear. "That these treaties did not deliver on the original intention of providing livelihood assistance for future generations in exchange for land can be demonstrated simply by the socio-economic disparity that continues to exist today. This disparity is likely to continue, unless solutions are rooted in deep historical understanding of the treaty relationships."[22]

Anderson concludes that the lack of a common understanding of treaties has tainted the modern relationship between Indigenous and non-Indigenous people, and that understanding the role of annuities was important.

"A re-imagining of the modern treaty relationship must not only recognize and respect the initial intent of the treaties to provide livelihood assistance, but also allow for interpretation of the treaties as living and forward-looking documents."[23]

It was unlikely treaty negotiators on either side saw any reason to concern themselves with the erosion of buying power through inflation. Government people were assuming Indians would figure out how to be self-supporting or would become assimilated, so that the livelihood assistance of the annuities would be temporary.[24] On the other hand, according to historians, Indigenous people considered their acceptance of an annuity payment each year as the renewal of a treaty relationship that was flexible and changeable. They were assuming that the livelihood assistance offered by annuities was subject to change as required, especially if the value of the ceded land increased.[25]

The whole impetus for the Robinson treaties was to clear the way for resource development, and certainly Ontario had benefited greatly from significant discoveries of copper and other minerals north of Huron and Superior lakes. However, the Huron chiefs did not trigger the escalator clause until 1874.[26] By then, not only had the annuities not been increased since 1850—despite the obvious wealth produced by mining on the ceded lands—the payment had shrunk to less than a dollar per person.

There was little argument that the Robinson bands were due increased annuities. The treaties were clear. If the land ceded in the two treaties could be shown to be producing an amount that allowed the government to increase the annuity payment without incurring debt, "the same shall be augmented from time to time, provided that the amount paid to each individual shall not exceed the sum of one pound provincial currency in any one year, or such further sum as Her Majesty may be graciously pleased to order."[27] The limit of the increase to a maximum of $4 appears to have been added later, without the consent of the chiefs.[28]

The augmented treaty issue came before the House of Commons for a vote in May 1878, and Parliament approved an increase "from 96 cents to $4 per head, for the year ending 30th June, 1879."[29]

There appears to have been no consideration of the "as Her Majesty may be graciously pleased to order" by the federal government, or an effort to set up a template for evaluating the increasing value of ceded lands as a basis for future increases. It simply read the limitations of the annuity as "up to $4" and set the annuity at that amount.

The issue of the annuity increases in the Robinson treaties came before the Supreme Court of Canada in 1895. It was not to argue the validity of the escalator clause because that was considered settled. Rather, the annuities were entangled with an ongoing dispute between the Ontario government and the federal government over who was responsible for the annuity arrears incurred prior to Confederation in 1867.[30]

In the summations, the Supreme Court affirmed the validity of the link between the increased value of ceded lands and the annuity, with one of the justices noting that "the consideration to the Indians for the ceding of their rights was threefold, the cash payment, the fixed annuity, and the further annuity up to a certain amount depending on the proceeds of the land."[31]

The Royal Commission on Aboriginal Peoples (RCAP) report of 1996, in describing the economic provisions in the treaties, referenced the Robinson annuities. "Among the clearest and most important provisions is that contained in the Robinson treaties, which contain promises of annuities to be tied to future Crown revenues from ceded lands… Despite the wealth generated from these vast lands, the annuity has been increased only once."[32]

This raises some important questions. Way back in 1895, the Supreme Court affirmed that the government had an obligation to augment annuities as proceeds from lands increased. Why didn't that happen? If annuities were intended as a form of family support, along with the freedom to pursue traditional vocations, why did the value of the annuity never increase again after Parliament voted its approval in 1878?

There are a few clues. When it came to the treaty annuities, the Dominion of Canada adopted a strict application of the monetary law called nominalism.[33] That meant the $5 stated in the treaties was $5 in 1880, $5 in 1980, and would still be $5 in 2080. The policy had the effect of freezing the annuities at the nominal amount of four dollars or five dollars and keeping it there. Over time, the livelihood support that was supposed to be secured and enhanced through the treaty relationship was devastated, not just by a failure to link the annuity to increasing prosperity, but by the effects of inflation. The loss of buying power of the annuity from the signing of the treaties was absorbed entirely by First Nations Treaty people, whereas the reduction in real benefits payable accrued to the Crown.[34]

There was, however, a much larger impediment that prevented Treaty people advocating for annuity increases as the buying power of the $4 or $5 shrank. Recall that the *Indian Act* was amended in 1929 to prevent Indigenous advocacy groups, band councils and others from hiring lawyers — or even raising money to hire lawyers — to challenge government policy, under threat of fines or imprisonment unless it was pre-approved by Indian Affairs.[35] That prohibition remained in effect until 1951.

The *Indian Act* of 1876 had little to say on annuities,[36] referencing annuities in only nine sections. For instance, an Indian woman marrying a non-Indian man "would cease to be an Indian in any respect within the meaning of this Act, except that she shall be entitled to share equally with the members of the band to which she formerly belonged, in the annual or semi-annual distribution of their annuities..." Similarly, enfranchised Indians[37] were no longer considered Indians under the *Indian Act*, but still retained the right to participate in annuities. In other words, eligibility for an annuity payment did not require remaining a treaty band member or even remaining an "Indian" as defined by the Act. Other sections of the Act authorized withholding annuities as a mean of punishment for immorality or imprisonment, with annuities seized and put towards covering legal and confinement costs.

The modern *Indian Act* of 1985 contains a single sentence[38] indicating that treaty moneys are the responsibility of the Government of Canada and are to be paid out of the Consolidated Revenue Fund. That's it. The words "annuity" and "annuities" are mentioned once each in reference to maintenance of dependents and to women who leave bands.

The Act is essentially silent on annuities, and does not define who is eligible for annuities or speak to rules for payment or distribution. The language varies slightly in the Numbered Treaties, but each specifies the amount of the annuity and that every man, woman and child of treaty bands is eligible. All the rest of the rules and regulations governing annuities are IA departmental policies, and those policies are subject to change depending on the objectives of the government of the day. The idea that annuities must remain $4 or $5 because that's the number used in the treaties is a policy, not a law.

The value of an annuity has long since degenerated to a point where it is meaningless as a livelihood support, but it has continued to be a powerful symbol.

Nearly three-quarters of people eligible to claim the annuity do so,[39] many showing up at Treaty Days on reserves or at a Treaty Tent set up in the urban centres to collect their five-dollar bills. Some, like those who have never lived on a reserve, consider the annuity as a link to the signing of the treaties and an affirmation that they are still officially Treaty people. Others might show up every few years or so when enough money has accrued to make it worth the effort. If it costs $2.50 for a bus ticket across the city to pick up a five-dollar bill, what's the point?

At the Treaty Tent at The Forks in Winnipeg in June 2017, a number of people who agreed to be interviewed seemed perplexed when asked why the annuity was still five dollars and had never been increased.[40]

"We don't even think about it," said a young mother from a northern reserve who lined up for the annuity payments with her small children. "Nobody questions it. Nobody asks why. We just accept what they give us. It makes the kids happy. The get their five dollars and they're excited."

An older woman who lived in the city got in line to pick up several years' worth of annuities. She didn't know why it was still five dollars either. "I've never thought about it. I guess it's always been that way." When asked who should be responsible for increasing the annuity, those who had an opinion agreed that it was up to "the government."

A reporter from the *The New York Times* attended the same event in June 2017, talking to people lined up at the Treaty tent about why the annuity payment was still $5 and what they thought about still receiving such a meagre amount.

"It's not about the money," said a seventy-one-year-old woman who collects payments every eight years. "I'm proud of being an Indian and this is a chance to see my people."[41]

A retired social worker said, "I come and get it because they owe me." He added that the five-dollar annuity should really be $5,000.[42]

The social worker might well have heard about the Treaty Annuity Working Group proposal for modernizing annuities. And so had others.

Unanticipated consequences

The lesson some FN leaders took from the idea of modernized annuities was that if it could be argued that annuities should be modernized today, then they should have been increased all along. Even if the increase was only for inflation, a claim for arrears could trigger a windfall of potentially billions of dollars, and all of it going to the band councils.

First out of the gate were two chiefs from Treaties 1 and 2 in Manitoba.[43] Their claim was for underpayment of annuities, and they were seeking certification for a class action lawsuit against the Crown. A class action suit is a legal mechanism for individuals who feel they have been harmed in a similar way to join together to seek compensation in a single court case. The certification in this case was denied because "Aboriginal claims pursuant to treaties can only be classified as giving rise to collective issues."[44]

Other legal claims followed, but went nowhere. The annuities are supposed to be an individual right, not a collective one. However, the arguments put forth by government lawyers in subsequent claims for arrears payments sought to have it both ways. If the claim was for class action certification for Treaty individuals, the lawyers argued that annuities were a collective right.[45] If the claim was made on behalf of the collective, government lawyers argued the opposite, saying that annuities were an individual right.[46]

Given the continuing confusion over whether treaty annuities are a collective right or an individual right, how did the Justice department's lawyers figure out what stand to take when arguing cases? A spokesperson for the Department of Justice Canada declined to answer and referred the question to Indigenous Affairs.[47]

A spokesperson for IA responded by stating, "Annuities are both a collective and individual rights issue in that an individual annuitant is entitled to collect the annuity by virtue of being a member of a collective, a First Nation treaty signatory."[48]

In other words, a Catch-22 situation had developed where annuities were both an individual *and* a collective right, and could be either/neither/both based on who was arguing which side of a legal case.

That changed when the Robinson Huron chiefs stepped through the door left open by the Supreme Court 120 years earlier. In 2014, the chiefs of twenty-one Anishinaabe bands filed a Statement of Claim with the Ontario Superior Court of Justice against the governments of Ontario and Canada for failing to live up to the terms of the treaty, citing the "escalator clause."[49] The claim put the onus on the courts to calculate the revenue generated from the treaty territory—from North Bay west to Sault Ste. Marie and north to Kirkland Lake, with Sudbury in the middle—since 1879.

The concept of increased treaty annuities tied to the value of the land was finally going to be tested in the courts.

Endnotes to Chapter 15

1. Harold Cardinal and Walter Hildebrandt, 2002, *Treaty Elders of Saskatchewan: Our Dream is That Our Peoples Will One Day Be Clearly Recognized as Nations*, University of Calgary Press, 69.
2. Rob McKinley, "Northern Alberta traditional chief passes away at 89," *Windspeaker*, Vol. 5, Issue 11, 1998.
3. Ibid.
4. *The Royal Proclamation*, October 7, 1763, reprinted in Clarence S. Brigham, *British Royal Proclamations Relating to America*, Vol. 12, Transactions and Collections of the American Antiquarian Society, 1911, 212–218.
5. John F. Leslie and Betsey Baldwin, 2006, *Indian treaty annuities: the historical evolution of government policy, from colonial times to Treaty 3*, Research and Analysis Directorate, Indigenous and Northern Affairs Canada.
6. R. Surtees, 1984, *Indian Land Surrenders in Ontario, 1763–1867*, Indian Affairs and Northern Development, 68.
7. Arthur J. Ray, 2013, "Shading a Promise, Interpreting the Livelihood Rights Clauses in Nineteenth-Century Canadian Treaties for First Nations," in *Volume 7: A History of Treaties and Policies*, Aboriginal Policy Research Series, Thompson Educational Publishing, 64.
8. Sheldon Krasowski, 2019, *No Surrender: The Land Remains Indigenous*, University of Regina Press, 24.
9. Bruce W. Hodgin, Ute Lischke, and David T. McNab, eds., 2002, *Blockades and Resistance: Studies in Actions of Peace and the Tamagami Blockades of 1988–89*, Wilfrid Laurier University Press, 79.
10. Treaty Texts: Robinson Superior and Robinson Huron treaties, https://www.aadnc-aandc.gc.ca/eng/1100100028978/1100100028982.
11. Hodgin, 79.
12. James Morrison, 1993, The Robinson Treaties of 1850: A Case Study, prepared for the Royal Commission on Aboriginal Peoples, Treaty and Land Research Section, 159.
13. Restoule *v* Canada et al, 2018, Court File C-3512-14, Ontario Superior Court of Justice, 28.
14. Ray, 64.
15. Morrison, 163.
16. Treaty Texts, Indigenous and Northern Affairs Canada, https://www.aadnc-aandc.gc.ca/eng/1370373165583/1370373202340 (accessed June 18, 2018).
17. A Historical Reference Guide to The Stone Fort Treaty (Treaty 1, 1871), Research Branch, Indian Affairs and Northern Development, 1980, 19, http://publications.gc.ca/collections/collection_2018/aanc-inac/R32-385-1980-eng.pdf.
18. Krasowski, 273.
19. Ray, 67.
20. Erik Anderson, 2009, "Treaty Annuities and Livelihood Assistance: Re-imagining the Modern Treaty Relationship," *Canadian Diversity*, Vol. 7, No. 3, 15.
21. Erik Anderson, 2013, "The Treaty Annuity as Livelihood Assistance and Relationship Renewal," in *Volume 7: A History of Treaties and Policies*, Aboriginal Policy Research Series, Thompson Educational Publishing, 74.
22. Anderson, 2009, 13.
23. Ibid., 17.
24. Ibid., 15.

25 Ibid., 14.
26 RCAP, Report on the Royal Commission on Aboriginal Peoples, *Volume 2: Restructuring the Relationship*, 542.
27 Treaty Texts: Robinson.
28 Hodgin, 82.
29 *Journals* of the House of Commons of Canada, 2nd May 1878, Vol. XII, 246.
30 Supreme Court of Canada, *In re* Indian Claims, 1895, The Province of Ontario v The Dominion of Canada and The Province of Quebec, May 15 and 16, 1895, *Supreme Court of Canada*, Vol. XXV, 541.
31 Ibid., 546.
32 RCAP, Vol. 2, 800–801.
33 Robert Metcs, 2008, "The Common Intention of the Parties and the Payment of Annuities Under the Numbered Treaties: Who Assumed the Risk of Inflation?," *Alberta Law Review*, 46:1, 42.
34 Ibid., 70.
35 Indian Legal Claims, *Looking Forward, Looking Back*, Vol. 1, Section 9.9, Royal Commission of Aboriginal Peoples, 272.
36 See Appendix E: Annuity language in the *Indian Act*, 1876 and 1985
37 In the context of *Indian Act* of 1876, an "enfranchised Indian" is a person who has lost or surrendered his or her official Indian status and has been enfranchised with the rights of ordinary Canadians, including the right of men to vote in municipal, provincial and federal elections.
38 Ibid.
39 *Evaluation of Indian Moneys, Estates and Treaty Annuities*, 2013, Aboriginal Affairs and Northern Development, 59, http://publications.gc.ca/collections/collection_2017/aanc-inac/R5-143-2013-eng.pdf.
40 Author's interviews with various Treaty people at the Treaty Tent at The Forks, Winnipeg, June 16 and June 20, 2017.
41 Dan Levin, 2017, "Canada's Treaty Payments: Meager Reminder of a Painful History," *The New York Times*, July 23, 2017, https://www.nytimes.com/2017/07/23/world/Americas/winnipegs-treaty-payments-meager-reminder-of-a-painful-history.html
42 Ibid.
43 Court of Appeal of Manitoba, Soldier *v* Canada (Attorney General), Vol. 13, No. 1, 2009, 174.
44 Ibid.
45 Horseman *v* Crown, 2015, Proposed Class Proceeding, Federal Court, Docket T-1784-12, October 15, 2015.
46 Special Claims Tribunal ruling, as cited in Horseman *v* Crown, 2015, Proposed Class Proceeding, Federal Court, Docket T-1784-12, October 15, 2015, 5.
47 Department of Justice Canada, email communication with author, August 30, 2107.
48 Indigenous and Northern Affairs Canada, email communication with author, September 8, 2017.
49 Restoule, et al. *v.* The Attorney General of Canada, The Attorney General of Ontario and Her Majesty the Queen in Right of Ontario, C-3512-14 and C-3512-14A.

16
CRUNCHING THE ANNUITY NUMBERS

The amount that the Indigenous Affairs (IA) department spends on annuities had gone up over the years as the number of eligible recipients increased, but it hadn't gone up very much. In 1966, the year that Indian Affairs became a department of its own, IA paid out $513,493 in annuities to just over 112,000 Treaty people.[1] In 2016, IA paid out some $1.9 million for annuities to about 579,000 Treaty people.[2]

Perhaps there is a very simple explanation for why treaty annuities have never been high on the agenda as an Indigenous issue. Just over half the bands are Treaty, and, due to changes in Status eligibility and IA's creation of new, non-Treaty bands like the Qalipu Mi'kmaq First Nation in Newfoundland, Treaty people now count for about 60 percent of Status Indians.[3] The majority live in Ontario, Manitoba, Saskatchewan and Alberta. However, one-third of Canada's bands are in British Columbia—making it the largest voting bloc in the Assembly of First Nation—but only a few bands in northern BC are in treaty territory. Pursuing an increased annuity would offer little benefit to non-Treaty First Nations people in BC. Neither would it benefit Quebec and the Maritimes.

Further, the annuity is considered a benefit paid to individuals, rather than a payment to the band government to distribute under its authorities. Historically, the treaties required that the annuity be paid in cash to eligible recipients in their communities,[4] but that has since been modified to include Treaty tents in urban centres and payments by mail.

IA did explore the idea of turning annuity payments over to the band councils in 2013 when it conducted a review of annuity payments. The department was trying to manage the increasing costs for Treaty Day events during which ceremonies were held to hand out five-dollar bills. In BC and Northwest Territories, the department was spending more on the delivery of the annuities than on the annuities themselves.⁵ Another concern was the cost of mailing annuity cheques. The report estimated that issuing and mailing out a single $5 annuity cheque cost the federal government between $50 and $60.⁶

IA considered reducing costs by, for example, making direct deposits; "making payments every two years; sending a cheque for the total amount to the band council for redistribution to members; or establishing a minimum amount of $20 for payments by cheque."⁷

In the end, IA did not move to paying annuities to band councils to distribute. Annuities were not band government business, any more than a bequest in a will was band government business. (It was, however, IA's business, since IA has "exclusive jurisdiction and authority over the estates of deceased First Nations individuals" living on Canada's reserves.⁸)

All other important aspects of the treaties have been modernized over the past fifty years. The nets, ammunition and other equipment itemized in the treaties have evolved into multi-million-dollar spending each year on economic development programs. The "medicine chest" clause in Treaty 6 has been modernized to mean providing health care services and benefits to all Status Indians at a cost of several billion dollars a year. And the "pestilence and famine" clause, which appeared only in Treaty 6, was modernized to mean social assistance for people in FN communities at a cost of about $1 billion a year.

However, Indigenous politicians—and non-Indigenous politicians, for that matter—have not bothered to champion the single provision of the treaties which directly benefits individuals and families.

Jean Allard argued in "Big Bear's Treaty" that, despite the harm done to Indian families by the Indian Residential School system and other misguided government policies, the tragic social breakdown on so many reserves can be better explained by 150 years of powerlessness, the last fifty years under the rule of their own leaders on reserves.⁹ The fact that the $5 annuity of 1873 was still $5 in 2019 was perhaps the most damning evidence available of just how voiceless and powerless ordinary First Nations people were.

Since annuities were intended all along to be a livelihood support and not just a symbolic gesture, it seems long past time to take another look at annuities as means of rebuilding families and empowering First Nations people to make their own choices, and see if it offers a meaningful path to reconciliation between Indigenous and non-Indigenous Canadians.

It is a move Harold Cardinal would agree with, if he were still around, fringed and beaded buckskin jacket and all. Cardinal died in the summer of 2005, right around the time the Kelowna discussions were going full-tilt. Cardinal had been admitted to the Bar of Alberta six months earlier, and just days before his death from cancer, he was awarded a Doctorate in Law. At a memorial service in Edmonton, former AFN leader Phil Fontaine acknowledged Cardinal as a true "Doctor, lawyer and Indian chief" and "an inspirational warrior and leader for First Nations for all of his life."¹⁰

When it came to a modernized treaty annuity, said Cardinal, "The livelihood arrangements of treaty must be the basis for bringing back on track the treaty relationship, which seemed to have become lost somewhere in the entrails of colonial history."[11]

However, the IA's policy on modernizing annuities, firmly embedded in the entrails of colonial history, was clear. For the government, "historic treaties are closed, non-negotiable agreements."[12]

A path of dignity

For some Treaty people such as Leona Freed, the annual payment was demeaning.

"I used to be ashamed to get the five dollars. It was an insult, a slap in the face."[13]

That's why she liked the idea of the modernized annuity from the time she first heard about it from Jean Allard.

"What appeals is the $5,000. For a family of four, that would get Indian people off welfare, get more self-esteem, and get people on their feet."[14]

Allard based that $5,000 figure by linking it to land values, but there are other ways to calculate a modernized annuity. Recall that the foundation of Allard's proposal is providing enough income so that family members could, together, have some degree of security and independence. At $5,000 per person, his land-based valuation for a family of five would mean an annual income of $25,000.

Demographer Stewart Clatworthy took a look at the annuities in 2007, and calculated what they would be, based on cost-of-living increases. He used the Consumer Price Index and the wholesale price index, both of which have relatively reliable data on the cost of living that date back to 1867.[15] By Clatworthy's calculations, the five-dollar annuity paid in 1871 for Treaties 1 and 2 would be worth $100.32 in 2007,[16] which translates into about $500 for a family of five. That $500 would be enough to buy one decent bolt-action rifle with a scope at a sporting goods store, or maybe winter boots for the whole family. In other words, an annuity increase based on inflation would not deliver security or independence.

Another technique for calculating annuities would be a wage-based comparison. The $25-annuity for a family of five in 1870 was considered to be the equivalent of about one-third to one-half of a year's wages for an unskilled labourer in Montreal or Toronto.[17] How would that compare to a minimum-wage, unskilled worker 135 years later in 2005 when the Treaty Annuity Working Group was studying this issue? Manitoba's minimum wage for that year was $7.25 per hour.[18] A person working full-time at 40 hours a week would earn just under $15,080 before deductions, and one-third of that would be $5,026. Multiply that by five people, and you've got a family income of about $25,130 which aligns with Allard's land-base valuation.

Basing an annuity increase on one-third of the minimum wage sounds a lot more like a poverty-related program, like enhanced welfare or a guaranteed basic income for First Nations people. Both miss the significance of the annuity being linked directly to the land through the treaties. Calculating an increased annuity based on land values is complex, but when Indigenous activists denounce Canada's failure to "share the wealth" derived from the land, this is a link they are making, too.

It might help to think of the treaties as an agreement between settlers and Indigenous people, where the Always people made space on the land as the "start-up" resource for this grand enterprise called Canada that would be rewarded through annuities. The country has flourished as a result of the sweat and toil of the many settlers who sought to make a better life for themselves and their families in this land, but the accompanying "return on investment" for Indigenous people didn't happen.

What would those "investor's fees" for the land have turned out to be, if they had actually been paid?

Allard used the price his grandparents paid for their good agricultural land in the Red River Valley as a benchmark for linking the annuity to land values. Canada is a vast country with a landscape of muskeg and black spruce swamps in the north, high-value agricultural land in the south, and even higher-value land for residential development in cities like Vancouver and Toronto. The value of farmland in the Red River Valley is somewhere in the middle, so let's work with that.

In 1871, Allard's grandparents' land was worth $5 for five acres. In 1871, there were just over 100,000 Status Indians in Canada, most of whom lived on reserves, although only about half lived in areas covered by treaties.[19] Many bands had not yet signed treaties by 1871 but would do so shortly, so we'll go with half of Status Indians being Treaty people. The $5 annuity paid out by the Government of Canada that year to some 50,000 eligible Treaty people on reserves would have totalled about $250,000.

If all the roughly 572,000 eligible Treaty people[20] had collected their $5 annuity in 2015, it would have come to a total of $2.9 million. So, just how much has the Government of Canada distributed in treaty annuities throughout the years?

Using Indigenous Affairs, Statistics Canada and other government data, the average population figures for Treaty Indians for the 145 years from 1871 to 2015,[21] the number of Treaty Indian recipients would have averaged about 214,000 per year.[22] At $5 per person for 145 years, the amount paid directly to Treaty people since 1871 until 2015 would be in the ballpark of just under $155 million. However, not all annuity monies have been collected. As of 2016, about $16 million remained unclaimed,[23] suggesting the payout figure is closer to $140 million.

To put that $140 million figure in context, in 2016, a Saskatchewan farmer sold his grain farm of some 7,900 acres for $26.5 million.[24] That would mean the return-on-investment for all Treaty Indians over 145 years for ceding half of Canada's landmass was, in total, the equivalent of about five large Saskatchewan grain farms.

The purpose of this exercise is to give a sense of what it would have meant to Treaty people, and to Canadian society, if the land-value-based annuity had been honoured after the vote in Parliament in 1878 and the affirmation by the Supreme Court of Canada in 1895.

What would have happened if the Government of Canada had elected to augment treaty annuities from 1880 onwards based on land values? What would Treaty people have earned in terms of "investor's fees"? Would it have been substantial enough to make a meaningful difference in the lives of families and Indigenous communities?

Making that calculation requires establishing a benchmark for annuity increases based on a consistent record of land-value increases over time. The benefit of using land values is that inflation is built in. Let's stay with Manitoba farmland because that's where Jean Allard began with a $5 annuity, which could buy five acres of land in 1880 (for about the same price as in 1871), and because those data are fairly reliable.

Taking the average number of Treaty Indians in Canada[25] and using the average value per acre of farmland in Manitoba from 1880 to 2015,[26] over those 135 years the federal government would have directed roughly $27 billion in augmented annuities[27] directly into the hands of Treaty people.

Now, consider a scenario where Canadian society, in an outburst of appreciation for the Always people and a willingness to share the wealth of the land, had chosen to extend the livelihood assistance provisions to all Status Indians, regardless of whether or not they signed onto the Robinson and Numbered Treaties. This is not as unrealistic as it might sound, since the federal government has, by policy, modernized and expanded Treaty benefits such as health care and economic development to cover all First Nations people.

If, over the same 135 years, the federal government had chosen to extend augmented annuities to all Status Indians, it would have resulted in sharing about $46 billion of Canada's economic wealth with First Nations people.[28]

The augmented annuity payments would certainly have added to the federal expenditures undertaken for providing education, economic assistance and other legally mandated Treaty obligations. If $46 billion for annuities sounds like a large expenditure, consider it in context of expenditures on programs, over time, specifically for Indigenous programs and services.

In 2013, a researcher for the Centre for Aboriginal Studies (Fraser Institute) tackled the question of how much money was spent by federal and provincial governments on programs specifically for Indigenous people from 1946 to 2011.[29] Municipal and territorial spending was not included, and provincial spending numbers prior to 1946 were not available. This calculation also did not include services paid for by Indian Affairs that all Canadians are eligible to receive, such as education and regular health care. The actual spending over those 65 years came to just under $235 billion.[30]

It is, perhaps, an apples and oranges comparison, but the point is that the federal government, through its policy choices, elected to ignore the means of building and strengthening families and FN governance through augmented annuities. It is impossible to assess how different the lives of Canada's Indigenous people would have been, then and today, if the country had elected to take a path of dignity and honoured the augmented annuity payment; if respect between Indigenous and non-Indigenous people had been knit into the fabric of society in Canada from the time it became a stand-alone country.

Instead, the government of the time chose an entirely different path, one of oppression under the *Indian Act*, assimilation policies, Indian Residential Schools, the systemic silencing of Indigenous voices, and building the vast empire of Indigenous Affairs Plus. We know how that policy choice turned out.

Before we leave the number crunching behind, let's see if we can draw a parallel between the significance of the annuity—which was meant to empower individuals and families within the collective by providing a degree of economic independence—as a percentage of the IA budget.

- According to Superintendent-General of Indian Affairs John A. Macdonald, in 1880, annuities for the Robinson Huron and Superior bands and Numbered Treaties 1–7 amounted to $303,242 out of a budget of $667,351.[31] Annuities accounted for 45 percent of the budget.
- According to Indian Affairs minister Arthur Laing in 1966–67, out of a budget for IA and its two co-delivery partners of $131 million, annuities for 112,132 Treaty Indians accounted for $587,862 in expenditures,[32] or just under 0.5 percent.
- By 2017–18, annuities amounted to about $2.7 million[33] for some 582,000 eligible Treaty First Nations people, out of a budget for IA and its 33 co-delivery partners of about $19 billion.[34] Annuities accounted for a little more than 0.01 percent of spending.

Over time, annuities had largely disappeared as a budget item. The wants, needs and controls of the collective fully dominated the concerns of FN band governments. However, those governments have, in turn, been thoroughly dominated by the vast, intrusive and ever-expanding powers of Indigenous Affairs Plus.

Endnotes to Chapter 16

1. Annual Report, 1966–67, Indian Affairs and Northern Development, 113.
2. Dan Levin, 2017, "Canada's Treaty Payments: Meager Reminder of a Painful History," *The New York Times*, July 23, 2017, https://www.nytimes.com/2017/07/23/world/Americas/winnipegs-treaty-payments-meager-reminder-of-a-painful-history.html.
3. Statistics Canada, 2016, Aboriginal peoples in Canada: Key results from the 2016 Census, https://www150.statcan.gc.ca/n1/daily-quotidien/171025/dq171025a-eng.htm.
4. Levin, 55.
5. *Evaluation of Indian Moneys, Estates and Treaty Annuities*, 2013, Aboriginal Affairs and Northern Development, p 64, http://publications.gc.ca/collections/collection_2017/aanc-inac/R5-143-2013-eng.pdf.
6. Ibid., footnote, 65.
7. Ibid.
8. Ibid., 39.
9. Jean Allard, 2002, "Big Bear's Treaty: The Road to Freedom," *Inroads*, Vol. 11, 131.
10. Dr. Harold Cardinal, Tribute, June 2005, Peter A. Allard School of Law, http://www.allard.ubc.ca/news-events/news-room/dr-harold-cardinal.
11. Harold Cardinal and Walter Hildebrandt, 2002, *Treaty Elders of Saskatchewan: Our Dream is That Our Peoples Will One Day Be Clearly Recognized as Nations*, University of Calgary Press, 47.
12. *Evaluation of Indian Moneys* 59.
13. Leona Freed, interview with author, August 2017.
14. Ibid.
15. Stewart Clatworthy, 2007, "Estimated 2007 Value of Original Annuity Amount, Adjusted for the Consumer Price Index, for Major Treaty and Adhesion Dates, as presented in The Treaty Annuity as Livelihood Assistance and Relationship Renewal," in *Volume 7: A History of Treaties and Policies*, Aboriginal Research Series, Erik Anderson, ed., Thompson Educational Publishing, 2013, 90.
16. Ibid.
17. Report on the Royal Commission on Aboriginal Peoples, 1996, *Volume 2-Restructuring the Relationship*, 76.
18. Historical Summary of Minimum Wage Rates in Manitoba, Government of Manitoba, https://www.gov.mb.ca/labour/labmgt/histmin.html.
19. Table of the Aboriginal Population of Canada, 1871, Statistics Canada, http://www.statcan.gc.ca/pub/98-187-x/4151278-eng.htm#part2.
20. Status Indian population in 2015 was 953,043. Sixty percent of that is about 572,000. Registered Indian Population by Type of Residence for All Canada, December 31, 1989 – 2016, https://www.aadnc-aandc.gc.ca/eng/1523286391452/1523286414623#tbc9.
21. Appendix C: Average Treaty Indian populations, 1871–2015.
22. Ibid.
23. Levin, 2017. By 2016, some $16-million in annuities had remained unclaimed.
24. Michael Raine, "Tisdale, Sask., farm sells for $26.5 million," *The Western Producer*, September 27, 2016.
25. Appendix C.
26. Appendix D: Average MB farmland value 1880–2015.

27 Calculation for total augmented annuity payments (Appendix C, Appendix D) for 1880–2015: 214,000 Treaty Indians/year x 135 years x $189/acre x 5 acres/Treaty Indian = $27.3-billion or $27-billion.

28 Calculation for total augmented annuity payments for all Status Indians (Appendix C, Appendix D) for 1880–2015: 356,637 Status Indians/year x 135 years x $189/acre x 5 acres/Status Indian = $45.5-billion or $46-billion.

29 Mark Milke, 2013, "Ever Higher: Government spending on Canada's Aboriginals since 1947," Centre for Aboriginal Studies, Fraser Institute, iii.

30 Ibid., 25.

31 Report of the Department of Indian Affairs, for the year ended 31st December 1880. Annuity payments for Treaties 1–7 were $218,002, p 316, and $85,242 for the Robinson Treaties (454). Expenses: 16.

32 Annual Report, Fiscal Year 1966–67, Department of Indian Affairs and Northern Development, 66.

33 IA does not list annuities as a line item in its Estimates, so exact figures are not available. For 2017–18, of the 970,562 Status, about 582,000 are Treaty. With a $5 annuity, the total is about $2.9-million, but some annuities are $4 and not all are collected. Estimate $2.7million.

34 See Appendix A.

17
FAILING UPWARD AT A SPECTACULAR RATE

The general public in Canada has little idea what actually goes on at IA, in part because it seems to suit the bureaucracy to shroud its operations in confusion, complexity and obscurity. While such obfuscation shields bureaucrats and politicians from uncomfortable questions, it also makes it nearly impossible for them to mount a defence against criticism and accusations that the public would understand.

Indeed, Indigenous Affairs is routinely beaten up in the media. It has been called "a vast bureaucratic black hole where hope disappears into a bottomless pit of inertia," "a giant government colon devouring good intentions and regurgitating them as waste," and a "stultifying swamp" where nothing gets fixed and no one is ever held responsible. And all of that was in a single 2017 Kelly McParland column in the *National Post*.[1]

There are many excellent IA staffers who are producing solid research into a range of Indigenous issues, adding to the body of knowledge needed to make sense of government policy. There are also stellar managers who run various departments within the IA purview who successfully hit the targets set by Plans and Priorities year after year, and who enjoy the respect and admiration of their staffers. They are exemplary bureaucrats, who are highly valued within the civil service. Yet their successes have little, if any, relevance to the on-the-ground suffering, abuses and hopelessness that pervade the lives of people on reserves. They seem, in fact, to operate in different realities.

Lambasting IA is a long-standing tradition in Indigenous politics. In 1969, twenty-four-year-old Alberta Cree activist Harold Cardinal launched his national political career with a scathing critique of IA and its ministers.

"Throughout the hundreds of years of the Indian-government relationship, political leaders responsible for matters relating to Indians have been outstanding in their ignorance of native people and remarkable in their insensitivity to the needs and aspirations of Indians in Canada... The question of paramount importance in the minds of successive ministers responsible for Indian Affairs appears to have been and continues to remain the defence of the gross ineptitude of their department."[2]

Jack Beaver was a little kinder in his 1979 report, entitled "To have what is one's own" but better known as the Beaver Report.

"There are some very able staff members who are genuinely committed to the search for new directions... They understand that the failure to deal with a change in the role and the function of the Department of Indian Affairs will ensure that the situation of demoralization and social disorder on reserves will not only continue but may get worse... [with] a consequent loss of faith in the institutions of the Government on the part of all Canadians for the abject failure of the Government to resolve the intransigent problems faced by Indian people."[3]

Jean Allard was far harsher in his criticism of "the abject failure" of the system that has evolved over the past fifty years, including government, Indigenous Affairs and Indigenous political organizations.

"The poverty and suffering of Indians allows the system to keep leveraging money out of the public pocket, and justifies the existence of a bloated bureaucracy. The system owes its continued life to ensuring the continued suffering of the most helpless and voiceless—without end."[4]

He painted an ugly picture of ordinary Indians being crushed under the weight of a bloated system, one where there was no motivation for the IA system to change.

"The whole system is against changes," said Allard, "because it is protecting its own interests, and it needs to keep Indians as their dependents, because the day Indians are independent, there is really no purpose for a whole number of those programs provided by Indian Affairs."[5]

This seemed like an appalling scenario that could not possibly exist in a country that prides itself on being one of the best places in the world to live. How could a government department, supported by taxpayers' dollars, institute and sustain a deliberate and cruel program of oppression under the Buffalo Jump policy? Yet despite facing constant criticism and being routinely slammed in the media, the department had been failing upward at a spectacular rate.

In Canada, in the years from 1966 to 2018, IA's client base grew six times larger, while spending on delivering Indigenous programs and services was 145 times larger, mushrooming from $131 million to more than $19 billion. Yet the issues of poverty and societal dysfunction plaguing Indigenous communities continued to sound exactly the same as in 1966, only more so.

In 2016, the country was shocked by the news that eleven children on the Attawapiskat reserve in northern Ontario had attempted suicide in one single day in April. More than 100 people in the community of about 2,000 on the west shore of James Bay had reportedly tried to commit suicide in the previous six months. The chief declared a state of emergency the following Monday when more than a dozen young people, including a nine-year-old, were overheard making a suicide pact.[6]

Suicide is a harsh reality in many Indigenous communities in Canada. First Nations males are ten times more likely to commit suicide than non-Indigenous males; First Nations females are twenty-one times more likely to kill themselves than non-Indigenous females.[7]

The response from government officials to the Attawapiskat crisis was predictable. Prime Minister Justin Trudeau tweeted that the situation was "heartbreaking," and that the government would "continue to work to improve living conditions for all indigenous peoples."[8]

The Ontario minister of Health said that the Ministry of Children and Youth Services had been contacted about "providing emergency life-promotion supports."[9] Federal Health minister Jane Philpott said she was working with the province to set up "a joint action table" to find solutions, and pointed to the need to improve socio-economic conditions in the community.[10]

The federal government had tried an even more extreme solution to the disastrous state of the Labrador coastal community of Davis Inlet in 1993, when video recordings went public showing children, aged eleven to fourteen, in the Inuit community openly sniffing gasoline fumes out of plastic bags and yelling that they wanted to die.[11] It was scandalous and drew international condemnation, and a close examination of the appalling living conditions in the community.

An addictions counsellor called to the scene that night said in an interview with *Time Magazine* that 95 percent of the adult population of Davis Inlet suffered from alcoholism and that a quarter of the community's population had attempted suicide over the past year.[12]

The Inuit community had been moved to Davis Inlet in the 1960s, and the federal government decided to move it again in 2002, this time to a brand new $159 million town built from scratch. The new community of Natuashish got 133 new homes, a $13 million school, a health centre, an airport, a fire hall and a concrete wharf.[13] It was supposed to be a fresh start, but not much really changed. The community of about 1,000 people was back in the news again in 2017 when two boys, aged eleven and seventeen, were seriously injured in a house fire where, according to police, they were sniffing gas. Community leaders said they were fighting yet another solvent-abuse epidemic, and were looking to the provincial government to provide a full-time mental health therapist.[14]

Inasmuch as officials called for improved mental health services and improved economic opportunities in Natuashish and in Attawapiskat, Caroline Tait, a Métis professor of psychiatry at the University of Saskatchewan, pointed out in 2016 how little had changed in the two decades since the Royal Commission on Aboriginal People.

"What do you find 20 years ago? The same conversations we are having now about suicide. The same conversation we are having now about the lack of mental health [services]. The same conversations that we are having around socio-economic development."¹⁵

If Indigenous people seem bitter and angry, Tait said, "it's because people have gone to the table over and over again."¹⁶

If the definition of insanity is doing the same thing over and over again,¹⁷ and expecting a different outcome, it is certainly demonstrated by the tragic stories of Attawapiskat and Natuashish crises. If the root cause of societal breakdown in Indigenous communities is the pervasive sense of helplessness and hopelessness, would it not make sense to address that issue head-on? Instead, what happened in both communities were calls for treating the symptoms—improved living conditions, emergency life-promotion supports, improved socio-economic conditions, more mental health services. However well-intentioned such ideas might be, it really amounted to announcing that things would continue on, just as they had for the past fifty years.

How could a federal government department have managed to fail so badly and not be called to task for it? All ministers in charge of government departments are accountable to cabinet and can be removed from their posting if they fail to deliver on behalf of the government of the day. Naturally, Indigenous Affairs is different.

The failures of IA have not been an impediment to the careers of IA ministers. For most IA ministers, the position was their first cabinet portfolio and a harbinger of political successes to come—in a different portfolio. Failure in IA was normal and expected. Success would have been unusual.

With the exception of Jean Chrétien and his seven-year tenure from 1968–1974, IA ministers rotated in and out of the department so quickly that a new minister barely had time to get on a first-name basis with the limo driver before dancing out the door on the way to a better posting. Ministers rarely stayed with the IA department more than a year or two. Recall that in 1965, Indian Affairs saw three different ministers in and out the door in the space of twelve months, and Jean Chrétien was the seventh minister in seven years when he was appointed.

The situation continued. Over thirty-eight months beginning in November 2015, there were three major changes in the ministerial appointments for the Indigenous portfolio, which included the splitting of the IA department into two separate entities.¹⁸

Deputy ministers are actually much more important for continuity and stability in any government department than ministers who come and go depending on the whim of the prime minister or the mood of the public on Election Day. Again, Indigenous Affairs is different.

IA deputy ministers tend to roll in and out of the department at just about the same pace as the ministers do. Ambitious civil servants typically put in two years at lesser government departments like IA to signal they've paid their dues, bureaucratically speaking, before moving to a more prestigious department. A recent exception was Michael Wernick, who put in eight years as DM from 2006 to 2014 before heading up the entire federal civil service as Clerk of the Privy Council Office. According to his colleagues, he insisted on staying on because he felt it was the only way he could make a real difference on seemingly intractable Indigenous issues. How much success did he have? It's hard to tell.

Without a firm hand at the top, the senior IA bureaucrats who have actually been running the show have been spectacularly successful at what every good bureaucracy does: it grows. More programs. More services.

It is the responsibility of Indigenous Affairs and its co-delivery partners to deliver and manage the many programs and services funded by its roughly $19 billion budget.[19] The vast role it plays in nearly every aspect of the lives of its client base would seem to be a recipe for failure. However, if you look beyond all the negative media stories, books and research papers written about how disastrous the department has been, you will find a remarkable success story. It's just not the success story you might be expecting.

Here are two key factors to consider about the department:

- IA is a very, very good department, based on Chrétien's assertion when he was IA minister that a department's success is based on how creative bureaucrats are in extracting money from the system for their projects, and the more projects, the better.[20]
- The IA official policy priority is to shrink the bureaucracy by devolving many of its responsibilities onto band and provincial governments, while entrenching federal control of First Nations lands through "self-government" agreements.

These two factors are antithetical. The department cannot deliver on both at the same time. Consider, however, that there are two faces to any government department — the public face seen in the media or at public hearings, and the "inside the bubble" face that is focussed on plans and priorities, budgets, deliverables and jurisdictional disputes, all of which are largely divorced from anything happening in the outside world.

From inside the Ottawa bubble, the IA department is a spectacular success. From outside the bubble, the department is viewed by many as a catastrophic failure.

It is perfectly legitimate for IA to be both a great success and a great failure at the same time, based on two different frames of reference. What IA cannot legitimately do is continue to grow at the same time it is attempting to deliver the department's devolution mandate to shrink itself. A bureaucracy cannot serve two mutually exclusive goals. However, it does help explain why the institution that is IA is so frustratingly difficult to understand.

The Indian Affairs department started down this path in the aftermath of the 1969 White Paper. IA bureaucrats had no idea that advisers in the Prime

Minister's Office were plotting to kill off the department. The "great thunderclap" of '69 awoke Indian politicians to the planned elimination of Indian rights, and it stunned bureaucrats with the news that their department had five years left to live. When the backlash from the White Paper forced the Trudeau government to back off, the IA department was given a reprieve. It makes sense, after such a close brush with death, that IA staffers would do their darnedest to turn IA into the best possible department it could be. And they had Chrétien cheering them on as he leveraged more and more money for them to spend.

To grow in the 1970s, IA already had a needy client base on reserves. Based on a stereotype of Indians that suited their purposes, bureaucrats could justify expanding services to fill ever more needs. In 1969 in *The Unjust Society*, Harold Cardinal denounced the willingness of IA bureaucrats to believe their own propaganda.

"They have fostered an image of Indians as helpless people, an incompetent people and an apathetic people in order to increase their own importance and to stress the need for their own continued presence."[21]

Cardinal did not attribute their motives to malice but rather to naïveté and the genuine belief that their solutions were necessary to the survival of Indians.

"For the most part they are not evil men. They have evolved no vicious plots intentionally to subjugate the Indian people. The situation for the Indian people, as bad as it is, has resulted largely from good intentions, however perverted, of civil servants within the Department of Indian Affairs."[22]

There is, of course, an old saying about good intentions.

Paradoxically, the devolution of programs to band councils offered IA a new vehicle for growth. As more and more chiefs and councils took over program delivery — what Dave Courchene called in 1974 "administering the suffering of our own people"[23] — there was much work to do managing the band governments delivering those programs. The continued failure of most programs could easily be explained away as band governments needing time to learn how to be little municipal governments. And those failures effectively reinforced the foundational premise of IA — that Indians were not capable of managing their own affairs. Successful programs would interfere with IA's growth. So would noisy Indian political activists.

After some initial resistance in the 1970s, Aboriginal Representative Organizations became accustomed to the financial largesse of IA's core funding and program money, and IA bureaucrats had the important role of managing the band councils that were running IA programs. Everyone was happy. IA was growing. The AROs had money to hire staff and researchers. Chiefs and councillors had good-paying jobs, useful work, and lots of side benefits because IA wasn't too worried about what they were doing with the money for programs. The department had little incentive to insist that the chiefs and councils produce good results. Failure was fine.

As long as chiefs and councils were suitably compliant in enacting IA's agenda, it didn't really matter all that much if band funds were spent on Caribbean cruises or high-stakes gambling in Las Vegas. The only time it became a problem was when such excesses turned into a public scandal and embarrassed the minister, who would then be forced to "do something."

In the same way that there was no incentive for IA to enforce accountability, neither was there any necessity for free and fair elections. How chiefs and councils were elected was of little significance. Those who were not suitably compliant could be unilaterally removed by the minister on advice from bureaucrats, and replaced with more pliable officials.

As a good department, IA was also advancing its policy priority of devolution. It was slow going, but bands were advancing inevitably towards municipal-style governance where Indians wouldn't need to worry about such amorphous concepts as inherent rights. They wouldn't have any.

That changed in 1982 when Aboriginal and treaty rights were enshrined in the Constitution. The government could no longer just extinguish Indigenous rights when and where it suited. That threw a monkey wrench into the machinery of devolution, because devolution negotiators were now constitutionally required to get bands to give up their rights *voluntarily*.

However tattered the reputations of some Indigenous political leaders might have become, they deserved full credit for acting swiftly to make sure the rights of their people had the best protection possible—written right into Canada's constitution.

IA's growing budget was, at this point, starting to become an issue within the federal government. A number of Supreme Court of Canada cases were also causing consternation in cabinet due to repeated rulings in favour of Indigenous rights.[24] The need to push harder on devolution and the ultimate goal of "self-government" became more urgent for the federal cabinet. The 1985 Nielsen Task Force review of IA (along with other departments) recommended cutting funding for a variety of IA programs, including the plan for training band governments to become municipal-style administrators. That task, noted the review authors, was largely completed. What was needed was "encouragement" for band governments to recognize the benefits of self-governance, and if a few could be herded in that direction, more would quickly follow and they could all be pushed off the rights cliff into the arms of provincial responsibility.

The review had been conducted behind a dense wall of suspicious secrecy, so when the "Buffalo Jump" memorandum was leaked by the media, it caused a great public furor. That is also when IA bureaucrats found out it contained another White Paper-style death sentence. According to the leaked memo, IA itself had become a problem because it was encouraging Indian dependence by offering them expensive social programs.[25] IA was going to be dismantled because it had become too successful! Once again, blowback from the leaked memo ended up giving IA a reprieve. However, if the powers-that-be wanted bands herded into self-government, IA would step up and do its part, once again proving itself to be a good department.

It was most helpful that the self-government process was shaping up to offer a whole new vista for growth. There would be negotiating tables with discussions and debates that could go on for as long as there was money in the form of government loans to keep band negotiators hooked into the process. Decades, even.

Modern treaties negotiated after 1975, which cover 40 percent of Canada's land mass, were much simpler to negotiate when it came to surrendering rights. They were explicitly negotiated so that it was clear that everyone at the table knew what was being surrendered, and in exchange for which concessions. When the Inuit treaties were signed, they specifically ceded "all their aboriginal claims, rights, titles and interests"[26] to lands and waters within Canada. The other modern treaties did the same, and all have surrendered their land rights. The only holdout was Nunavut, which, in 2019, still didn't have a final devolution agreement on land and resource management.[27]

The bands that signed historic treaties prior to 1975, an area covering half of Canada's landscape, have proved to be more difficult for IA to herd towards self-government. People who viewed the treaties as their protection were not going to give them up easily. Even though most of the Robinson and Numbered Treaties contained land-surrender language, the courts have made it clear that even explicit surrender language is subject to interpretation and must be considered in its cultural and historical context.[28] The duty to consult has also increased uncertainty for governments and industries with an eye on land development. The IA imperative to push chiefs and councils into negotiating "self-government" grew stronger as court cases muddied the waters over rights.

From the 1970s onward, the poverty and suffering of Indians on reserves had a larger political utility than just bolstering IA's client base. If the lives of people on those reserves didn't get any better or, say, actually got worse, would that not help band politicians to see the light and the necessity of sitting down at the negotiating table? It would be for their own good, wouldn't it?

There may not have been any confirmed official federal government policy that explicitly stated that dialling up the level of suffering on reserves was an approved tactic. But the evidence on the ground—the continuing problems of boil-water orders on reserves, rotting houses and children killing themselves—was much the same as if it were official policy.

It's about jobs

And still IA grew and grew, and so did the number of federal co-delivery partners. Based on estimates and extrapolations (in the absence of the IA being able or willing to provide data about its co-delivery partners), by 2017–18, Indigenous Affairs Plus could well have been employing roughly 12,000 federal civil servants delivering Indigenous programs and services.[29] That may seem like a significant number of federal employees, but it was a small fraction of the civil service in 2018 of about 280,000 people (not including the RCMP and Armed Forces members).[30]

The Aboriginal Representative Organizations (AROs), their seventy-some regional, provincial and territorial counterparts[31] were serving as the Indigenous co-delivery partners for IA+. There were 100 people employed in the Assembly of First Nations Secretariat and National Chief's Office in 2017,[32] but accurate employment numbers for the ARO national and regional operations were not readily available.

Another source of Indigenous employment courtesy of IA+ were the approximately 4,000 arts, culture and sports groups funded by Canadian Heritage and Indigenous Affairs programs,[33] with support for executive directors, artists, Indigenous women and many more positions. Again, data on employment numbers is fragmented.

The really big employment numbers based on IA+ funding are in First Nations communities themselves, and there are data to back them up.

In early 2019, the Brandon University Rural Development Institute and two regional chiefs' organizations produced an unusual report. This exercise, called Indigenous Contributions to the Manitoba Economy,[34] reversed the usual practice of studying how much Indigenous people cost the economy. Instead, the report quantified spending by Indigenous and First Nations people in Manitoba in order to calculate their contributions to the province's economy. The analysis, paid for by Indigenous Services and the Manitoba government, showed the province's Indigenous people contribute about 3.9 percent of Manitoba's gross domestic product for 2016, a bit less than agriculture and a bit more than manufacturing. It also addressed a common misconception that FN people do not pay taxes: Manitoba Indigenous people paid about $231 million in federal, provincial, corporate and sales taxes in 2016.[35]

Inside the report were also details on employment in First Nations communities and tribal councils. According to the report, Manitoba's sixty-three FN governments and eight tribal councils provided 19,821 jobs in 2016, with 96.5 percent of those jobs (19,130) in the government sector.[36] In other words, nearly all the employment by band governments and tribal councils was in government administration and the delivery of programs and services. This is not surprising, since band governments *are* governments and tribal councils are cooperative organizations made up of band governments with shared interests.

How would the numbers translate at a national level? If we assume a similar employment level for the 632 First Nations band governments and eighty tribal councils across Canada as in Manitoba, the number of IA+ funded jobs for First Nations people would approach 200,000.[37] While a handful of First Nations communities have own-source revenues from their businesses and other ventures that are profitable enough to contribute to governance costs, the vast majority are dependent on IA+ for funding their governance, as well as the programs and services delivered to band members. On small, remote reserves, band government jobs are sometimes the only jobs.

Given that about 373,500 FN people lived on reserves in 2016,[38] Indigenous governance employment of 200,000 across Canada would mean about 54 percent of people on reserves were employed in the governance sector. It would appear that FN band governments and tribal councils had collectively become the largest co-delivery partner for IA+, at least in terms of jobs numbers.

Recall that at the federal level, power and money flows downward from the Indigenous Affairs department to the band and tribal council level, with some of that power and money channelled down through the AROs to the regional counterparts to the band level. The downward flow of power ends at the band council level, where FN government officials allocate resources (and jobs) to the band membership as they choose.

IA+ is a significant employer of Canada's Indigenous people, either directly or indirectly through the band governments and organizations it funds. It might not be too big a leap to suggest that some 250,000 people in Canada—mostly Indigenous—owe their employment to IA+. It helps to explain where some of its substantial spending is going: jobs for Indigenous and non-Indigenous Canadians. It also clarifies the challenge facing Indigenous leaders who see economic independence as the means of freedom from IA controls. It will take a great deal of economic progress to replace IA+ funding when half of the people living on reserves are, for all intents and purposes, in the employ of IA+.

The end game

Despite repeated pronouncements over the past fifty years that the Indian Affairs department was going to be shut down as programs and services were devolved to band governments, it was not going to happen, and staffers knew it.

As one senior manager put it, "All knew that even if [IA] was abolished, a new bureaucracy would be required to transfer resources to and support new Indian governments, and to perform the many land and resources management functions that had nothing to do with aboriginal peoples as such. Thus a disparate, committed and high-spirited group of people were consistently being told by their political masters what all knew to be a pack of self-serving lies."[39]

Wayne Helgason, the co-founder of the Treaty Annuity Working Group, was equally doubtful of IA disappearing any time soon.

"There's a little bit of a joke," said the Ojibway activist. "If you got rid of all of the Indians, it would still take Indian Affairs about a hundred years to wind down."[40]

Based on past history, every time the Indigenous Affairs department was handed down a death sentence, it just grew bigger. That's what happened in 2017 after the Trudeau government split the Indigenous Affairs into two departments, with the new Indigenous Services department immediately slated for termination. Some day. Thereafter, Indigenous people in Canada had two federal departments and two ministers closely managing just about every aspect of their lives. As per the growth trend, in 2018 and 2019, the government added nearly $10 billion in new spending over six years to IA and its federal co-delivery partners, bumping its annual spending for 2019–20 to an estimated $21 billion.[41] The Indigenous Services department might have been slated for eventual termination, but the new Crown-Indigenous Relations department, assigned the responsibility of overseeing "self-government" was not going anywhere.[42] In fact, there were big plans in the works.

Endnotes to Chapter 17

1 Kelly McParland, "A bigger Indigenous bureaucracy isn't necessarily better," *National Post*, September 6, 2017.

2 Harold Cardinal, 1999, *Unjust Society* (1st edition, 1969, originally published by MG Hurtig Publishers), Douglas & McIntyre, 6.

3 Jack Beaver, 1979, *To have what is one's own*, The National Indian Socio-Economic Development Committee, prepared on behalf of the Department of Indian Affairs and Northern Development and the National Indian Brotherhood, 44.

4 Jean Allard, 2002, "Big Bear's Treaty: The Road to Freedom," *Inroads*, Vol. 11, 151.

5 Jean Allard, interview with author, May 6, 2000.

6 The Canadian Press, "Attawapiskat First Nation declares state of emergency after 11 suicide attempts in one day," *National Post*, April 10, 2016, https://nationalpost.com/news/canada/attawapiskat-first-nation-declares-state-of-emergency-after-11-suicide-attempts-in-one-day.

7 Laurence Mathieu-Léger and Ashifa Kassam, "First Nations community grappling with suicide crisis: 'We're crying out for help,'" *The Guardian*, April 16, 2016.

8 Justin Trudeau, tweet, April 10, 2016, https://twitter.com/justintrudeau/status/719308218803965952?lang=en.

9 The Canadian Press, 2016.

10 Ibid.

11 Brenda Craig, "A heart-wrenching cry for help in Davis Inlet," *Prime Time News*, CBC TV, January 28, 1993.

12 Gavin Scott, "I can't cry anymore," *Time Magazine*, February 22, 1993.

13 Editorial: "Shishatshuiu's request," *The Globe and Mail*, March 13, 2004, A18.

14 Sue Bailey, "New gas-sniffing 'epidemic' grips Labrador's Innu community," *The Star*, May 15, 2017, https://www.thestar.com/news/canada/2017/05/15/new-gas-sniffing-epidemic-grips-labradors-innu-community.html.

15 Geraldine Malone, "Canada had all the information it needed to predict Attawapiskat suicide crisis," *Vice*, April 28, 2016, https://www.vice.com/en_ca/article/5gqapx/canada-had-all-the-information-it-needed-to-predict-attawapiskat-suicide-crisis.

16 Ibid.

17 The quotation seems to have been used by Alcoholics Anonymous for many decades, and is likely attributable to someone from that organization like Bill Wilson, possibly as far back as the 1930s. www.quora.com/Did-Einstein-really-define-insanity-as-doing-the-same-thing-over-and-over-again-and-expecting-different-results.

18 Carolyn Bennett was appointed Indigenous and Northern Affairs Minister in November 2015. She was appointed minister of Crown-Indigenous Relations in August 2017. Jane Philpott was appointed minister of Indigenous Services in August 2017, and was replaced by Seamus O'Regan in January 2019.

19 See Appendix A.

20 Jean Chrétien, 1985, *Straight from the Heart*, Key Porter Books, 72.

21 Harold Cardinal, 1969, *The Unjust Society*, Hurtig Publishers, 9.

22 Ibid., 10.

23 Dave Courchene, as quoted in *Paper Tomahawks: From red tape to red power*, by James Burke, 1976, Queenston House Publishing, 73.

24 For example: R *v* Marshall (No 1) [1999] 3 S.C.R. 456; R *v* Marshall (No 2) [1999]; R. *v.*

Badger, [1996] 1 SCR 771; R. v. Sparrow, [1990] 1 SCR 1075.

25 Menno Boldt, 1993, *Surviving as Indians: The Challenge of Self-Government*, University of Toronto Press, 295.

26 Allistair Campbell, Terry Fegne, and Udloriak Hanson, 2011, "Implementing the 1993 Nunavut Land Claims Agreement," *Arctic Review on Law and Politics*, Vol. 2, No. 1, 2011, 1.

27 Nunavut Department of Executive and Intergovernmental Affairs, https://www.gov.nu.ca/eia/information/frequently-asked-questions-devolution.

28 For example: Delgamuukw v British Columbia, [1997]; Calder v British Columbia (AG) [1973] S.C.R. 313, [1973] 4 W.W.R. 1; Grassy Narrows First Nation v Ontario (Natural Resources), 2014 SCC 48.

29 INAC full-time equivalents (FTEs) 2017–18: 4,627; Health Canada Indigenous programs FTEs 2017–18: 3,668 (including Internal Services FTEs for Indigenous programs). INAC+HC FTEs: 8,295. Since INAC+HC made up some 70 percent of IA+ spending for 2017–18 (See Appendix A), we can postulate that it also made up 70 percent of FTEs, meaning IA+ would be employing roughly 12,000 FTEs in the federal civil service. Sources: Indigenous and Northern Affairs Canada, 2017–18 Departmental Plan; Health Canada, 2017–18 Departmental Plan.

30 Population of the federal public service, Treasury Board of Canada Secretariat, Government of Canada, https://www.canada.ca/en/treasury-board-secretariat/services/innovation/human-resources-statistics/population-federal-public-service.html.

31 The five AROs are: Assembly of First Nations, Métis National Council, Congress of Aboriginal Peoples, Inuit Tapirit Kanatami, and Native Women's Association of Canada. Based on their respective websites in March 2019, they collectively identify 69 regional, provincial and territorial counterparts.

32 Assembly of First Nations Organizational Structure, 2017, PowerPoint presentation, 25.

33 Yale D. Belanger, David R. Newhouse, and Kevin Fitzmaurice, 2008, "Creating a Seat at the Table: A Retrospective Study of Aboriginal Programming at Canadian Heritage," *The Canadian Journal of Native Studies*, XXVIII, 1 (2008), 41. Prior to 2012, Canadian Heritage was funding some 4,000 Indigenous groups and organizations, primarily Indigenous women's and artists' organizations, friendship centres, and cultural and media organizations. After 2012, many of those programs were transferred to Indigenous Affairs.

34 *Indigenous Contributions to the Manitoba Economy*, January 2018, Brandon University, Rural Development Institute, Manitoba Keewatinowi Okimakanak (MKO), Southern Chiefs' Organization (SCO), https://www.brandonu.ca/rdi/projects/indigenous-economy/.

35 Ibid., 36.

36 Ibid., 20.

37 According to the *Indigenous Contributions to the Manitoba Economy* report cited above, 96.5% of 19,821 jobs or 19,130 jobs are for 63 First Nations (FN) and 8 Tribal Council (TC) governance. This averages to 270 jobs/FN+TC. Extrapolating the same average to Canada's 634 FNs and 80 TCs works out to 192,377 jobs, or about 200,000 jobs nationally.

38 IA's number for the on-reserve population in 2016 is 436,780, but on-reserve numbers are often inflated due to reliance on per capita funding. A report on urban FN populations calculates the on-reserve number at 373,500. Sources: INAC, 2017, Registered Indian Population by Sex and Residence, https://www.aadnc-aandc.gc.ca/eng/1523286391452/1523286414623#tbc7; Urban Paper re ASETS Renewal Issues regarding the Indigenous Urban Population, Report to the minister, Employment and Social Development Canada, March 2017.

39 Harry Swain, 2010, *Oka: A Political Crisis and Its Legacy*, Douglas & McIntyre, 35.

40 Wayne Helgason, *A Rethink of Indigenous Funding*, December 27, 2018, YouTube video, https://fcpp.org/2018/12/27/a-rethink-of-indigenous-funding/.

41 The 2018 and 2019 budgets announced $4.757B and $4.730B respectively in new Indigenous program spending over a total of six years. Government of Canada, Budget 2018 Chapter 3-Reconciliation, https://www.budget.gc.ca/2018/docs/plan/budget-2018-en.pdf ; Budget 2019, Chapter 3-Advancing Reconciliation, , https://budget.gc.ca/2019/docs/plan/chap-03-en.html.

42 Prime Minister's Office, *New Ministers to support the renewed relationship with Indigenous Peoples*, August 28, 2017, http://pm.gc.ca/eng/news/2017/08/28/new-ministers-support-renewed-relationship-indigenous-peoples.

18
BUFFALO JUMP 2.0

The Mulroney era Buffalo Jump policy of 1985[1] promised the elimination of the *Indian Act*, gradually doing away with Indian Affairs department, devolving responsibilities to other levels of government and to bands that would have been turned into self-governing ethnic municipalities. All that was required from band governments was to sign away their peoples' rights in exchange for five-year block funding.

Fast forward to 2017 and the promise of a new nation-to-nation relationship between the Crown and First Nations that calls for the elimination of the *Indian Act*, gradually doing away with the Indigenous Services department, and devolving responsibilities to self-governing "nations," all under the management of Crown-Indigenous Relations. All that is required of "nations" at the negotiating table is to sign away their peoples' rights in exchange for ten-year block funding.[2]

The self-government process that Justin Trudeau announced in the summer of 2017 was supposed to be the way to make "our national journey of reconciliation a reality."[3] It looks more like Buffalo Jump 2.0.

The Mulroney Buffalo Jump policy, for instance, sought to download the responsibility for fixing all the problems on reserves to the local communities to solve for themselves.[4] The Trudeau policy seeks to download to First Nations communities the responsibility for figuring out for themselves how to finally hold their own governments accountable to them.[5]

There are, however, significant differences between the Buffalo Jump of the 1980s and Buffalo Jump 2.0.

Recall that the Mulroney Buffalo Jump policy was primarily motivated by cost-cutting at IA to "contain the rapid escalation of future costs that would derive from leaving existing programs unchecked."[6] It called for a fresh approach "to deal with the growing needs and native aspirations for more local control while curtailing the unbridled growth of more *ad hoc* social policy programs."[7]

The Trudeau effort, announced in 2017, called for significantly more spending on programs and services, promising "a new fiscal relationship will ensure sufficient funding,"[8] and "will underpin progress toward the elimination of socio-economic gaps between First Nations citizens and other Canadians."[9] It was backed up by new spending announcements in early 2018 of $4.8 billion for clean water, education, employment, children's services, health and creating new Indigenous governance structures,[10] followed by the announcement of $1.7 billion in spending on the Indigenous Early Learning and Child Care Framework.[11]

The new Indigenous Services minister, Jane Philpott, acknowledged at the time, "There is an incredible amount of important work ahead—work to be done in partnership with Indigenous peoples—to address the inequities and priorities of First Nations, Inuit and Métis Nation."[12]

Unlike the Mulroney government, which in 1985 feared that spending on Indigenous programs and services by IA and its co-delivery partners would expand over the next five years from $2.4 billion to more than $5 billion by 1990, the Trudeau government seemed comfortable with continuing to expand Indigenous Affairs and its co-delivery partners (IA+), bumping spending to reach approximately $21 billion per year.[13]

A major difference between Buffalo Jump 1.0 and Buffalo Jump 2.0 was the role of Aboriginal Representative Organizations (AROs). The Mulroney policy sought to rein in AROs, with an eye to giving ARO funding to the bands instead.[14] It tasked the IA minister, in consultation with the Justice minister, to review whether funding selected Indian political groups constituted a possible contravention of the Charter of Rights.[15] The Trudeau version, on the other hand, elevated one ARO, the Assembly of First Nations (AFN), to the status of a "nation" in its nation-to-nation negotiations.[16] The AFN, despite not being the legitimate voice of ordinary First Nations people, was negotiating as if it, alone, had the authority to sit at the table in negotiating future FN governance with the Crown.

However, one of the biggest differences was the suggestion by Trudeau that his government might consider the possibility of replacing its policy of requiring extinguishment of Indigenous rights in exchange for modern treaty/self-government agreements.[17] That is a very big maybe, and FN leaders were skeptical in the absence of information about what form this policy change might take.[18] At the time of writing, the extinguishment policy was still in place.

With Indigenous Affairs divided into two departments, the federal government plan was to gradually devolve the responsibilities of the new Indigenous Services department to band governments (or to provincial and municipal governments) so that, in theory, sometime in the future the department would no longer be needed. However, the IA client base was growing. The number of Status Indians was predicted by IA to grow dramatically. In 2012, IA was predicting a 46 percent growth in the number of Status Indians in Canada over the twenty-five years from 2009 to 2034.[19] It figured there would be more than 1.2 million Status Indians by 2034, with a growing number (56 percent) living off-reserve. IA attributed the growth projection, in part, to its creation of the new bands, and the continuing impact of changes in gender discrimination laws.[20] Nonetheless, Indigenous Services was the department that is intended for elimination under the Buffalo Jump 2.0 policy.

The future planned for the Crown-Indigenous Relations (CIR) was quite different. It was set to grow dramatically as it expanded the modern treaty-making process to encompass all aspects of band governance and new governance institutions.

There were, in 2017, about 100 "negotiating tables" at which First Nations representatives were attempting to work out land claims and self-governance issues, some of which had been going on for decades.[21] There was one practical reason for band governments to consider IA's version of "self-government." Instead of filling out a multitude of forms and waiting every year to find out what funding the band had, the funding would come in five-year blocks. And there would be no more *Indian Act* constraints to contend with. The same would be true for agreements after 2017, except with ten-year block funding.

However, as IA had learned in negotiating post-1975 treaties, the process of arriving at a negotiated "self-government" agreement was enormously complex. And it still is.

The alchemy of modern treaties

Here's how the modern treaty process works. A band, or a group of First Nations bands, begins the work of developing an Agreement in Principle with IA bureaucrats. Arriving at this agreement can take a decade or so, depending on the issues in contention and the funding. (Indigenous Affairs had long been providing loans to band governments so they could pay the professional researchers, consultants and negotiators who would sit on the band's side of the table. The consequence of this debt financing was that many bands could not abandon the process once it had started because they were too deeply in hock to IA.)

Arriving at an agreement involves parties on both sides of the table. On IA's side is the implementation negotiator, along with IA regional staff from the province/territory where the band is located, and representatives from Other Government Departments (OGDs) who have a stake in the agreement.[22] Once there is a serious chance of an agreement, the process gets kicked upstairs to the Main Table for the implementation planning phase. That's when the real work begins.

It can take a long time for the two parties sitting on opposite sides of the table to iron out all the details of the implementation plan, but it is the "road map" that will govern the future of the newly "self-governing" band. That is why it is so important.

Once the implementation plan has been sorted, there is an even busier time ahead for government bureaucrats, who must make sure all the details are taken care of, including making sure all the Cabinet documents get signed off and Treasury Board and the Justice Department approve submissions for legal authorization and funding. This is all in aid of arriving at the "effective date" of implementation.[23] The effective date is where it gets real, where the new rules that will change life in the FN community kick in.

In theory, after the agreement is signed and sealed and takes effect, it should be up to the community to make "self-government" work. In theory, the community is self-governed, with the officials of the Nation in control and making decisions for the community. But in reality, that is not what is happening.

Post 2017, Crown-Indigenous Relations (CIR, formerly IA) bureaucrats will have just begun a long and fruitful future for themselves.

Every agreement comes with a requirement for multiple boards to look after various responsibilities on the new nation's land base, but mainly for resources, water and dispute resolution. It's about the land, and control over what happens on the land, and the CIR minister has got his/her fingers in all of it.

Modern treaties signed after 1975 impact primarily the North, BC and Quebec. In 2015, there were nearly three dozen boards and panels created as part of the treaties for managing environmental impact and renewable resources, land use and water, and dispute resolution and arbitration.[24] Of the 389 positions on those boards, 175 were appointed by the minister. It is worth noting that the minister appoints *every single member* of the boards mandated by the modern treaties that control water, surface rights, land planning, environmental assessment and other land-specific issues.[25] (There are a couple of exceptions where the minister appoints the majority of the board but not all its members.)

As author Thomas King said in his best-selling *The Inconvenient Indian*, it is all about the land. "If you understand nothing else about the history of Indians in North America, you need to understand that the question that really matters most of all is the question of the land... Land contains the languages, the stories, and the histories of the people... And land is home."[26]

It's about what non-Indigenous people want, said King, and they want the land.[27]

Arthur Manuel, who had followed in his father George's footsteps to become a widely respected Indigenous leader in his own right, said the same in *The Reconciliation Manifesto*, a book he completed just prior to his death in 2017. "The overriding objective in all of the government's dealing with Indigenous people is to have continued, unfettered access and control over Indigenous lands. Today, they have armies of civil servants working on new schemes to get us to surrender our title and rights and whatever they come up with, they are certain to call it 'reconciliation.'"[28]

According to the department's handbook for federal officials on implementing self-government agreements,[29] once an agreement came into effect, there was much yet to be done in working out the kinks that were inevitable in applying the implementation plan in the real world, with real people. There would be tensions and misunderstandings in the new government-to-government relationships, and multiple boards with appointments for the minister to fill.

But even when "self-government" was implemented, CIR's regional offices remained responsible for "day-to-day management and administration of fiscal arrangements,"[30] retaining control of the day-to-day financial issues related to the new "nation."

The financial part of the "self-government" agreement would have to be reviewed every five years.[31] The overall implementation plan would have to be renegotiated every ten years. This is what CIR bureaucrats described as the "enduring phase."[32] The bureaucrats intended to remain involved for a long, long time. CIR recommended that bands begin the renewal process in year seven or eight to be sure there was enough time to complete the new implementation plan by year ten.[33] The band government administrators would barely have time to take a deep breath after the financial review was over before they had to start prepping for the next implementation plan renewal.

CIR considered the renewal process as a new career path for bureaucrats. "Because the standard term for negotiated implementation plans is ten years, and five for financial documents, the renewal of these documents will undoubtedly be an expanding business line for implementation practitioners."[34]

Critics of the modern treaty-making process called it an outright fraud. Mohawk policy analyst Russell Diabo condemned the negotiation tables as "termination tables," since the objective is ultimately to terminate Indigenous rights, one band at a time.

"Self-government agreements," said the Kahnawake activist, "will be manipulated to modify, convert and extinguish the inherent sovereignty of First Nations. More self-government agreements will be signed with bands formed under the *Indian Act*. The political effect will be to convert these bands into a kind of ethnic Indigenous municipality rather than self-determining nations. The Crown continues to set the parameters for how First Nations peoples are to live on their land, even once they opt out of the *Indian Act*."[35]

AROs do not escape blame either. According to Arthur Manuel, the organizations had become useful tools of the federal government in its agenda of terminating Indigenous rights.

Government policy, he said, has penetrated right into BC reserve communities without band members understanding the insidious effect and how their participation may actually be hurting them. But some bands are financially on the hook.

"It sometimes seems that those who are negotiating cannot stop because they are dependent upon the money they get through treaty loans from the federal and provincial governments. But continuing at these termination tables is the single greatest injury that we inflict on ourselves and our future."[36]

Ordinary Indigenous people, he said, cannot look to the Assembly of First Nations or the chiefs and councils to find a path out of the termination trap.

"This is complicated by the fact that our establishment organizations have disappeared so far down the path for our termination that it seems they can no longer find their way back to the grassroots and their needs."[37]

Former Nuu-chah-nulth Tribal Council treaty manager Cliff Atleo, Jr. agreed with Manuel and Diabo that negotiation tables are more accurately called "termination tables." After more than six years working on the BC treaty process — a separate category of treaty-making process that differs from the rest of the country — Atleo said he saw no evidence of a willingness to actually negotiate treaties or any sign of flexibility from provincial or federal government officials.

"They had, for all intents and purposes determined a formula for calculating 'treaty' agreements and applied that template everywhere. The governments have shown an unwavering desire to diminish Indigenous claims to land, water and rights as quickly and cheaply as possible."[38]

There is no place for sovereignty or self-determination in IA's version of "self-government." There wasn't in the 1990s with the failed Manitoba Framework Initiative, and there isn't now.

While IA has delivered on the "self-governance" agenda for non-Treaty communities in the North, it has so far failed to make meaningful inroads into extinguishing Indigenous rights in Treaty areas, BC and the Maritimes. Recall that IA's Buffalo Jump policy begun in the Mulroney era used the misery and suffering of ordinary First Nations people as leverage to advance modern treaties or "self-government." It still does. The impact of the policy on the people themselves was well-articulated in 2012 by former BC regional chief for the Assembly of First Nations, Jody Wilson-Raybould:

"Far too many of our people are poor, dispossessed of their lands, uneducated, dependent upon state services and generally unhealthy.... Sadly, for a lot of our citizens there is still a sense of hopelessness. This sense of hopelessness can be overwhelming at times and is evidence of a far greater pathology that many of our citizens need to overcome — namely apathy, alienation, dependency and powerlessness...."[39]

The Buffalo Jump 1.0 policy exacerbated First Nation poverty and suffering and trapped bands into remaining in negotiations due the accumulated debt to IA. In the 2019 federal budget, the government announced that those loans, valued at over $1 billion,[40] would be forgiven. However, an updated Buffalo Jump 2.0 that failed to address the root causes of poverty and suffering, even if it came with a great deal more money and loan forgiveness, was obviously not a solution.

Endnotes to Chapter 18

1. Erik Nielsen, 1985, Memorandum to Cabinet: Report of the Ministerial Task Force on Native Programs, https://www.scribd.com/document/330654416/Memo-to-Cabinet-on-Native-Programs-Buffalo-Jump-of-1980-s-April-12-1985

2. ISC (Indigenous Services Canada), 2017, *A New Approach: Co-development of a New Fiscal Relationship*, 2, https://www.aadnc-aandc.gc.ca/DAM/DAM-INTER-HQ-ACH/STAGING/texte-text/reconciliation_new_fiscal_rel_approach_1512565483826_eng.pdf.

3. Prime Minister's Office, *New Ministers to support the renewed relationship with Indigenous Peoples*, August 28, 2017, http://pm.gc.ca/eng/news/2017/08/28/new-ministers-support-renewed-relationship-indigenous-peoples.

4. Nielsen, 1985, 19.

5. Gloria Galloway, 2017, "Ottawa to give 10-year grants to First Nations, with less reporting on how money is spent," *The Globe and Mail*, December 28, 2017, https://www.theglobeandmail.com/news/politics/feds-to-give-10-year-grants-to-first-nations-with-less-reporting-on-how-money-is-spent/article37438522/.

6. Nielsen, 1985, 9.

7. Ibid., 8.

8. ISC 2017, 8.

9. Ibid.

10. Government of Canada, Budget Plan 2018–19, p 145–146, https://www.budget.gc.ca/2018/home-accueil-en.html

11. Employment and Social Development Canada, 2018, Media Release: Assembly of First Nations, Inuit Tapiriit Kanatami and Métis National Council announce the first Indigenous Early Learning and Child Care Framework, September 17, 2018, https://www.canada.ca/en/employment-social-development/news/2018/09/government-of-canada-assembly-of-first-nations-inuit-tapiriit-kanatami-and-metis-national-council-announce-the-first-indigenous-early-learning-and-.html

12. Rachel Gilmore, "Philpott unveils ambitious to-do list for new Indigenous Services department," *ipolitics*, January 23, 2018, https://ipolitics.ca/2018/01/23/philpott-unveils-ambitious-list-new-indigenous-services-department/

13. The 2018 and 2019 budgets announced $4.757B and $4.730B respectively in new Indigenous program spending over five years. Government of Canada, Budget 2018 Chapter 3-Reconciliation, https://www.budget.gc.ca/2018/docs/plan/budget-2018-en.pdf ; Budget 2019, Chapter 3-Advancing Reconciliation, , https://budget.gc.ca/2019/docs/plan/chap-03-en.html.

14. Nielsen, 1985, E:42, 35.

15. Ibid., E:7, 21.

16. Hayden King, and Shiri Pasternak, 2018, *Canada's Emerging Indigenous Rights Framework: A Critical Analysis*, Yellowhead Institute, 9.

17. Jorge Barrera, "First Nations leaders react with caution to Justin Trudeau's Indigenous rights plan," *CBC News*, February 14, 2018, http://www.cbc.ca/news/indigenous/first-nations-reaction-trudeau-indigenous-rights-plan-1.4536098.

18. Ibid.

19. Registered Indian Population, Household and Family Projections, 2009–2034, Strategic Analysis Directorate, INAC, 2012.

20. Ibid.

21. Marcia Nickerson, 2017, Characteristics of a Nation-to-Nation Relationship: Discussion Paper,

Institute on Governance, 29.

22 *Implementation of comprehensive land claims and self-government agreements: A handbook for the use of federal officials*, INAC, 2003, 15.

23 Ibid., 14.

24 INAC *Ministerial Transition Book: 2015*, Northern Context: Co-management of Northern Resources, https://www.aadnc-aandc.gc.ca/eng/1450197908882/1450197959844.

25 Ibid.

26 Thomas King, 2012, *The Inconvenient Indian: A Curious Account of Native People in North America*, Anchor Canada, 218.

27 Ibid., 216.

28 Arthur Manuel, and Ronald Derrickson, 2017, *The Reconciliation Manifesto: Recovering the Land, Rebuilding the Economy*, James Lorimer and Company, 204.

29 *Implementation*, 2003.

30 Ibid., 26.

31 Ibid., 33.

32 Ibid., 24.

33 Ibid., 32–33.

34 Ibid., 36.

35 Russell Diabo, "When moving past the Indian Act means something worse," *Policy Options*, September 22, 2017. http://policyoptions.irpp.org/magazines/september-2017/when-moving-past-the-indian-act-means-something-worse/.

36 Manuel and Derrickson, 141.

37 Ibid., 147.

38 Cliff Atleo Jr., "*Unsettling Canada*: A review," *Decolonization: Indigeneity, Education & Society*, Vol. 5, No. 1, 2016, 75.

39 Jody Wilson Raybould and Tim Raybould, 2012, *BCAFN Governance Toolkit: A guide to Nation Building, Part 3: A Guide to Community Engagement*, British Columbia Assembly of First Nations, 14.

40 Budget 2019, Government of Canada, Chapter 3-Advancing Reconciliation, https://budget.gc.ca/2019/docs/plan/chap-03-en.html.

19
BREAKING THE TYRANNY OF SILENCE

If people on First Nations reserves are so oppressed, you might ask, why don't they rise up and demand change? They don't because many remember what happened when all the angry mothers and grandmothers rose up in protest in 1999. They saw those women labelled as liars, Satanists and terrorists. They saw them punished by being evicted from their homes, fired from jobs, and forced to leave their home reserves for their physical safety. They had to take the death threats seriously. Those women had their families' safety to consider, too.

People on First Nations saw at the time who came to the women's defence, and who didn't. It is true that some politicians, particularly in the Reform Party, used their positions to amplify the women's voices and raise their concerns in the House of Commons and the Senate. Political pundits added their voices. But a year later, the media had wearied of stories of band corruption and election fraud. They moved on to other issues. People on reserves also saw who didn't defend the women and rally behind them. The Assembly of First Nations dismissed the women as troublemakers who were just making Indigenous people look bad, and a number of band chiefs threatened the women with lawsuits.

People on First Nations saw what happened after all the shouting and finger-pointing died down and the RCMP and Indigenous Affairs investigations ended. A few people were charged with crimes like fraud and misappropriation of band funds, but it seemed like the worst punishment faced by most chiefs, councillors, band administrators and consultants suspected of wrongdoing was the temporary embarrassment of being held up as bad examples by the media. If ordinary Indigenous people still harboured a lingering hope that they could make their voices heard, the results of the women's protests pretty much killed it. What was the point of going up against IA or their own political leaders? Nothing was going to change. It was better to stay silent. It was *safer* to stay silent.

Well, you might ask, why didn't they leave the reserves if life there was so bad? Many did, but nearly half stayed. It has to do with the land. For people who have walked the land for Always (or about 10,000 years), the land is their connection to everyone who came before. The attachment to the land can be powerful, and not just for Indigenous people.

In the early 1990s on the Prairies, many farmers whose land had been in their families from not long after the land was ceded in treaties were facing bankruptcy. High interest rates were killing them, and some farmers were killing themselves. It was so bad that Manitoba, Saskatchewan and Alberta set up crisis hotlines specifically for farmers. These were men who would rather commit suicide than face being the one who failed the generations who had gone before and lost the land.[1] People who experience the pull of the land understand just how powerful it can be. Now, imagine being the person who gives up the land that had been in your family for several millennia. That's why people stay.

It is the land, again, that is at the nexus of the conflict between Indigenous and non-Indigenous people, just as it has been from the start.

"The issue that came ashore with the French and the English and the Spanish," said author Thomas King, "the issue that was the *raison d'être* for each of the colonies, the issue that has made its way from coast to coast to coast and is with us today, the issue that has never changed, never varied, never faltered in its resolve is the issue of land. The issue has always been the land."[2]

It would seem fitting that the value of modernized annuities should also be about the land.

It is a testament to the spirit of Indigenous people living under the *Indian Act* that they have endured for more than 150 years, but not without casualties. Overlooked in all the attention that is paid to the ugly side of reserve life—high unemployment, band corruption, crime, suicide and social dysfunction relative to mainstream society—are all the people in reserve communities who are employed, raising their families, drumming and dancing, and simply getting on with their lives. All but the most desperate reserves seem to have a core of quiet, steady people who are the backbone of their communities. You won't hear much about them because they're not the ones involved in the crises that attract media attention. And you won't hear much from them on the political scene, either. They have deliberately avoided the toxic internecine warfare between the families who battle it out every election to see who will control the money and power devolved to the band by IA, and all the jobs that go with it. And they haven't involved themselves in the political power struggles in the provincial and national representative organizations either, as those entities were often viewed with suspicion.

The AFN has long been sensitive to accusations that it does not represent ordinary First Nations people. National Indian Brotherhood leaders knew their legitimacy was questionable as far back as 1973 when Jack Beaver helpfully pointed it out to them.

The AFN might have officially declared itself the sole voice of all First Nations people, but there have always been some obvious holes in that claim. Status Indians who were not members of a band had no means of representation within the AFN structure. Neither is there a place for other First Nations organizations to have a say in AFN policy or get their voices heard in policy negotiations with IA or the government. In 2004, the AFN undertook a renewal process, with a $2 million consultation across the country that involved twenty-seven meetings and about 1,000 grassroots participants.[3] The results produced by the renewal commission were delivered to the AFN in December 2004 in a report called "A Treaty Among Ourselves."[4]

The commission recommended that the AFN not alter its membership structure, but rather that the organization work on developing a positive working relationship with groups representing other Indigenous voices. There would still be no place for Status Indians without band membership.[5]

The contentious question of allowing individuals to have voting powers was addressed in the report, with the commissioners noting that the unresolved issue was creating tension within the AFN. The commission recommended "that the National Chief be elected to office for a four-year term through the process of a universal vote of eligible First Nations citizens."[6]

The report laid out the process for electing the National Chief with voting on reserves and in urban areas, although individuals would have no say in nominations. The chiefs would continue the same process of nominating a National Chief as they usually did.[7] Grassroots people would get to choose only among the chiefs' selected candidates.

There was considerable excitement and anticipation in First Nations communities that they would be allowed to vote for the National Chief in the July 2006 elections.[8] However, the hope that grassroots people would finally have a say in electing the national voice for the AFN was quickly dashed. A 2008 review of the restructuring efforts indicated that, while options for electoral models were completed, extensive consultations would be required before any change could be made. And it would cost a lot of money.[9] And that was that.

Of course, the problem did not go away. Following the 2009 AFN elections, a journalist for the *Montreal Gazette* noted that the National Chief who claims to be the spokesperson for all First Nations people is not elected by them; he is elected by the chiefs.

"What's needed is simple: Direct election of a national chief by all status and treaty Indians across Canada, bypassing the chiefs. The Assembly of Chiefs, as it should properly be called at present, has fought ferociously against even simple reforms."[10]

While it is understandable that the chiefs would want to retain control of the organization that represents them, it is illogical for the "Assembly of Chiefs" to continue to claim that it speaks for all First Nations people, while at the same time silencing them. The AFN knew it was not the legitimate voice of ordinary First Nations people. So too did Indigenous Affairs bureaucrats, the IA minister, the federal cabinet, First Nations people on and off the reserve, other Indigenous groups, and the chiefs. The only people who did not know were ordinary non-Indigenous people. They heard the AFN National Chief declare that he was speaking for all First Nations people and had no reason to doubt that it was true. If it weren't, surely the AFN would be called out on it.

Maybe that's the point. It was, after all, the tens of millions of ordinary non-Indigenous people who had the power to sway elections and influence the priorities of the federal government of the day. If the general public could be led to believe that AFN was the legitimate voice of First Nations people, then it was as good as being true. There's a saying, attributed to George W. Bush, that you can fool some of the people some of the time, and you can fool some of the people all the time, and those are the ones you want to concentrate on.[11] It would seem that IA and the AFN were placing their bets on continuing to fool the public. However, that tactic only works as long as the public isn't paying attention, and the interest across the country in participating in reconciliation was fuelling a desire by non-Indigenous people to learn about Indigenous issues. There was a risk they would not be fooled any longer.

If the AFN did not represent the grassroots, how did band chiefs themselves measure up as legitimate representatives of the people who elected them? In 2008, a report by the National Centre for First Nations Governance noted that just over half of First Nations were still running elections under the *Indian Act* rules, which had no provision for independent oversight. The rest had custom codes.[12] However, the custom codes did not have a requirement for an independent electoral officer either. In advising bands on how to write their own codes, the National Centre stressed the importance of electoral-officer impartiality in ensuring that election results be accepted as legitimate.

"As the person charged with overseeing the election process, the electoral officer carries a heavy responsibility. Because of this, a number of communities have looked at ways of helping to ensure the impartiality of this position. While the majority of codes give council the role of selecting the electoral officer, at least one code requires electoral officers to be selected by a show of hands at a meeting of voters."[13]

The Centre's analysis of band codes showed that only one of the 276 codes in effect in FN communities across Canada in 2008 required that the electoral officer be someone from outside the community. A number of others required that the electoral officer, once chosen by council (whose members might be running in that same election), had to promise to be fair and neutral.[14]

The problems with elections on reserves got a thorough hearing in 2010 by the Senate Standing Committee on Aboriginal Peoples. It was led by Senator Gerry St. Germaine, a Métis who hailed from the same French village west of Winnipeg where Jean Allard's grandparents bought their farmland.

There were multiple issues raised by the resulting St. Germaine report, including IA's control over the election process on reserves and its authority to nullify elections, a deeply flawed appeals process for challenging disputed election results, a mail-in ballot system open to abuse and fraud, the constant election mode created by holding elections every two years, and the lack of band government accountability to members.

The senate committee recommended that more First Nations move toward adopting community-designed election codes, which "offers a satisfying way to address the weaknesses of the *Indian Act* electoral system, while respecting the great diversity of circumstances, priorities and aspirations of First Nations."[15]

During the Senate hearing, it was noted by several presenters that there was little provision for governance models that did not involve elections. Law professor Bradford Morse, a specialist on Indigenous governance issues, said that the absence was notable because First Nations had once been global leaders in democracy—before the *Indian Act*.

"Democracy in my mind does not mean elections with ballots; it means the voice of the people in the selection of their leaders and in the decision-making of governments. First Nations were extraordinarily democratic."[16]

Morse was talking about the traditional forms of governance. It would seem to make sense for FN communities to develop their own election codes. However, custom codes approved by IA were not necessarily offering much change, mainly because IA required they align closely with the *Indian Act* model. One of the serious flaws in band elections remained—the lack of any requirement for free and fair elections overseen by an independent electoral officer. The incumbents were in charge of election machinery. A band chief could appoint her brother to be the electoral officer overseeing the election she was running in, and there was nothing community members could do about it.

By 2014, only about a third of bands were still operating under the *Indian Act* electoral system. Indigenous Affairs updated the election rules to allow elections every four years, but there was still no requirement for an independent electoral officer. Nor was there any suggestion that elections should be free and fair.

As time passed, it became apparent the custom code elections were actually turning out to be worse for some communities. As soon as a custom code was approved, IA divested itself of any further responsibility for how the elections were managed. Or mismanaged.

A 2017 review of custom codes suggested they were a double-edged sword. Some bands, such as the Mississauga First Nation, had successfully developed their own codes. In the Mississauga case, the community had created a constitution, and defused the monopolistic power of council through creating parallel councils and other governance institutions, thereby reducing its ability to do harm or abuse its power.[17]

Under the control of IA, said researchers Joseph Quesnel and Kayla Ishkanian, band governments have lacked the checks and balances of other governments that are generally taken for granted, and those imbalances have been continued in many custom codes.

"The executive and legislative functions are fused in the chief and council and there is no official opposition to hold the government to account. And not only are the voluntary and private sectors underdeveloped, but there are few independent review mechanisms such as ombudspersons, First Nations-run courts, auditing agencies, or ethics commissions. Finally, media in First Nation communities… are not independent of First Nations governments."[18]

It is exactly the kind of climate that is likely to continue nurturing Harold Cardinal's "village-level tyrants."

The lack of any requirement that band elections be free and fair serves to further entrench the sense of hopelessness for people who must live under such regimes. The whole system leans towards abuse instead of democracy. As American theologian and ethicist Reinhold Niebuhr once said, "Man's capacity for justice makes democracy possible, but man's inclination to injustice makes democracy necessary."[19]

Just before Arthur Manuel died in early 2017, he shared his view on Indigenous political organizations and their lack of leadership. He didn't pull any punches.

"Indian organizations are led and staffed by an Indian elite who have used our people's poverty to leverage their own government-funded jobs. In their eagerness to please the ones who are paying them, they have forgotten about the people who they are supposed to be serving. Our leaders have abandoned our people and many of them have simply boarded the Trudeau train and disappeared from Indian country into cushy jobs in Ottawa. They are no longer hanging around the Liberal fort, they have disappeared into it."[20]

However, times are changing. In an era of high-speed internet and cell phones, information is much more readily accessible for those seeking it. Indigenous people are generally better educated than ever.[21] There is a new generation of Indigenous leaders who are looking for new solutions to old problems, who want to empower their people, and to take back power from the AROs.

In 2017, IA minister Carolyn Bennett conducted a consultation on transparency and accountability with elected and administrative officials from FN bands and tribal councils in twenty-seven meetings held across the country.[22] Ordinary FN people could attend the meetings as observers. The problem with government consultations is that the people invited to speak are often those who will say what the government wants to hear, so the conclusions are preordained to fit the government's agenda. This may well have been the case with the accountability consultations. However, it is noteworthy that the AFN did not participate in the meetings but rather filed a separate report prepared in consultation with Indigenous Services.[23]

Up for discussion at the accountability consultations: an ombudsman, free and fair elections, and FN band government accountability to FN people. Yes, these were the exact same issues at the heart of the protests by the angry women some twenty years earlier when FN leaders had denounced the women and tried to silence them. This time, it was the leaders putting those important ideas on the table, resulting in a consultation report with recommendations that included the following:[24]

- an accountability framework must recognize First Nations governments' primary accountability to their members, first and foremost,
- a mutual accountability framework must be put in place that holds both First Nations and the Government of Canada to account, and
- consultation must be carried out to determine an independent ombudsperson and Aboriginal Auditor General.

The FN and tribal council leaders were explicitly acknowledging the need to be accountable to their people. For the AFN's part in the accountability consultations, its separate report made no mention of an ombudsperson or free and fair elections.

But it's not enough to say the right words. The means of empowerment so that the people can hold their leaders accountable has to be there, too.

Rating the politicians

It isn't often that ordinary Indigenous people get their voices heard, but they did in a survey by Probe Research in 2017, aptly called Indigenous Voices. The 500 Indigenous people surveyed by telephone in Manitoba were asked to rate their political organizations. About 60 percent of respondents were First Nations and 36 percent were Métis. A handful of people identified as Inuit.[25]

The political and government organizations being rated were the Assembly of Manitoba Chiefs, the Manitoba Métis Federation, "your Chief and council," and the federal and Manitoba governments.

When asked to rank the effectiveness of the organizations in helping Indigenous people overall in Manitoba, only 16 percent of First Nations people ranked their chief and council as helpful, and only 18 percent ranked the AMC as helpful. As low as that might sound, it was still better than the ranking of both the Manitoba and federal government by all respondents at 12 percent.[26] The Manitoba Métis Federation performed better, with a 29 percent helpful rating, but that may be attributable to the fact that the organization has limited control over the lives of most Métis people, other than having the authority to issue Métis harvesting licences for hunting, trapping and fishing.

The takeaway from this survey is that ordinary Indigenous people are not very happy with their political organizations, the federal government or the Manitoba government. Although the survey applied only to Manitoba, it is not difficult to believe that surveys in other provinces might reveal a similar result. Indigenous political groups have generally proved themselves to be disappointments to the people they claim to represent.

Endnotes to Chapter 19

1 Sheila Jones Morrison, 1993, Documentary: Farm Suicide, *Radio Noon*, CBC Radio Winnipeg, September 30, 1993.

2 Thomas King, 2013, *The Inconvenient Indian: A Curious Account of Native People in North America*, Anchor Canada, 217.

3 Paul Barnsley, 2006, "One person, one vote for grassroots," *Windspeaker*, Volume 23, Issue 11.

4 AFN Renewal Commission: Report of Recommendations, 2005, A Treaty Among Ourselves: Returning to the Spirit of Our Peoples, prepared for the Assembly of First Nations.

5 Ibid., 30.

6 Ibid., 29.

7 Ibid., 100.

8 Barnsley, 2006.

9 AFN Renewal: Review, Analysis and Recommendations, prepared for the Assembly of First Nations, April 2008, 7.

10 Patrick Lamontagne, "New AFN chief must reform organization," *Montreal Gazette*, July 27, 2009.

11 The original quotation, attributed to Abraham Lincoln, is: "You can fool all of the people some of the time, and some of the people all of the time, but you cannot fool all the people all of the time."

12 Custom leadership selection codes for First Nations, 2008, National Centre for First Nations Governance, 7.

13 Ibid., 28.

14 Ibid., 44.

15 Gerry St. Germaine, 2010, First Nations Elections: The Choice is Inherently Theirs, Report of the Standing Senate Committee on Aboriginal Peoples, 43.

16 Bradford Morse, as quoted in St. Germaine, 32.

17 Joseph Quesnel and Kayla Ishkanian, 2017, Custom Election Codes for First Nations: A Double-Edged Sword, prepared for the Fraser Institute, 8.

18 Ibid., 2.

19 Reinhold Niebuhr, 1944, *The Children of Light and the Children of Darkness*, Charles Scribner's Sons, xi.

20 Arthur Manuel and Ronald Derrikson, 2017, *The Reconciliation Manifesto: Recovering the Land and Rebuilding the Economy*, James Lorimer and Company Inc., 140.

21 In 2016, nearly half of First Nations people, on and off reserve, had earned a college diploma, compared to 34 percent of non-Indigenous people, although university attainment was about 20 percent lower. *Post-Secondary Education Attainment* Fact Sheet, Assembly of First Nations, with data from the 2016 Census. https://www.afn.ca/wp-content/uploads/2018/07/PSE_Fact_Sheet_ENG.pdf.

22 Summary engagement report on a new approach for mutual transparency and accountability, 2017, INAC, 2017, https://www.aadnc-aandc.gc.ca/eng/1535402416096/1535402477042.

23 *A New Approach: Co-development of a New Fiscal Relationship*, 2017, Assembly of First Nations and Indigenous Services Canada, https://www.aadnc-aandc.gc.ca/DAM/DAM-INTER-HQ-ACH/STAGING/texte-text/reconciliation_new_fiscal_rel_approach_1512565483826_eng.pdf.

24 Summary, 2017, INAC.

25 Indigenous Voices Omnibus Survey 2017, Probe Research Inc., Winnipeg; selected data shared by Probe Research with author, October 5, 2017.

26 Ibid.

20
LET THE PEOPLE SPEAK

There is no such thing as the "voiceless." There are the deliberately silenced and the preferably unheard. —Arundhati Roy, 2006

Ordinary Canadians are the "preferably unheard" for a federal Indigenous affairs system that seems to deliberately confuse and obfuscate so people just give up asking questions. Announcing funding for Indigenous programs and services, but without identifying how much is going to which of the many co-delivery partners, makes it difficult to know who should be held to account. Trying to nail down how much is being spent on Indigenous programs and services and where it is being spent can feel, at times, like the federal government is operating under Heisenberg's Uncertainty Principle.[1]

According to the German physicist,[2] it is impossible under the rules of quantum physics to know with certainty where an atomic particle is located *and* how fast it is moving. Testing to determine location destroys the information about speed, and vice versa. In the realm of IA+ (Indigenous Affairs plus its many co-delivery partners), understanding spending is fraught with uncertainty. At times, it seems possible to know much is being spent, but not where. Or to know where money is being spent, but not find reliable figures on how much. It is no wonder that Canadians—Indigenous and non-Indigenous—might become frustrated and angry at a system that seems to defy comprehension.

Ordinary Indigenous people continue to be the "deliberately silenced." Since the 1970s, their voices have been assumed by government-sanctioned organizations over which they have no power or control. The result of sustaining the illusion that ordinary Indigenous people have plenty of councils, groups and organizations to legitimately speak for them has been to entrench systemic oppression.

However complex and confusing the issues surrounding Indigenous affairs in Canada, it should now be clear that the system in place at the federal level cannot be sustained. Since the 1960s, the system has been built on the premise that Indian people are "uniquely impoverished and disorganized"[3] and "somehow not competent enough to decide for themselves."[4] The evidence was there for all to see in the poverty and social pathologies in so many Indigenous communities. The growth of the Indian Affairs department was fuelled by that misery, but also dependent on it to sustain public support for more and more programs and an ever-expanding budget.

Indian leaders knew in the 1970s that they, too, were administering the suffering of their own people as they delivered more and more programs on behalf of IA,[5] but what choice did they have? Some jobs were better than no jobs. Some power, however compromised it might be, was better than no power at all.

It is unlikely that anyone could have foreseen what would happen over the next fifty years. Indian Affairs grew from a small department in 1966 with 3,000 employees (mostly non-Indigenous), a budget of $131 million, and two co-delivery partners. By 2019, it had been transformed into two departments, each with its own cabinet minister. The budgets for the two departments and their more than thirty co-delivery partners had mushroomed to some $21 billion in spending on delivering Indigenous programs and services, along with jobs for some quarter million people (mostly Indigenous).

But this vast system was built upon a foundation of continued suffering of a core group of First Nations, Inuit and Métis people. Without them, the justification to the public for its continued financial support would collapse.

The thousands of people working inside the federal bureaucratic bubble can go home at the end of a workday, satisfied with the job they're doing, without any awareness of the human costs embedded in their paycheques. Indigenous leaders have long known the system for what it is, but they remain trapped inside it. Indigenous leaders and workers in First Nations and Inuit communities do not have the luxury of obliviousness. They live where the poverty and suffering is plainly visible, but they are powerless to change the system. Over the years, the only option for leaders seemed to be demanding more money in the hope it might do some good.

"I'll always say we need more," said AFN National Chief Perry Bellegarde in an interview on CBC's *The House* in February 2018. "That's almost automatic from First Nations people…"[6]

However confused and perplexed the Canadian public may be about Indigenous issues, they have known for a long time that there is something very wrong with a system that has been unable to solve the issues of Indigenous poverty and suffering, no matter how much money was spent over the past fifty years. Or will be spent in the future.

The way out of this conundrum must, however, be one that does not deepen the existing poverty and suffering, or pull the supports out from under the thousands of Indigenous people who are dependent on the system for their livelihood. That is where the modernized treaty annuity comes in; it was intended as a livelihood support for First Nations families.

A modernized annuity would quickly put an end to the poverty of so many FN people—although the healing of suffering will take time—and it would serve to transition FN people away from their dependency on jobs funded by IA+. Ordinary FN people would be empowered to hold their leaders accountable to them, a shift in power that good leaders would welcome. In turn, this would empower the leaders to authentically speak for their people.

A modernized annuity offers a workable and dignified solution to a seemingly intractable problem, but it offers much more than that.

Recall that in 2004, Jean Allard, Wayne Helgason and the Treaty Annuity Working Group (TAWG) recommended that annuities be:

- increased from $5 to $5,000 for every man, woman and child, based on land-values, and extended to all Status First Nations people, wherever they live in Canada.
- payable directly to recipients through a mechanism similar to the Canada Child Benefit that is outside the control of Indigenous Affairs and band governments.
- funded from current or planned allocations to IA+ so that it is revenue neutral.

As much as a modernized annuity sounds like a form of guaranteed annual income, it is not. The annuity was historically intended to provide livelihood support for families by linking its value to the land ceded in treaties. It is a mechanism for honouring the treaties by sharing the prosperity of the land with First Nations people.

It should be noted that farmland values in Manitoba have increased significantly since TAWG worked out its calculations. How to establish the value an annuity based on land values is one of the big questions that will need to be addressed, as well as questions about taxation, distribution to minors, education on money management, and many more.

In fact, there is a great deal to be discussed.

We have to talk

Shuswap leader Arthur Manuel hoped there might soon be a time when the general public in Canada would understand and respect the Indigenous right to self-determination, and to respect the rights and benefits from the shared lands.

"At this point," he wrote in *The Reconciliation Manifesto*, "we can finally sit down together for the long grown-up talk about who we are and what we need, and who you are and what you need, and we can then begin to sort out the complicated questions about access to our lands and sharing the benefits. These talks can, indeed, lead to reconciliation, but only after our rights as title holders and decision makers on the land and our economic and cultural needs are met. We in turn will ensure that your very real human right to be here after four hundred years is respected and your economic and cultural needs are also met."[7]

Manuel died in 2017 before he could see his hope realized.[8]

The problem with talking as a vehicle for advancing reconciliation is that one side of this conversation has no political voice. It means that those who do have a voice need to help those without a voice to find their own. Given a chance and somebody willing to listen, Indigenous people are more than capable of speaking for themselves. As Harold Cardinal pointed out some fifty years ago, if you want your voice to be loud enough to influence government policy, you need money. The source of funds for ordinary Indigenous people to make themselves heard is right there in the treaties in the form of annuities.

Modernized annuities: the immediate implications

Families in First Nations communities are often entirely dependent on the band government for social assistance, housing, employment, etc. A modernized annuity would provide a degree of economic independence for individuals and families that would act to rebalance the power dynamic within the collective. It would also contribute to the healing and strengthening of families by eliminating social assistance dependency and its accompanying destructive effects in First Nations communities, which would have the effect, particularly in urban centres on the Prairies, of lifting nearly half of Indigenous children out of poverty.[9]

With the stable support of a modernized annuity, Indigenous families would have:

- the resources to choose for themselves how and where to live that are in the best interests of their families and their communities.

- the resources to "vote with their feet," by moving to a community with better leadership and opportunities, as their ancestors did in pre-settlement times.

- sufficient economic independence to be able to challenge the dominance of band governments and demand accountability from them.

- the ability to join and support political organizations at the community and national level that are legitimate voices for the people and are accountable to them rather than to Indigenous Affairs bureaucrats.

- positive economic assets in FN communities, which families can bring with them if they choose to move to a different community.

- financial equity that will help make families attractive clients for mortgages, business start-up loans, etc.

Modernized annuities: the national implications

A modernized treaty annuity would have immediate implications for a wide range of economic and social issues currently facing Canadian society:

- Because their annuity payments go with them, wherever they go, women and girls are empowered to escape exploitive situations.[10] This would directly address the Economic Security recommendations in the Missing and Murdered Indigenous Women and Girls (MMIWG) Inquiry Final Report, by providing support "during critical times of transition in the lives of Indigenous women, girls, and 2SLGBTQQIA people, such as moving out of their home communities into larger cities, or aging out of care."[11]

- The security of annuity payments would empower women and girls, and men and boys, to escape abusive and exploitive relationships.

- It would kick-start Canada's first Poverty Reduction Strategy by directly addressing the finding that half of all children living in First Nations communities live in poverty.[12] The federal government states that $22 billion has been invested in a range of poverty reduction efforts since 2015, lifting some 650,000 Canadians out of poverty by 2019.[13] The modernized annuity could potentially double that number.

- It addresses the issue of inequitable support for First Nations children as identified by the Canadian Human Rights Tribunal Decisions on First Nations Child Welfare and Jordan's Principle[14] in 2016 by providing the necessary economic support to strengthen families through annuities to allow more children to remain in the care of their families. An estimated 70 percent of children are taken into care because of economic issues.

- An annuity linked to land values provides a tangible, monetary link between the benefits of resource development on traditional lands and the well-being and prosperity of First Nations people and their communities, whether via pipelines, hydro-electric projects, or diamond mines.

- It responds to the criticism of the federal government by two-thirds of Canadians who feel that the amount of attention and funding for Canada's Indigenous peoples has mostly been ineffective,[15] by acting on a simple but effective policy change that can produce immediate, measurable and understandable results for Indigenous people.

- It addresses a long-standing political embarrassment for Canada over international accusations of persistent violations of the rights of Indigenous people[16] by honouring treaty rights, respectfully sharing the land and resources, and empowering people to speak for themselves and to decide for themselves how they want to live.

- It responds to the Calls to Action from the 2015 Truth and Reconciliation Report[17] and the spirit of the recommendations in the 1996 Report of the Royal Commission on Aboriginal Peoples.[18]

Modernized annuities are coming, whether the public gets behind the idea or not. The courts are already addressing claims that annuities should have been increased all along. The *Restoule v Crown* case brought by the Anishinaabe of the Robinson Huron and Superior treaties was heard by the Ontario Superior Court of Justice and a ruling delivered in December 2018. The justice found that "the Crown has a mandatory and reviewable obligation to increase the Treaties' annuities when the economic circumstances warrant. The economic circumstances will trigger an increase to the annuities…"[19] The ruling did not address how the increase would be calculated, or how to address the claim for arrears and interest.

Once Indigenous people can speak for themselves, we can hold real discussions about what to do about annuity valuations, arrears, interest and issues such as governance. It would serve the cause of reconciliation if we—where "we" includes our elected federal officials—choose to modernize annuities rather than waiting for it to be ordered by the courts.

There's an old saying (yes, another one) that the best time to plant a tree is twenty years ago; the second best time is now. The best time to have modernized treaty annuities was 150 years ago; the second best time is now.

At the time of this writing, the Province of Ontario had appealed the *Restoule* decision. Ottawa did not, which appears to be aligned with a Practice Directive issued by Attorney General of Canada, Jody Wilson-Raybould.[20] Justice department lawyers were directed to strive for reconciliation with Indigenous claimants, rather than approach cases from the usual adversarial perspective. Thus, the Crown might not appeal a judge's decision, even if it opposed the decision or thought it mistaken, in aid of advancing reconciliation. While the AG's directive may seem to heavily weight court claims to the benefit of Indigenous claimants, it limits one of the few mechanisms for bringing Indigenous issues into public view as they are argued in the courts. Negotiations and settlements arrived at behind closed doors reinforce the troubling issue of secrecy, and muddy the waters about who is representing the interests of ordinary Canadians—Indigenous and non-Indigenous—on issues that could affect their lives.

The Attorney General of Canada can order federal lawyers to go easy on claims by Indigenous groups; the RCMP can make eagle feathers available for swearing legal oaths; and NHL hockey games played in Treaty territories can start with an acknowledgment that the event is being held on Treaty lands. Each advances reconciliation in its own way. However, modernizing treaty annuities would fundamentally redefine the relationship between Indigenous and non-Indigenous Canadians right across the country.

Yes, Indigenous issues are undoubtedly complicated, but it is not necessary to try to figure out how to fix all the problems at once. Start with just this one thing: help ordinary Indigenous people find their voices so they can speak for themselves. Accomplishing just this one change would be amazing. And it is something all ordinary Canadians can do, together.

Let us not waste this rare and precious opportunity for reconciliation.

Endnotes to Chapter 20

1. Sheilla Jones, 2008, *The Quantum Ten: A story of passion, tragedy, ambition and science*, Oxford University Press, 231–232; David C. Cassidy,1992, *Uncertainty: The Life and Science of Werner Heisenberg*, W.H. Freeman and Company, 228–229.
2. Physicist Werner Heisenberg developed the Uncertainty Principle in 1927.
3. Yale D. Belanger, David R. Newhouse, and Kevin Fitzmaurice, 2008, "Creating a Seat at the Table: A Retrospective Study of Aboriginal Programming at Canadian Heritage," *The Canadian Journal of Native Studies*, Vol 28, No. 1, 37.
4. Ibid., 26.
5. James Burke, 1976, *Paper Tomahawks: From red tape to red power*, Queenston House Publishing, 73.
6. Perry Bellegarde, National Chief of the Assembly of First Nations, interview on *The House*, February 22, 2018, 5:00, https://www.cbc.ca/player/play/1169035843851.
7. Arthur Manuel and Ronald Derrickson, 2017, *The Reconciliation Manifesto: Recovering the Land and Rebuilding the Economy*, James Lorimer and Co., 276.
8. Jody Paterson, 2017, Obituary: B.C. aboriginal leader Arthur Manuel fought tirelessly for rights, *The Globe and Mail*, January 19, 2017, https://www.theglobeandmail.com/news/british-columbia/bc-aboriginal-leader-arthur-manuel-fought-tirelessly-for-rights/article33679268/.
9. David Macdonald and Daniel Wilson, 2016, *Shameful Neglect: Indigenous Child Poverty in Canada*, Canadian Centre for Policy Alternatives, 18, https://www.policyalternatives.ca/sites/default/files/uploads/publications/National%20Office/2016/05/Indigenous_Child%20_Poverty.pdf.
10. Statistics Canada, 2016, Homicide in Canada, reports that the homicide rate for Aboriginal females in 2016 was five times that of non-Aboriginal females. https://www150.statcan.gc.ca/n1/daily-quotidien/171122/dq171122b-eng.htm.
11. *Reclaiming Power and Place: The Final Report of the National Inquiry into Missing and Murdered Indigenous Women and Girls*, 2019, Executive Summary, 33.
12. David Macdonald, and Daniel Wilson, 2013, *Poverty or Prosperity: Indigenous Children in Canada*, Canadian Centre for Policy Alternatives, 12.
13. ESCD, 2018, Media Release, Government of Canada launches first Poverty Reduction Strategy, Employment and Social Development Canada, https://www.canada.ca/en/employment-social-development/news/2018/08/government-of-canada-launches-first-poverty-reduction-strategy.html.
14. Canadian Human Rights Tribunal Decisions on First Nations Child Welfare and Jordan's Principle, Information Sheet, 2016, Case Reference CHRT 1340/7008, 2.
15. David Korzinski, 2018, *Truths of reconciliation: Canadians are deeply divided on how best to address Indigenous issues*, Angus Reid Survey, 19, http://angusreid.org/indigenous-canada/.
16. World Report 2018: Canada, Human Rights Watch, https://www.hrw.org/world-report/2018/country-chapters/canada.
17. Truth and Reconciliation Commission of Canada: *Calls to Action*, 2015, Sections 45.iii and 45.iv, 5.
18. Report on the Royal Commission on Aboriginal Peoples, 1996, Volumes 1–5, https://www.bac-lac.gc.ca/eng/discover/aboriginal-heritage/royal-commission-aboriginal-peoples/Pages/final-report.aspx.
19. Restoule *v* Canada (Attorney General), Ontario Superior Court of Justice, 2018, [3].
20. Attorney General of Canada issues Directive on Civil Litigation Involving Indigenous Peoples,

Justice Canada, January 11, 2019, https://www.canada.ca/en/department-justice/news/2019/01/attorney-general-of-canada-issues-directive-on-civil-litigation-involving-indigenous-peoples.html.

APPENDICES

APPENDIX A

Estimate of IA+ spending on Indigenous programs and services 2017–2018

	Indigenous program spending	2004–2005	2017–2018	Increase factor
	(millions)			
1	Indigenous Affairs	$5,832	$10,057	1.72
2	Health Canada	$1,795	$3,364	1.87
3	12 co-delivery partners	$1,183	$2,130	1.80
4	20 more co-delivery partners		$3,550	
5	Total program spending	$8,810	$19,101	

Sources

1. Indigenous Affairs: INAC Plans and Priorities, 2004–2005; INAC Main Estimates 2017–18
2. Health Canada, co-delivery partner, INAC Plans and Priorities, 2004–2005, Health Canada: 2017–2018 Departmental Plan[1]
3. Co-delivery partners (12): INAC Plans and Priorities, 2004–2005
4. Co-delivery partners (20) 2017–2018: unidentified co-delivery partners[2]
5. Total program spending: INAC Plans and Priorities, 2004–2005; estimate of 2017–2018 total spending based on extrapolation methodology

Methodology

IA (Indigenous Services and Crown-Indigenous Relations) was unable to provide a list of the names and spending figures for co-delivery partners for 2017–2018, as it stated that no such "official" list exists. This calculation uses spending figures from Indigenous Affairs (IA) and Health Canada (HC) Estimates for 2004–2005 and 2017–2018. The spending figure for the 12 co-delivery partners in 2004–2005 is taken from IA Estimates. The spending by 12 co-delivery partners in 2017–2018 assumes a similar increase in spending from 2004–2005 to 2017–2018 as for IA and HC. In the absence of data on

---

1 Health Canada Programs 3.1, 3.2 and 3.3 ($3,134M) plus 80% of Internal Services costs ($230M)=$3,364M.
2 INAC stated that there were 34 federal departments and agencies, including INAC, delivering Indigenous programs and services in Canada in 2017. INAC, HC and 12 known co-delivery partners leaves 20 unidentified. INAC's Mandate, Presentation to the Natural Energy Board Modernization Expert Panel, January 20, 2017, Indigenous and Northern Affairs Canada, 2.

spending for the remaining 20 co-delivery partners, an estimate is extrapolated as follows:

- Average increase factor for 12 co-delivery partners from 2004–2005 to 2017–2018: 1.72 + 1.87 = 3.59/2 = 1.80
- Estimated contribution of 12 co-delivery partners in 2017–2018: $1,183M × 1.80 =$2,130M
- Estimated contribution per 12 co-delivery partners for 2017–2018: $2,130M/12= $177.5M
- Estimated contribution of 20 more co-delivery partners for 2017–2018: $177.5M × 20 = $3,550M
- Total program spending for IA+ of $19,101 million includes IA non-Indigenous spending of about two percent for 2017–2018, but does not include new Indigenous program funding of announced in the months after the Estimates were published.

APPENDIX B

Federal transfers to IA+, provinces and territories, 2017–2018

	Federal Transfers* (billions)	Per Capita Spending ($)
Quebec	22.7	2,710
Ontario	21.1	1,489
Indigenous Affairs Plus	19.1	16,609
British Columbia	6.7	1,388
Alberta	5.9	1,388
Manitoba	3.7	2,751
Nova Scotia	3.1	3,292
New Brunswick	2.8	3,703
Saskatchewan	1.6	1,388
Nunavut	1.6	41,745
Northwest Territories	1.3	29,044
Yukon	1.0	25,299
Newfoundland Labrador	0.7	1,388
Prince Edward Island	0.6	3,958

* Finance Canada, Federal Support for Provinces and Territories (2009–2019), https://www.fin.gc.ca/fedprov/mtp-eng.asp

APPENDIX C

Average Treaty Indian populations, 1871–2015

Year	Status Indians
1871	102,358
1901	107,000
1921	113,724
1931	133,000
1941	125,521
1951	165,607
1961	220,121
1981	289,175
1991	511,791
2001	690,101
2011	868,206
2015	953,043
	4,279,647
	divided by 12

Average Status pop.	**356,637**
Percentage of Treaty*	x 60%
Average Treaty pop.	**213,982**

- Some early population numbers include Inuit people, which account for about 6% of the "Indian and Eskimo" population.
- 1871: Table of the Aboriginal Population of Canada, 1871. These numbers include "Eskimos," which represented only a small portion of the Indigenous population Statistics Canada, https://www150.statcan.gc.ca/n1/pub/98-187-x/4151278-eng.htm Note: A different page in Stats Can data gives the Aboriginal population in 1871 as 23,000. https://www65.statcan.gc.ca/acyb01/acyb01_0007-eng.htm
- 1901 and 1931: Anatole Romaniuc, 2000, *Aboriginal Population of Canada*, 108, http://www3.brandonu.ca/cjns/20.1/cjnsv20no1_pg95-137.pdf

- 1941, 1951, 1961: These numbers include "Eskimos," which represented only a small portion of the Indigenous population. Statistics Canada, https://www65.statcan.gc.ca/acyb02/1967/acyb02_19670197014-eng.htm
- 1981: Number is for Status Indians. Statistics Canada, https://www150.statcan.gc.ca/n1/pub/89-503-x/2010001/article/11442/tbl/tbl003-eng.htm
- 1991, 2001, 2011, 2015: Registered Indian Population by Type of Residence for All Canada, Table, December 31, 1989–2016, Indigenous Affairs
- https://www.aadnc-aandc.gc.ca/eng/1523286391452/1523286414623#tbc9
- *Treaty Indians as a percentage of Status Indians: In 2011, IA reported 503,635 Treaty Indians out of 868,206 Status Indians (58%) or about 60%. Sources: Registered Indian Population; Evaluation of Indian Moneys, Estates and Treaty Annuities, Final Report, AANDC, April 2013, 55, https://www.aadnc-aandc.gc.ca/eng/1382702626948/1382702680155#chp6

APPENDIX D
Average MB farmland value, 1880–2015

Year	$/acre	Year	$/acre	Year	$/acre	Year	$/acre	Year	$/acre
*1880	1	1907	27	1934	15	1961	59	1988	304
1881	1	^1908	27	1935	15	1962	59	1989	328
1882	1	1909	29	1936	15	1963	59	1990	359
1883	1	1910	28	1937	15	1964	59	1991	357
1884	1	1911	28	1938	15	1965	59	1992	360
1885	1	1912	28	1939	15	1966	59	1993	373
1886	5	1913	28	1940	15	1967	59	1994	388
1887	5	1914	31	1941	20	1968	59	1995	413
1888	5	1915	30	1942	20	1969	59	1996	443
1889	5	1916	32	1943	20	1970	59	1997	483
1890	5	1917	32	1944	20	1971	176	1998	501
1891	8	1918	32	1945	20	1972	176	1999	510
1892	8	1919	32	1946	20	1973	176	2000	518
1893	8	1920	26	1947	20	1974	176	2001	525
1894	8	^1921	26	1948	20	1975	176	2002	547
1895	8	1922	26	1949	20	1976	176	2003	581
1896	10	1923	26	1950	20	1977	176	2004	605
1897	10	1924	26	1951	34	1978	176	2005	636
1898	10	1925	26	1952	34	1979	176	2006	664
1899	10	1926	26	1953	34	1980	176	2007	706
1900	10	1927	26	1954	34	1981	350	2008	804
1901	12	1928	26	1955	34	1982	350	2009	890
1902	12	1929	26	1956	34	1983	350	2010	981
1903	12	1930	26	1957	34	1984	350	2011	1035
1904	12	1931	15	1958	34	1985	350	2012	1137
1905	12	1932	15	1959	34	1986	344	2013	1388
1906	27	1933	15	1960	34	1987	325	2014	1583
								2015	1749
								Total	25,505

Land value average per acre: ($25,505/acre for 135 years)/135 years=**$188.93/ acre or $189/acre**

- Figures for 1880–1905 are estimates. See Homestead Files c1870–1930, M2001-3248 at Archives of Manitoba
- Figures for 1908–1916, Statistics Canada, https://www65.statcan.gc.ca/acyb02/1917/acyb02_191702017-eng.htm
- Figures from 1921–2015 from Manitoba Agriculture Value per Unit of Farmland and Buildings, https://www.gov.mb.ca/agriculture/market-prices-and-statistics/ndex.html

APPENDIX E

Annuity language in the *Indian Act, 1876* and *1985*

Indian Act of 1876:

3.1. The term "band" means any tribe, band or body of Indians who own or are interested in a reserve or in Indian lands in common, of which the legal title is vested in the Crown, or who share alike in the distribution of any **annuities** or interest moneys for which the Government of Canada is responsible...

3.3(c) Provided that any Indian woman marrying any other than an Indian or a non-treaty Indian shall cease to be an Indian in any respect within the meaning of this Act, except that she shall be entitled to share equally with the members of the band to which she formerly belonged, in the annual or semi-annual distribution of their **annuities**, interest moneys and rents; but this income may be commuted to her at any time at ten years' purchase with the consent of the band.

69. No presents given to Indians or non-treaty Indians, nor any property purchased, or acquired with or by means of any **annuities** granted to Indians or any part thereof or otherwise howsoever, and in the possession of any band of such Indians or of any Indian of any band or irregular band, shall be liable to be taken, seized or distrained for any debt, matter or cause whatsoever.

71. Any Indian convicted of any crime punishable by imprisonment in any penitentiary or other place of confinement, shall, during such imprisonment, be excluded from participating in the **annuities**, interest money, or rents payable to the band of which he or she is a member; and whenever any Indian shall be convicted of any crime punishable by imprisonment in a penitentiary or other place of confinement, the legal costs incurred in procuring such conviction, and in carrying out the various sentences recorded, may be defrayed by the Superintendent-General, and paid out of any **annuity** or interest coming to such Indian, or to the band, as the case may be.

72. The Superintendent-General shall have power to stop the payment of the annuity and interest money of any Indian who may be proved, to the satisfaction of the Superintendent General, to have been guilty of deserting his or her family, and the said Superintendent-General may apply the same towards the support of any family, woman or child so deserted; also to stop the payment of the **annuity** and interest money of any woman having no children, who deserts her husband and lives immorally with another man.

88....[The Indian Act] shall cease to apply to any Indian, or to the wife or minor unmarried children of any Indian as aforesaid, so declared to be enfranchised, who shall no longer be deemed Indians within the meaning of the laws relating to Indians, except in so far as their right to participate in the **annuities** and interest moneys, and rents and councils of the band of Indians to which they belonged is concerned...

92. Any Indian, not a member of the band, or any non-treaty Indian who, with the consent of the band and the approval of the Superintendent-General, has been permitted to reside upon the reserve, or obtain a location thereon, may, on being assigned a suitable allotment of land by the band for enfranchisement, become enfranchised on the same terms and conditions as a member of the band; and such enfranchisement shall confer upon such Indian the same legal rights and privileges, and make such Indian subject to such disabilities and liabilities as affect Her Majesty's other subjects; but such enfranchisement shall not confer upon such Indian any right to participate in the **annuities**, interest moneys, rents and councils of the band.

93. Whenever any band of Indians, at a council summoned for the purpose according to their rules, and held in the presence of the Superintendent-General or of an agent duly authorized by him to attend such council, decides to allow every member of the band who chooses, and who may be found qualified, to become enfranchised, and to receive his or her share of the principal moneys of the band...by his or her exemplary good conduct and management of property, proves that he or she is qualified to receive his or her share of such moneys, the Governor may, on the report of the Superintendent-General to that effect, order that the said Indian be paid his or her share of the capital funds at the credit of the band, or his or her share of the principal of the **annuities** of the band, estimated as yielding five percent.

Indian Act of 1985:
15. (5) Where, prior to September 4, 1951, any woman became entitled, under section 14 of the Indian Act, chapter 98 of the Revised Statutes of Canada, 1927, or any prior provisions to the like effect, to share in the distribution of **annuities**, interest moneys or rents, the Minister may, in lieu thereof, pay to that woman out of the moneys of the band an amount equal to ten times the average annual amounts of the payments made to her during the ten years last preceding or, if they were paid for less than ten years, during the years they were paid.

68. Where the Minister is satisfied that an Indian

(a) has deserted his spouse or common-law partner or family without sufficient cause,

(b) has conducted himself in such a manner as to justify the refusal of his spouse or common-law partner or family to live with him, or

(c) has been separated by imprisonment from his spouse or common-law partner and family,

the Minister may order that payments of any **annuity** or interest money to which that Indian is entitled shall be applied to the support of the spouse or common-law partner or family or both the spouse or common-law partner and family of that Indian.

Treaty Money

72. Moneys that are payable to Indians or to Indian bands under a treaty between Her Majesty and a band and for the payment of which the Government of Canada is responsible may be paid out of the Consolidated Revenue Fund.

DEFINITIONS

Indigenous Canadians: Canadians who identify as Indian (First Nations), Inuit and Métis, the three groups identified as Aboriginal (Indigenous) in the *Constitution Act* of 1982.

Non-Indigenous Canadians: Canadians who do not identify as Indigenous.

Indian Affairs Branch: Prior to 1966, the Indian Affairs Branch, which was part of the Department of Citizenship and Immigration.

Indian Affairs/Indigenous Affairs (IA): In 1966, Indian Affairs became a stand-alone federal government department, with the responsibility for overseeing the *Indian Act*, administration of Crown-Indigenous treaties, and delivering Indigenous programs and services. Since then it has changed names: Department of Indian Affairs and Northern Development (DIAND); Aboriginal Affairs and Northern Development Canada (AANDC); Indigenous and Northern Affairs Canada (INAC); and, after the department was split in 2017, Indigenous Services Canada (ISC) and Crown-Indigenous Relations Canada (CIRC). To avoid drowning in acronyms, IA (Indian Affairs or Indigenous Affairs, in modern terminology) will refer to the department from 1966 onwards. Indigenous Affairs will also describe the combined departments of ISC and CIRC, unless otherwise indicated.

Indigenous Affairs Plus (IA+): all the federal government departments and agencies collectively delivering programs and services for Canada's Indigenous people and communities. This includes IA, plus more than 30 federal departments and agencies that act as IA's co-delivery partners.

Aboriginal Representative Organizations (AROs): Indigenous organizations funded by the federal government after 1971 to advocate on behalf of their designated Indigenous group. There are currently five AROs: Assembly of First Nations; Inuit Tapiriit Kanatami; Métis National Council; Congress of Aboriginal Peoples; Native Women's Association of Canada. AROs are sometimes referred to as Indigenous National Organizations or Indigenous Representative Organizations.

Tribal Councils: representative bodies created by First Nations with shared geography, culture or interests to advocate for specific support and advisory services for their members.

First Nations: communities with band members on reserve land set aside by the Crown for the use and benefit of First Nations people, and FN communities with band membership that do not have a land base.

First Nations people: Indigenous people who are not Inuit or Métis, historically referred to as Indians. This is collective term that encompasses some 60 tribal identities.

First Nations band or band council: the governance structure under the *Indian Act* or by custom code that administers and manages First Nations community affairs.

Indians: the term collectively describing Indigenous people in Canada who are not Inuit or Métis. The term Indian has largely been replaced by the term First Nations; however, the federal government continues to use the terms Status Indian, non-Status Indian and Treaty Indian to identify specific groups of First Nations people.

Status Indian: people whose names are on the Indian Register maintained by IA. Only Status Indians are recognized as Indians under the *Indian Act* and entitled to certain benefits and rights under the Act.

Non-Status Indians: people who are not recognized by the Government of Canada as Status Indians, even though they may identify as Indian or are members of a First Nation.

Treaty Indians: people who are descendants of Indians who were members of bands that signed treaties with the Crown, and who are currently members of a treaty band.

Métis: the broad term used to describe "mixed blood" people with First Nations and European ancestry. There is considerable dispute among Métis political organizations over who is considered eligible to call themselves Métis.

Inuit: the collective term for the Inuit and Innu, the circumpolar people traditionally inhabiting Alaska, Canada and Greenland, and those inhabiting Quebec and Labrador.

ABOUT THE AUTHOR

Sheilla Jones is a Senior Fellow with the Frontier Centre for Public Policy, leading the Treaty Annuity/Individual Empowerment Initiative. She has been researching Indigenous politics for more than 20 years, serving as a facilitator for the Treaty Annuity Working Group, a special committee of the Social Planning Council of Winnipeg, which focused on modernizing First Nations treaty annuities. Sheilla is an award-winning Canadian journalist and author of several books, including an examination of the troubled early years of the Manitoba Métis Federation, as well as books on cosmology and quantum physics. Sheilla has a deep settler history. Her French and British ancestors have been settling Canada for nearly 400 years. She lives in Winnipeg.

ACKNOWLEDGEMENTS

I would like to express my deep appreciation for the many people who, over the past twenty years, have helped me to understand the complexities of treaty annuities and to build a picture of the vast, seemingly immutable entity called Indian Affairs. First and foremost, I would like to thank Jean Allard for the many hours spent arguing, laughing and challenging each other's points of view on treaty annuities. I also want to acknowledge the persistence of Peter Holle, president of Frontier Centre for Public Policy, who has wanted the idea of modernizing treaty annuities to be part of Canada's public policy conversation for just about as long as Jean and I have been talking about it.

Researching and writing about complex public policy issues can consume enormous amounts of time and energy. I offer a heartfelt thank you to the Lotte & John Hecht Memorial Foundation in Vancouver for being financial leaders and visionaries and supporting this critical public policy research. Without such support and leadership, research and the public dissemination of such significant public policy would not be possible. Thanks also those who work for the Frontier Centre for Public Policy, across Canada, for their insights and support in helping see this book project through to completion.

Thank you to the team of advisers from the former Treaty Annuity Working Group—Jean Allard, Wayne Helgason, Guy Savoie and Paul Walsh, along with Leona Freed—who shared their wisdom during the writing process.

And thank you to Sheila North for contributing the foreword to this book, and for her enthusiastic support of the idea of modernizing treaty annuities.

Finally, I would be most remiss if I did not acknowledge my husband Jim Burns and daughter Kate Morrison for their unstinting support. They know how important they've been to me.

INDEX

A

Allard, Jean 52, 54, 55, 76, 80, 85, 89, 90, 104–106, 108, 116, 120, 122, 123–124, 126, 128, 132–134, 135, 141, 142, 143, 144–145, 147, 148, 154, 165, 166–167, 170, 173, 183, 197, 204
Anderson, Erik 156–157, 162, 170
Assembly of First Nations, AFN 19, 20, 32, 86, 87, 130, 131, 135, 138, 139, 140, 146, 147, 150, 165, 187, 195–196, 199, 200, 201, 203
Atleo. Jr., Cliff 191, 193

B

Balan, Bill 124
Beardy's & Okemasis First Nation 29, 32, 34
Beaver, Jack, IA Advisor 73–74, 76, 81–86, 90, 133, 136, 139, 147, 173, 183, 195
Beaver Legitimacy Test 75, 140
Beaver Report, "To have what is one's own," 1979 83, 173
Bellegarde, Perry, National Chief, AFN 203, 209
Big Bear, (Mistahimaskwa) 44, 80, 89, 134, 135
Blakeney, Allan 132, 135
Boldt, Menno 93, 99, 184
Buffalo Jump of the 1980s, Nielson Task Force Report, 1985 16, 93, 186
Burke, James 48–49, 55, 65, 66, 68, 89, 183, 209
Butler, Kelly Anne 28

C

Camsell-Blondin, Violet 124, 128
Cardinal, Frank 63
Cardinal, Harold 47, 49–50, 52, 54, 55, 57–64, 66, 67, 68, 71, 77, 78–82, 85, 87, 89, 90, 117, 120, 126, 128, 154, 162, 165–166, 170, 172, 177, 183, 199, 205
Chonkolay, Harry 45–47, 62, 154
Chrétien, Jean, IA Minister 16, 50–51, 56–57, 59, 61, 62, 63–65, 67, 70, 88, 92, 149, 175, 176, 177
Chrétien, Jean, Justice Minister 87
Chrétien, Jean, Prime Minister 15, 24, 91, 95, 134, 137, 141, 143, 145, 146, 148, 183
Chrétien, Wellie 63
Clatworthy, Stewart 166, 170
Congress of Aboriginal Peoples, CAP 24, 87, 113, 150, 151, 184, 223
Connelly, Robert (Bob), ADM, Indian Affairs 73, 76, 133, 135, 147
Coon Come, Matthew, National Chief, AFN 139
Courchene, Dave, President, Manitoba Indian Brotherhood 50, 51, 52, 53, 62, 63, 81, 132, 149, 153, 177, 183

Crombie, David, IA Minister 94
Crown-Indigenous Relations 16, 26, 27, 37, 39, 42, 89, 182, 183, 186, 188, 189, 213, 223

D

Deiter, Walter, President, Federation of Saskatchewan Indians 50, 62
Denechoan, Willie 46
Diabo, Russell 99, 190, 191, 193
Dumont, Yvon 122

E

Epp, Jake, IA Minister 83

F

Falcon Ouellette, Robert, Liberal MP 22, 25
Faulkner, Hugh, IA Minister 81, 82
Flanagan, Tom 133, 135
Fontaine, Phil, National Chief, AFN 53, 81, 95, 97, 165
Freed, Leona 110–114, 116–117, 118, 120, 125, 126, 129–131, 136, 144, 147, 166, 170, 227

G

Galloway, Rita 113, 116, 117
Gibson, Gordon 133–134, 135, 144
Gladstone, Jim, Senator 48

H

Harper, Stephen, Prime Minister 17, 37, 99, 152
Heisenberg's Uncertainty Principle 202, 209
Helgason, Wayne 141–143, 147, 148, 181, 184, 204, 227
Hurtig, Mel 58

I

Indigenous Affairs Plus (IA+) 36–40, 43, 180–181, 184, 187, 202, 204, 213–214, 215, 223
Indigenous Services Canada 42, 43, 192, 201, 223
Inuit Tapiriit Kanatami, ITK 24, 43, 150, 184, 192, 223
Irwin, Ron, IA Minister 95
Ishkanian, Kayla 198, 201

J

Jordan's Principle 206, 209

K

Kelowna Accord 149, 151, 152, 153
King, Thomas 189, 193, 195, 201
Kuhn Boudreau, Lynda 78, 89, 101, 108

L

Laing, Arthur, IA Minister 42, 51, 55, 133, 169
Lynch, Kevin, DM, Finance 144–145

M

Macdonald, John A., Prime Minister 29, 41, 169
Mahoney, Steve, MP, Liberal Party of Canada 129, 135
Manitoba Framework Agreement 95–97
Manley, John, Minister, Finance Canada 145
Manness, Clayton 142
Manning, Ernest, Premier, Alberta 46
Manuel, Arthur 90, 147, 189, 190–191, 193, 199, 201, 204–205, 209
Manuel, George, President, National Indian Brotherhood 65, 87
Martin, Pat, MP 139, 147

Martin, Paul, Prime Minister 17, 32, 35, 143, 144, 145, 146, 148, 149, 151, 152
Martin, Sr., Paul, Liberal MP 62
Maytwayashing, Eileen 125, 128
McParland, Kelly 172, 183
Membertou, Henri, Grand Chief 102, 108
Merasty, Ben 124, 128
Métis Nation 28–29, 31, 33, 39, 43, 76, 95, 187
Métis National Council, MNC 24, 43, 87, 113, 150, 184, 192, 223
MMIWG, Missing and Murdered Indigenous Women and Girls Final Report 206
Mulroney, Brian, Prime Minister 16, 17, 24, 28, 29, 92, 94, 95, 99, 113, 186, 187, 191

N

National Indian Brotherhood, NIB 65, 66, 67, 72, 73, 74, 82, 83, 84, 86, 87
Native Women's Association of Canada, NWAC 87, 139, 140
Nault, Robert (Bob), IA Minister 137–140, 143–144, 145, 146, 148, 150
Niebuhr, Reinhold 199
Nielsen, Erik, Conservative MP 16, 24, 91, 92, 99, 192
Numbered treaties, Treaties 1-11 45, 80, 126, 156, 159, 162, 163, 165, 168, 169, 179

P

Paul, Pamela 139
Pelletier, Gérard, Minister, Secretary of State 59–60, 70
People of Always 121–122
Philpott, Jane, Minister, Health Canada 174
Philpott, Jane, Minister, Indigenous Services 183, 187, 192
Price, Frank 132, 135
Prince, Rufus 110, 118

Q

Qalipu Mi'kmaq First Nation 27–28, 31, 34, 35, 164
Quesnel, Joseph 198, 201

R

Red Paper, Citizens Plus, 1970 60–61, 62, 64, 65, 67, 68, 77, 101, 126
Restoule decision 207
Richards, John 134, 144
Riel, Louis 29–30, 72, 106, 108, 122, 123
Robertson, Heather 46–47, 54
Robinson treaties, Robinson Huron, Robinson Superior treaties 155–158, 161, 162, 163, 168, 169, 171, 179, 207
Royal Commission of Aboriginal Peoples, RCAP 108, 113, 118, 158, 163

S

Schreyer, Edward (Ed), Premier, Manitoba 52–53, 104–105, 123, 144
Simpson, Wemyss 156
Stanbury, Robert, Minister Without Portfolio, Secretary of State 69, 70, 72, 123
Starblanket, Noel, President, NIB 82, 83
Starlight, Bruce 111–112
Stewart, Jane, IA Minister 97, 111, 113, 114, 117, 118, 140
St. Germaine, Gerry, Senator 197, 201

T

Tait, Caroline 174–175

Thompson, Myron, MP, Reform Party of Canada 113–114, 116, 117, 118, 129, 130, 135, 136
Treaty Annuity Working Group, TAWG 142, 144–146, 148, 154, 204
Trudeau, Justin, Prime Minister 16, 17, 21–22, 24, 41, 43, 174, 183, 186, 187, 192
Trudeau, Pierre, Prime Minister 16, 17, 50, 58, 59, 60, 61, 62, 63, 65, 67, 69, 70, 71, 85, 92, 133, 154
Truth and Reconciliation Commission Report, TRC 10, 209

U

Uskiw, Sam 142, 143–144, 148

W

Wastesicoot, Jennie 99, 100, 107, 108
Wernick, Michael, DM, Indigenous Affairs 176
Wheeler, Jordan 140, 147
White Paper, Statement of the Government of Canada on Indian Policy, 1969 24, 57–63, 64, 65, 66, 67, 68, 71, 85, 92, 94, 95, 115, 127, 133, 134, 138, 140, 149, 176, 177, 178
Wilson-Raybould, Jody, Attorney General of Canada 191, 193, 207
Wuttunee, William 52, 55, 68